ASYLUM

ASYLUM

Hollywood Tales from My Great Depression:
Brain Dis-Ease, Recovery, and
Being My Mother's Son

Joe Pantoliano

WEINSTEIN
BOOKS

ISBN: 978-1-60286-135-0

First Edition
10 9 8 7 6 5 4 3 2 1

For Nancy Sheppard Pantoliano,
and the man who married us, Charlie Rocket

The mass of men lead lives of quiet desperation and go to the grave with the song still in them.

—Attributed to Henry David Thoreau

Acknowledgments

To the people who inspired me on my creative journey—the weavers of my magic carpet. Thanks for the ride.

Ron Abbott
Alan Arkin
Jon Avnet
Alec Baldwin
Ed Begley Jr.
Herbert Berghof
Leo Bookman
Sully Boyer
Richard Bradford
Martin Brest
Paul Brickman
James Burrows
Red Buttons
Mary Cahoon
Francis Campbell
Joe Carbone
Rachelle Carson
Harris Cattleman

John Cazale
Mary Centrella-
   Pantoliano
David Chase
Ellen Chenoweth
Michael Chinch
Harry Columbi
Tom Cruise
Donna Damiano
Andy Davis
Dino De Laurentiis
Rebecca de Mornay
Pam Dickson
Charlie Durning
Robert Duvall
David Evanier
Mike Feinberg
Mickey Finn

John Ford Noonan
Robert Forster
David Foster
Eddie Foy III
John Fredericks
Gail (my singing
   teacher from
   73rd Street)
Vincent Gardenia
Bill Gersh
Bobby Gersh
David Gersh
Vincent Gogliati
Howard Goldberg
Alisa Halliman
Annette Handley
Mike Hartos
Nico Hartos

Jeff Harris

Dick Harvey

Patrick Hearley

Harriet Helberg

Alice Hermmes

Peter Hines

Jack Hofsiss

Michael Howard

Tony Howard

Florio Isabella

Anne Jackson

Sheila Jaffe

James Jenter

Mattie Jordan

Jack Keegan

Michael Kell

Max Kennedy

Robert Kennedy Jr.

Lyle Kessler

Jim Kiernan

John Kimbel

Gleb Klioner

Nancy Klopper

Bernie Kukoff

Buzz Kulik

Bobby Lewis

Marlene Mancine

Kenny Marino

Penny Marshall

Rino Mascarino

Lillah McCarthy

Pat McQueeney

Nick Mele

Bobby Moresco

Chris Nolan

Emma Nolan

Michael O'Neal

Patrick O'Neal

Al Onorato

Joseph Peck

Penny Perry

Don Phillips

Bruce Postman

Michael Rado

Steve Railsback

Vic Ramos

Rob Reiner

Ralph Ricci

Rita Riggs

Fred Roos

Daniel Roth

Joe Roth

Gerald Saldo

Lee Sankowich

Alex Schifel

Richard Serfaffien

Eileen Shaw

Al Sinkys

Lain Smith

Elaine Smith

Lynn Stalmaster

Maureen Stapleton

Joe Stern

Clifford Stevens

Nick Stevens

Stephen Strimpell

Brandon Tartikoff

Frank Tidy

Steve Tisch

Rosemary Tishler

Harry Ulfland

Bill Unger

Robert Wagner

Eli Wallach

Peter Wallach

Roberta Wallach

Georgianne Walken

J.T. Walsh

Natalie Wood

Contents

No Kidding, Me Too!

"I am now the most miserable man living . . . Whether I shall ever be better I cannot tell; I awfully forebode I shall not. To remain as I am is impossible; I must die or be better . . ."

I read those words aloud, but in a stage whisper so the passengers boarding past me wouldn't think I was talking to myself. From the luxurious embrace of my first-class seat, compliments of a flight attendant I'd charmed on the way to business class, I held my cell phone up to my ear and waited for a response from my wife, Nancy.

A pregnant pause. Then Nancy said, "Joe, did you just say 'awfully forebode'?"

Far from being the most miserable man living, at that moment I was actually the most grateful man on the plane. An ice-cold bottle of water between my legs, my laptop on my foldout table, I was on my way home to my beautiful wife of twenty years.

Nancy must have thought I'd lost my mind. Well, I had. After all, I was returning from a nine-day "Stomp the Stigma" tour in

Iraq, where I was comically billed as the "Bob Hope of the Mentally Challenged." I took the trip against the wishes of several of my children, my friends, my doctor, and even my lawyer. My agent supported it (anything for a buck! da prick!), so did Nancy and my son Marco, bless them. Oh, Nancy, sweet, darling Nancy. Everyone was so scared, me most of all! The whole thing was crazy. Me flying around in Black Hawks. Then aboard C-130s, cargo planes, flying into Bagdad in a corkscrew rotation, experiencing weightlessness, as if I were John F'n Glenn! I even broke bread with a four-star general! But at this moment my mind felt more intact, and I felt more serene than ever before.

Nancy had called knowing I was on my way home and she was eager to hear how the trip from Baghdad had gone.

"Hey, Joe, everything OK?"

"Yeah babe, everything's A-OK. That's military talk, hon. Nancy, if we were on Skype you'd see my canary-eating grin." I was going through my e-mails before Nancy called and I was in the middle of reading an article sent to me by a friend. It was about a man and his lifelong depression. And it made me really happy.

Nancy and I chatted and said goodbye. I reread the words: "Whether I shall ever be better I cannot tell; I awfully forebode I shall not." The source of the quotation had surprised me: Abraham Lincoln.

A few years before this trip, I was diagnosed with the same thing Lincoln suffered: clinical depression, or "melancholia," as it was called in Lincoln's time. *Melancholia* . . . a charming term.

I'm familiar with his feeling of endless misery. I've lived on that same bleak block for much of my life. I, too, reached the point of saying, either this shit gets better, or it ends. Of course, I never put it as eloquently as Lincoln; my usual brand of expression was brewed in a world where the importance of something said is directly proportional to the number of four-letter words needed for a punch line.

The military invited me to Iraq because of nkm2.org—a.k.a. No Kidding, Me 2!—the organization I created to end the stigma and shame around brain dis-ease, and create equal rights for the All-American Brain.

Since 2002, the suicide rate among our soldiers has grown 350 percent. Suicides have actually outnumbered combat deaths in Iraq and Afghanistan since at least 2009—and that's not counting the failed attempts. Let me repeat that so it really sinks in: suicides have outnumbered combat deaths. From 2005 to 2010, active service members took their own lives at a rate of approximately one every 36 hours. The Department of Veterans Affairs estimates that a veteran dies by suicide every 80 minutes. That's a lot of shame, and that is why I went: to take shame out of the closet, to meet with hundreds of our men and women stationed there. I went with my two-person team: psychiatrist Dr. Bob Irwin, and actress and model Lisa Jay—how else could we get the GIs to show up! Dr. Bob talked to the troops about the importance of sharing feelings rather than keeping the secrets inside, festering like an emotional cancer of the soul. They could tell a battle buddy and surrender to the feelings, getting their peace of mind back. Surrender to win. I shared sad and funny stories about my struggles with depression and I listened as they told theirs.

The common thread I have with so many of those soldiers is that feeling of embarrassment and shame. And that's why I'm writing this book: to eliminate the shame and obliterate the blame. That's why Lincoln's words made me happy. I recognized myself in them. What's the first thing we think about when it comes to Abe Lincoln? That he was depressed? Had "melancholia"? He's honest Abe, the guy whose face is carved into the side of Mount Rushmore. He should be our posterboy to abolish bigotry, discrimination, and shame. The guy who wrote the Gettysburg Address on the back of a fucking napkin, and was dyslexic to boot! Him! He should be the 2012 poster boy for the equal rights of our all-American brain, for Christ's sake. One in four Americans live with a brain dis-ease, just like the one in four Americans up on that rock.

This is the last great frontier of civil rights in our country. Why is brain dis-ease the kind of diagnosis you get yelled at for having? Why? Why all that stigma, shame and bigotry? Our brain has as many treatable maladies as our other vital organs. They might send you to the hospital, but you won't be getting The Fruit Cake! Why all this fear, bigotry, and shame surrounding three pounds of fat?

It's the civil right of all Americans to not walk with shame because of a sadness that lurks inside them, with a secret hidden in a closet, when according to the National Alliance on Mental Illness there is a 75 percent recovery rate for people suffering from a brain dis-ease. Those are great odds, better than cancer. The disease can be stomped. It ain't forever, as I once thought.

Honest Abe wrote honestly about his dis-ease. I will too. I know now that if you—or maybe someone you know—has a BD, you can survive and succeed and live through it, as millions do, as Lincoln did, as I did.

I plan to wear my dis-easiness on my sleeve, to share my life experience, my strengths, and my weaknesses. *Yes,* even those dirty little weaknesses! I'll be as open with you as I can, except when to do so could hurt or injure loved ones I held hostage before my emotional rescue. (Note: Some of the names in this book have been changed to protect the guilty.)

By the time I'm done, you'll see how cool it is to be out there, to admit the truth! We're all a little nuts! Won't that be nice. I long for the day when talking about having BD is not a matter of courage, but simply "a matter of fact."

—⚏—

For me to finally get how my depression worked—to understand that my black moods and my behaviors were born out of my disease, and not a character flaw—well, my man, that information was like hitting the $500 trifecta, on the *nose!* MY OH MY! I've known for years now how my dyslexia and my ADHD worked, that I was different. I learned about ADHD only after my youngest two children were diagnosed with it. They got it from me! I knew that I was neither stupid, nor lazy, nor crazy. But why does my brain work the way it does? It was when the doc said, *It's not your fault.* That's when things started to finally make sense. Finally, I was getting answers! Answers about me, my kids, my mother.

Let me get this out of the way right now: I loathe the term *mental illness.* It implies that something in my brain is permanently broken, and that I or that anyone like me is "less than." Well I got news for ya! Our brains are not broken! They're just human! So let's cross out ~~mental illness~~. In this book let's choose to identify these moods as my "uneasiness," or "dis-ease." "Brain dis-ease." There—BD, if you like. 'Cause I like!

It is safe to say I'm an ordinary person who has led a charmed life. But *why me*? I'm a likable guy. It's taken me forty years to discover that Hollywood was no different than Hoboken. Just a more expensive zip code! I could be your best friend if you had something I needed to fill my emptiness. If you got in the way of it then I was your worst nightmare. I was a chameleon. Just like I flirted my way into that first-class seat, I spent my whole life working the rooms, sneaking in the back door and leaving through the front like I owned the joint, mimicking the moves my mother taught me, that her father taught her, our Neapolitan legacy. I probably shouldn't confess this so early in the book!

Louis B. Mayer once said, "The most important thing about acting is sincerity. . . . Once you learn to fake that, you got it made." That's what my depression felt like—like I was faking it. Faking sincerity. Faking serenity. Faking life.

Even after I had acquired all the things I wanted, all the collateral of success, I still lived in fear of being found out as a "facazy"—that's what Cousin Curly the jeweler called a phony stone. It gnawed at me, that I didn't earn my success fair and square. Actor Joe Pantoliano, that wildly charming and unpredictable young man? That phony fuck was just a front man for the depressed sack of shit cowering behind, the man behind the curtain, whom nobody was supposed to pay attention to. I was the guy who, because of undiagnosed dyslexia, could barely even read or write! I owned the patent on the emptiness I felt. That feeling that my life would be perpetually unfinished. I dared not share that feeling with another soul. The shame I felt fueled my isolation. I imagined I was the only soul who felt that way.

—m—

My dark moods sprouted into all kinds of other behaviors that I now understand were really forms of self-medication. We'll call these behaviors the Seven Deadly Symptoms.

MY SEVEN DEADLY SYMPTOMS

1. Food (either overeating or starving myself)

2. Vanity (status symbols, popularity, hanging with the cool kids)
3. Shopping and shoplifting (either compulsively spending or getting "the five finger discount" to feel better)
4. Success (seeking fame and admiration to avoid nihilistic thoughts, to end my soul sickness)
5. Sex (or masturbation, other ways to distract from dark thoughts)
6. Alcohol (to remind me to be on, to wind down, and of course, to have more sex)
7. Prescription drugs (to numb pain, avoid the calories of white wine spritzers, to help me enjoy success, and to make myself too tired to worry about losing what I now had)

Nobody chooses to become an alcoholic. And nobody wakes up one day and says, "I think I'll get myself hooked on Vicodin. That sounds like fun." But the experts tell me that there's a huge correlation between BD and substance abuse. For most of my life, I didn't know that.

My Seven Deadlies made me feel great. These behaviors worked for a time. They were quick and on the spot! But no matter who you are, no matter what your poison—meditation, medication, masturbation—no matter what people use to make themselves feel better, it will work for a while, but then it stops working. It's like shaving with a dull butter knife.

I became an alcoholic, an addict, a compulsive shopper, a kleptomaniac. And a maniac! I had family and friends, but I was a ghost, lost and alone, held hostage by the things that I always felt would set me right. Now that I had them, I lived in constant fear of losing them, losing the things that never worked to stop the psychic pain! My despair was a rush of shame and sadness flooding through my bloodstream, invading my psyche like a cancer. I was afraid of the future and obsessed with my past. Most of all, I was afraid to ask for help. I was numb, only I could not compartmentalize my sadness without also numbing my joy. I would get hit by this black mood when my kids were happy just being children! The alien inside me wanted to make them feel as miserable as I did. I grew contemptuous of the suckers who loved me. I was emotionally as numb as a sack of hammers; I knew the lines in the play, but who said them? I was alone and isolated, and I liked it! I liked sleepwalking through the most prolific period of my life in Hollywood. I remembered Jimmy Jenter saying that hurt people . . . hurt people!

I imagine some people will hear about this book and say,

WANNABE #1:"Hey, you hear about what Pantoliano wrote in his new book?"

WANNABE #2: "Joey Pants?—What's he hawkin' now?"

WANNABE #1: "How he got over his depression."

WANNABE #2: Well ain't that rich! Joey Pants? The guy can't read, can't write, and positively can't act his way out of a wet paper bag! He's crying about how he's making a living out of lying, doing what he loves! What's that Dough got to be depressed about?"

Yeah, that's exactly how I felt.

Like them, what I couldn't understand was *why*. Why, with all my success, was I so unhappy? Why weren't these feelings going away? Why were they more acute? Jesus Christ! Everything I'd ever wanted or worked for was working out. How was I able to get that lucky? My wildest dreams had come true! I'm making a living as a professional actor. I got what I prayed for. Not just a shot at the brass ring—I got the brass ring! I'm among two percent of the 120,000 members of the Screen Actor's Guild who make a good living purely from what we are paid to do: act. Hi fiddly dee, motherfucker! For 28 consecutive years I've been one of only a few hundred blessed with the good fortune of being able to say that. Ninety-five present of the SAG membership in a twelve month period make zero dollars. And still I'm miserable—what a nightmare. Why was I so unhappy? What was wrong with me? It wasn't my mother's, father's, or stepfather's fault, not anybody's, hell, not even mine! There was nothing bad going on.

—m—

I had no understanding of what BD was before my own diagnosis. I thought my feelings defined who I was, that my brain *was* busted, I *was* defective, like the broken toys in the trunk of Sammy the Peddler's car, the ones my mother could buy us for twenty cents on the dollar.

Growing up, I can't recall the expression *mental illness* ever being used, mentioned, or even whispered. If you had a problem—and were dumb enough to mention it—the response would be: "What! There's nothing wrong with you! Nothing that a swift kick in the ass or a hundred dollar bill couldn't cure. You ain't crazy! That shit's all in your head. Snap out of it!" It's in your head, all right . . . too bad you can't snap out of it. As I write this, I'm sitting at my desk in the apartment I still keep in Hoboken, peering out my parlor window, no more than forty yards from the parlor window across the street at Fialla's Funeral Parlor, where my mother was laid out thirty years ago. My father worked there until his death in 1987. For most of my life I was so ignorant about our family history of brain dis-ease. I didn't know my mother had it; I had condemned her simply for not caring enough. I thought Mommy could change if she worked hard enough at it, that she could have snapped out of it if she really wanted to. But I was wrong, she couldn't. Just like I couldn't.

It's been a decade since my first book, *Who's Sorry Now?* came out. It was a tour through my Hoboken upbringing, full of real-life characters straight out of *Mean Streets* running head-on into *It's a Wonderful Life*. I grew up surrounded by a large and colorful extended family of Italian-Americans but nevertheless always at the side of the alluring and enigmatic Mary Centrella Pantoliano—seamstress-bookie-housewife, a.k.a. the boss of me and every other male in her life. The book made people laugh, and it made the *New York Times* Best Sellers list. When I told these stories, I thought they were funny. It was all a joke. Today, I would tell those stories differently, because while they're still fun stories, I now understand the dis-ease that motivated my mother's ways and the ways of other characters.

My mother was never officially diagnosed with anything. The closest she ever came to a shrink was the gypsy fortune-teller in Jersey City. Mommy was a little wacky, but so was everybody else in the neighborhood. She cooked supper, yelled at her husband, and then went off mumbling to bingo.

It took my own diagnosis for me to wake up to how wrong I was about Mommy. I thought that she was willful and refused to find the joy in living. I thought Mommy was self-centered, maybe a little selfish, and that she could have changed if she wanted to, but never that she was crazy. I didn't know crazy meant *crazy*! I didn't know the power of one's traumatic past or the monstrous nature of my mother's father. I just thought she was a drama queen who wasn't happy unless she was miserable. She designed the craziness and made it her life. I didn't understand the hold our dis-ease had on her; I thought she was faking her way through the four strokes and the heart attack that finally killed her. I thought it was her recipe for attention. It wasn't.

If crazy didn't mean *crazy*, I could also pass the buck on to my Italian-American culture. We are known to be boisterous, fun-loving, and passionate, quick-tempered and forgiving, with a zest for life. *Mommy was Italian, she wasn't a lunatic. She wasn't crazy—she, was Italian-American!* My mother was born in 1915, almost one hundred years ago! She had to quit school in the seventh grade to go to work. (Daddy, born in 1911, had to quit in the fourth.) That was the norm. Think about the stress of being first-generation Italians, of having three jobs to have enough food to feed their family then pissing half of it away on gambling. This was not crazy. This was just simply living. I thought everybody in the world operated like this.

—m—

As a kid, I decided the antidote to all my unhappiness lay inside a black and white TV set in my mother's bedroom. I had to get inside that TV set. All those actors—James Dean, Errol Flynn, Judy Garland, Lesley Howard, John Garfield, Marilyn Monroe, Francis Farmer, Vivien Leigh, Lee Marvin, Richard Burton, Natalie Wood, Spencer Tracy . . . they were there, and they had their pain too. You could see it in their close-ups. Their ambiguous pain made them special, it was a divine gift. Watching Clift, Dean, and Monroe, Judy Garland singing "Over the Rainbow," my heart in my throat and my stomach aching, churning, even now. They had me by the nuts. My favorites: Montgomery Clift, Marlon Brando, Harpo Marx, Cary Grant, Buster Keaton, W.C. Fields, Abbott and Costello, ZaSu Pitts, Humphrey Bogart. They inspired me to dream. My dream kept me warm at night, protecting me from my frigid fear of failure! The fear that I'd wind up back in the projects. That I'd never be good enough.

Early on, I decided that Hollywood would be my asylum. I would exile myself!

The word *asylum* evokes images of crazy people in restraints, undergoing lobotomies, salivating; middle-aged men and women in blue gowns sipping apple juice out of Dixie cups—scary stuff. But an asylum is also a sanctuary, a place of relief. A safe haven.

I saw a refuge and secure retreat inside our Zenith TV. It would be my retreat from the real world, a place to pursue my passion. I planned my escape from Hoboken to Hollywood. With success I'd have eternal life. When I made it to Hollywood, life would be great. And I was happy there for a long time. Then the real world broke down the door to my sanctuary. The fact is that ultimately, my asylum couldn't protect me. It wasn't a cocoon in which I could turn my tattered self into a star and then emerge and feel great forever. I couldn't just live off the initial high of success. If you aren't truthful to yourself, if you don't have a strong foundation, you're never happy to be happy.

When you grow up like I did, in a blue-collar working-class town, a mile-square city of about 38,000 people, you learn a lot of lessons from the stories you hear or overhear. People were always telling stories, sharing the news of other people's failures and accomplishments, talking about their own dreams. If you listened, that I always tried to, you could always discover something interesting to help you chart your own route. There were the stories that we told each other firsthand, and then there were the stories that we heard through song, watched on television, or read in a book. Those other stories didn't necessarily have to be learned firsthand. Somebody else could have watched the show; or maybe it was their husband or sister who'd read the book. The point is that if the information was available, it was valuable, and because somebody that you knew had access to it, it would eventually make its way to you. And you could absorb the information in your own time, in your own way. That's the kind of book I want *Asylum* to be, the kind that has a story that people want to talk about in the corner store, on the subway, during the repast after a big funeral for a family member. While my first book told of my early Hoboken upbringing, this book will bring you down the rabbit hole into my Hollywood asylum. That is where I wrestled with the things in my head for nearly four decades until, ironically, I was in a movie about brain dis-ease, and the first layer of the onion came off.

I want this book to examine what drove me from Hoboken to Hollywood. We will venture into the murky world beneath my glimmering bald noggin, inside its three pounds of fat. It can get weird in there, like a Tim Burton movie. Bats. Gooey stuff dripping from the ceiling. We'll need flashlights and guns, maybe even hand grenades, pepper spray, tire irons, and salami sandwiches. Headgear and switchblades are optional, but an extra $49.95 plus tax. This pilgrimage is not for the faint of heart. We will travel to my humble beginnings. Then to the Hollywood career that God cursed me with. We'll visit my successes, follies, and failures (I learned most from the failures). We'll travel my river of discontent and see how my seven deadlies showed themselves in my personal life and in the parts I've played.

Over the past decade, I've matured as an actor, I've had some big successes in Hollywood, and I've been recognized for them. Far more important, I've been discovered by *me*. I've begun to see me for what I really am. All my life I've studied human nature, and now I'm studying my nature. It's taken me thirty years to fully understand just this one challenge and manage it. I'm still learning.

These days I manage, monitor, and regulate my sanity daily, whether through the 12-step program, walking, yoga, or meditation . . . even masturbation. BD still lives inside of me, donning its mad hat every now and again. Believe me, I am not a saint. It's hard, but I'm taking baby steps, one at a time.

Today, with the help of different angels, I'm learning to direct my mind to good places, to see the events of my life happening not to me, but for me. To understand that not everyone is out to get me, but rather, is likely on a journey similar to mine. "No kidding, me too!" people often say to me when I tell the story of my BD. That's the reaction I hope you have to this book. I want people to understand (a) what happened to me and why, (b) how to avoid what I went through, and (c) what I'm doing today to regulate my dis-ease. That's it! That's my message.

This journey, my resurrection, has its own healing powers. A hundred years of my family's Neapolitan past, my mother's secrets, her DNA—that's what was handed down to me like an heirloom. I'm finding pieces of me still; it won't ever be over until, you know, it's over. There's still a lot I don't understand about my past, things that I still wonder about. I wonder what quality of life my mother would have had if she'd been diagnosed and had the kind of treatment I can afford. A lot of treatment options have been developed in the last forty years. Might Mommy have been a happier person? I blamed her for so much before I learned about BD. In the epilogue of my first book, I said that book was a love story for Mommy. It was. This book, then, is my amends to her and me for what I didn't know.

CHAPTER ONE

Abandon All Hope for a Better Past

Some fuckin' birthday!

The day was sunny and unseasonably warm for September. It was September 12, 1961, my tenth birthday to be exact, and I was fucking pissed! In an act of defiance, I had run away from home. From my very own birthday party, thrown by my very proud parents who, just moments ago, had tried to swindle their only son.

Mommy had called a meeting of the minds at our kitchen table, away from our birthday guests, who were scattered around the apartment, inside and out. A little block party, a crowd of aunts and uncles and cousins; I could see some of my chums through our kitchen window while Mommy explained how the numbers didn't lie. She showed me the math on the back of an unpaid bill.

JOEY, *trying to grab the envelope full of birthday cash out of Mommy's hand.* No! It's my money!

MOMMY. Are you fuckin nuts?! This party cost us $30. You made $45 in presents, so you cleared $15.

1

JOEY. Fuck you! You fuckin' fuck!

MOMMY. Watch your mouth, you little sumanabitch!

JOEY, *turning away*. I hate this house!

MOMMY. Well, click your heels. Then go kiss my ass in Macy's window.

MONK *(a.k.a. Daddy)*. Joey, will you get back here.

We see Joey running out of the ground-floor apartment past well wishers and family members yelling out, "Let it go, kid. You know how you mother gets." Joey is noticeably upset. We see JP crossing in front of the kitchen window and hear Monk yelling at Mary.

MONK. You had to start, right? You couldn't let the kid alone on his birthday?

Exterior. Wide overhead shot as Joey jogs across Adams Street toward the enormous staircase leading to P.S. 8. Mary dialogue overlapping.

MOMMY. What? And where are we gonna get the $5 for my sister Patty's boy's birthday next month too? Whose birthdays are next month? We still gotta give Poppi's Anthony the same $5 for his. Money don't grow on trees ya know!

MONK. For Christ's sake, Mary, can't you leave the kid alone!

I could still hear them yelling from across the street. They too had attended this particular institute of hardly learning. My school was usually a place to be avoided, but today it gave me an excellent vantage point. From there I could see my confused party guests milling around inside our apartment at 701 Adams Street. I could hear Mom ranting, and see her smoking her cigarette. No doubt she could see me too, but she wasn't letting on.

At that very moment in time, over fifty years ago now, a vision of my future formed in my brain. I made a promise to myself then and there. A *malocchio*, the Neapolitan curse! On myself! God willing, I would do whatever was in my power not to be anywhere within the mile square of Hoboken number eight school on Seventh and Adams when I was my parents' age. I hadn't quite hashed out the exact details of my plan, but I had a pretty good idea about how I wanted things to work out.

I remember it was a hot afternoon, and I sat on the school stoop plotting my escape. I was wearing my good luck baseball cap, the one I'd worn when we won our Little League playoff. Our team, the Troyes S.& L., were the city champs. The sun was against my back and my shadow on the street looked like a spaceman who'd dropped in from another planet, or perhaps the future. As I watched him, this character started coming out of me in that free, spontaneous way things happen for kids. The spaceman was doing a commercial. It might as well have been a commercial for my future life, because just then I made a pact with myself that I would grow up to be somebody famous and important, rich, like an actor, and that would get me out of this very scary place called Hoboken.

Life was hard. Money was scarce, our household chaotic. Survival was a daily concern. The glass was worse than half empty—somebody took a piss in it. About two years later my father would have a heart attack, and because he wasn't working, we'd have to go on welfare and move to the projects. We lived day to day, always broke. But so was the rest of the world—I thought everybody's parents gambled and fought over money.

I grew up surrounded by SYMPTOMS in big capital letters. It was a Symptomatron of symptoms. In our house we had obesity, alcoholism, gambling addictions, and behavioral risk choices like organized crime, or, in some cases, disorganized crime. My parents were degenerate gamblers; they couldn't stop. While I thought show business would pull me out of the gutter, they thought a horse named Gutter would do it, or the numbers. Strike it rich, that's what we'll do—the exacta, the mutuel field, and the daily double.

Our character foibles were threatening to undo us on a daily basis. But through sheer will and ingenuity, insulated by a wicked sense of humor and unshakable family loyalty, we inexplicably managed to keep our ship from going under, despite throwing missiles at one another.

Back then Hoboken was a town where everybody knew each other, but you learned fast that nobody should know everything about you. I was told not to say nothin' about anything that happened in our house. *Don't say nothin' and don't ask nobody nothin' either.* I don't know how much we had to hide. My mother taught us how to build our secrets, usually about money—where it came from, how we'd lost or spent it. We were great pretenders. When we had it, we didn't. When we didn't, we said we did. Mommy and I kept secrets from Daddy and then Daddy and I kept them from her. My mother monitored the flow of information in our house because she had to control everything. She didn't like surprises.

She was quite the character, my mother. I miss her very much. I used to feel like there weren't enough adjectives to describe the kind of person she was or the kinds of things she used to do. Mommy embraced her contradictions and expressed them continuously. If finding the right words to describe my mother was difficult, you couldn't say that it was for lack of trying. She was at the heart of most of my dinner-table anecdotes and the laughter-drenched stories I used to tell when I was out with my friends.

"Noooo—your mom really said that?" my friends asked, their mouths open and eyes wide in amazement. "She said that?" Stories about Mommy never failed to get that level of reaction. She was not for the weak of heart or stomach. She defied categorization, the woman you expected, even wanted, to see in a novel or on the screen, but not in your neighborhood, where the status quo prevails and lives are neatly contained.

I didn't want to be relegated to the predetermined roles of those other men in her life. Daddy (Dominic/Monk) Pantoliano, was a soft-spoken guy, a workaday fellow who was always broke and always behind, and—just like Mommy—blew through his wages and his chances at the track, hoping and betting that one day he would win and it would put us ahead. Eventually she kicked him out, and Florie moved in. Florie was an honest-to-God, card-carrying wise guy, and like my father, he quickly earned my mother's disapproval. Florie (who also happened to be my cousin, though his relationship with my mother was not really official because she and my father never got divorced) had easy access to large sums of cash, a luxury that came with chronic nightmares and the very real possibility of being sent to sleep with the fishes or thrown back in the can perpetually hanging over him. Flo was a career criminal. At the time of his release from prison, circa 1964 at age forty-nine, he had spent twenty-one years of his life in different federal prisons. A "no-good sumanabitch" was what my mother called every male in her life who was old enough to have hair on his balls, because, in her mind, we were all selfish shits every bit deserving of her disdain.

Reflecting back on my first decade, I can see that even as a ten-year-old kid I knew that "money didn't grow on trees." I had to grow my own, which meant, what the fuck was I gonna do? I didn't know what exactly the challenges would be, I just knew in my heart that I would do whatever it took to get far away from Seventh and Adams.

I knew education wouldn't be my ticket out. At that point I didn't know that I had dyslexia. Just that everybody thought I was stupid. My parents were frustrated and thought I wasn't trying hard enough. None of us knew what those particular letters in the alphabet, ADHD, might signify.

At age ten, I was one week into my second run in the fifth grade. Having been held back, I was already nervous, feeling this mounting anxiety about reading and writing, and not being able to deliver. More would be asked of me in each coming year, and if I couldn't even hack elementary school, how could I expect to achieve greatness? Even now it's hard for me to go back to that painful, uncertain time.

My growing anxiety led to spiraling depression—though my ten-year-old brain didn't know to call it that—and a feeling of emptiness that had to be filled. I thought the hole inside of me was a character defect, a chink in me, a dented tin can. Even as a kid I knew there were things that could fill that hole. Food would do it. I'd be at home crying about something, and my father would say, "What's the matter? Jesus Christ! Let me make you a sandwich. You want a sandwich?" So I'd eat a salami sandwich with provolone and roasted peppers, and stuff those feelings down. By the time I was ten years old I was on my way to becoming a fat fuck. On my next birthday every kid in Hoboken would be outdoing themselves, making jokes at my expense. "Ah, here he comes. Look at this fat fuck. Hey, tubby, come here, what'd you swallow, a basketball?"

The birth of a symptom! Being fat was only humiliating when I was reminded of it, which I constantly was. I was always the last guy to be picked for a game of stickball, or Johnny on a Pony. I was the guy no girls would look at. The big target for bullies. They would pick on me and at some point I would blow up. I'd be so enraged I'd just see white, and the next thing I knew they were tearing me off somebody, or they were tearing him off me.

By the time I was twelve or thirteen, enough people had made fun of me that I decided I was going to lose weight. And the feeling I got from starving myself was better than the feeling I was getting from stuffing myself! Instead of stuffing those feelings down, now I was starving those feelings down. I would continue to have food issues for decades to come, but neither feast nor famine ever worked as a permanent solution.

One thing led to another—dyslexia and ADHD and depression led to the eating, dieting/starving, fighting, and alcohol, then the drugs came later. The behaviors that would later undo me took root. Memories of my past that were too painful to keep in my conscious mind ended up stored in my unconscious mind, waiting to resurface years later when I was at my most vulnerable.

Only after a lot of therapy did I understand the genesis of my thick Neapolitan noggin and how it works. But even back then I knew one thing: I was headed for Hollywood. Acting was going to cure me, lift me up, and get me out.

—m—

As a kid, I'd run down those flights of stairs two at a time, the school bell still ringing in my ears. Still out of breath from my long run home, I'd break off the best end of a loaf of Gustozo's crusty bread and fill it with salami and mozzarella cheese drenched in olive oil, vinegar with a pinch of salt then pepper *and* my secret weapon (don't tell nobody) . . . oregano! Then I'm seated and ready to begin my after school ritual on the floor watching Mommy's TV, my back resting against her bed, the crumbs dusting my folded legs. Gazing into that box, I'd wonder, *How?*

I'd see an actor whose name ended in a vowel—Frank

Sinatra, Lou Costello, Jimmy Durante, Perry Como, and another Monroe Street buddy, Jimmy Roselli. My Italian-American colleagues knew what it was like to live in poverty not much different from my own, and they became somebody. (Even Sammy Davis Jr., my Italian brother from another mother, who was Sicilian! Until he became Jewish.) *But they did it!* Why not me? If I could only get inside Mommy's TV like Sinatra! Mommy knew him. He came from the same street as me, Monroe Street.

But Mary's Joey? Was he tough enough to make it? Deep down inside, I never felt tough, I never even felt Italian. I felt the coward. Having been tested in the gutters of Monroe Street and having failed miserably, I was a chicken, a target. I was no tough guy. But stick me in them nice clothes—those suits and silk shirts and ties—I could fool them all. I was a hustler, a born charmer, and a natural liar. I knew that if I sported the right wardrobe, and the right mannerisms, and greeted the world with bluster and bravado, then it might not see the scared and moody little boy playacting with cues from his genes and upbringing.

Once inside that refuge called television, I would use the pain and anger and confusion I experienced in my own life to breathe life into characters that other people created from their own pain and confusion. I'd find people with the same need to be in the TV—to be somebody—whether through their acting or lighting or sound or directing. All of us in a box. That box would be my asylum. I had no money and was low on education. What I did have was blind ambition. I was relentless; I was never going to give up. My bank account demanded I forge ahead. I learned I had to hustle to survive. Call me crazy, but I'm not stupid. In high school, I was buying T-shirts legit at wholesale for two bucks each, then I charged the kids ten bucks, telling them the shirts were SWAG (Stolen Without A Gun)! Me crazy? Like a *fox*! I am my mother's son. It's true. In so many ways: the good, the bad, even the indifferent. She was as passionate as she was cunning. Never went to college, never took a business course, but she knew how to work people's emotional clocks and re-gifted that to me. I'm a button pusher. You don't learn that in school, anyway, so it's probably good we never wasted much time there.

When my family lived in Hoboken we moved eight times. Then I went to high school in Fort Lee (for six months), then we moved to Cliffside Park (for three weeks), then to Fairview, then back to Cliffside Park until graduation, and then in short order we moved four more times between three towns; always one step ahead of the rent collector. That was a lot of new people to meet, assess, and use to my advantage.

My ambition knew no limits. I didn't know how, I just knew I'd make *it* happen. I would earn respect through the quality of my work. When I was rich and famous, success would prove to me—who cares about anybody else—I didn't need people to love me. I'd show them I WAS NOT A PIECE OF SHIT! I would buy the things that would define me, and never worry or fight over money again. I'd have "the stuff that dreams are made of."

All the pain and sadness, the hunger that lived in me would disappear because I'd have it all.

—〰—

My mother didn't want me to leave home, and she was afraid to dream. That had been beaten out of her. A child of the Depression, she was afraid she'd be left all alone, with nothing and nobody. "What are you crazy? Don't ask for too much, don't get your heart broken." She didn't want me to love anyone or anything more than her. Not even acting. "And what if you get hurt?

Better not take that chance." Always: "Don't go up there, don't do that. What are you going to do? Move to New York? What are people gonna say? Stay here where it's safe. Stay here where we have control over our existence."

Florie, on the other hand, encouraged my ambition. He always told me, "Sinatra did it and so can you. Remember that these people wipe their ass when they shit just like you. They are no different. But you have to work really hard, and you have to put your mind to it." He knew that going to Hollywood was a major risk. We had no money to take chances on a glamorous career—thanks to him, of course.

Florie was one of the few people who supported my dream of being an actor, but he also warned me and put a curse on me. He assured me that if I failed, it would be my own damn fault. He used to say, "Every chance I had, I fucked up. Nothing bad that ever happened to me just happened to me. Remember: every hour I spent in prison I earned. I was no fuckin' victim, I created the chains that bound me! Every move I made? The wrong move. You want to get something out of this life? Then break your fuckin' back and get it. There is no easy money, Joey. You put your heart and soul into this. Into your dreams! Always remember, IT'S AN INSIDE JOB! *You* make it happen. If it don't? Well fuck 'em all, you tried. How many people can say that? Don't wind up like me, kid!"

I wasn't the only one who sought an asylum. There are 120,000 members of the Screen Actors Guild, and Hollywood was going to save us all. We were all going to get everything we wanted. We were all gonna be somebody. And when we got everything we thought would fill us up, it was never enough.

You don't have to go to Hollywood to find an asylum. We

all want to be important. We all want the world to remember us by name. We are all trying to fill an emptiness.

The asylum could be money. It could be politics. Somebody said politics is show business for ugly people. It could be YouTube. Everybody thinking, I could be somebody! I could be a contender!

In that great Depression-era movie *My Man Godfrey*, there's a scene in the ballroom at the Waldorf-Ritz Hotel. All the glittery people are there. At the bar two men are observing.

BLAKE. This place slightly resembles an insane asylum.

BULLOCK. Well, all you need to start an asylum is an empty room and the right kind of people.

—m—

In 1973 I had high hopes, but at the same time I prided myself on knowing my limitations. Take for example, Cary Grant. Loved him, love his work; he is by far, my favorite movie star/actor ever. I knew I could never fill Cary Grant's canoes, but if I could act like he did in *Arsenic and Old Lace* or *His Girl Friday* and have his comic sensibility, I'd be set! The man born Archibald Leach was a clown. Well shit, so was I! He was self-effacing, fearless too. And he certainly knew what it was like to be poor and sing for your supper.

Show business is a lot like Hoboken. To survive you have to win over and over again! At all costs. For me two things were blatantly clear. In order for somebody to win a role, somebody had to lose. Kill or be killed. My chosen profession was not that far removed from being a longshoreman. My father used to go down to the docks for the shape-up, when longshoremen were picked for a day's work. I went to all the cattle calls hoping I'd be lucky enough to get the job. Every time I did, what mattered most was getting the next job, expecting that the next big break would keep the misery inside me at bay.

—m—

Two score years and some 196 IMDB credits ago, I thought I'd made the escape of the century when I broke out of Hoboken. At the age of eighteen, I was a boy on the cusp of becoming a man, living on the island of Manhattan, liberated from my unfortunate genetic bonds to that particularly cursed New Jersey breed: the Y-chromosome Pantoliano-Centrellas. In this new world, I was dedicated to the proposition that not all men are created broke, imprisoned, and destined to degradation by Mary "Mommy" Centrella—the single-handed first, second, third, and fourth horsewoman of the apocalyptic inevitability for all the men in her life.

I left our family's apartment in Jersey, my mother sobbing behind me in the pouring rain as I made my great escape, running to an acting career that would erase all my misery. Failure was not an option.

Leaving New Jersey behind I had this naïve belief that I would also be leaving behind the dangers and vulnerabilities I had experienced growing up in a scary place like Hoboken. Drug and alcohol addiction were dangers that would affect me only in that environment. I was convinced that I was heading for a different world. Once I escaped, I couldn't go back. I would never go back. I was certain that by becoming an actor I would redefine not only my destiny, but also myself. I could invent a brand-new me. Hell, maybe I would even be able to finally get rid of that stupid nickname, "Joey Pants," that had plagued me my whole childhood.

In the final chapter of *Who's Sorry Now*, I wrote about what it took for me to be able to leave home, and by that I don't mean anything so esoteric as courage or internal resolve. I'm talking about having to find a way to move physically past my mother, who had absolutely no intention of letting me pursue life as an actor. She closed, then locked, the front door and used her body as a blockade, all the while screaming the lyrics to Connie Francis's breakthrough song, "Who's Sorry Now?" at the top of her lungs in a gravelly voice, as the smoke from the Chesterfield she was inhaling and exhaling laced her lips and her beautiful Neapolitan nose. But I did manage to leave! And believe me, at the time what I was feeling was far from sorrow. The last two lines of that chapter are: "I had broken free, and I was alive. Joey Pants, meet the world. World, this is Joey Pants."

What I did not comprehend when I left my mother's house for good, and to be honest not even when I wrote my last book, was that even though I did leave in many ways, I didn't break free; I didn't escape. The Hoboken of my childhood made me who I am. I didn't know I would always be my mother's son. And even though I was keen on introducing myself to the world, there was still so much about myself that I didn't know or understand. There were things about me that I had not yet learned to recognize, things I carried with me, in me. Things that sometimes stood like a blockade between me and the life I wanted; the future I'd envisioned for myself. Either that or else they pulled me back in time, back home, to New Jersey and Mommy and all the things that she was and all the things that she handed down to me.

CHAPTER TWO

Lying for a Living

The dream is always the same.

I'm flying; that's how I usually know I'm dreaming. I love that feeling. In my younger years, I flew a lot. Never too high—nothing too scary—maybe thirty feet, tops. I'm flying, floating, ya feel me? I'm also looking sharp, wearing a very nice cocoa brown silk tuxedo with tails. Think Liberace. I got my top hat with brown velvet trim and I got patent leather kicks.

So I'm dreaming in living color—I'm floating above the freeway, getting the lay of the land.

I'm going to the Academy Awards. I've been nominated for Best Actor! (Now I'm sure I'm dreaming!) This dream, each time I have it's a little different. Today I'm floating above a big white stretch limo provided by my studio. But one thing remains the same: I'm always late. And if you've ever been to a movie theater you know that being late guarantees you're gonna run into trouble.

From my point of view I see that traffic's moving slowly, and that my limo's sunroof is opening, and *there she is*! God love her—Mommy's dead now, over twenty years, but out she comes. Now she's banging on the roof of the limo, screaming to the driver as they head south on the 101. Wait, south? What the fuck? He's going the wrong way! The Kodak Theatre is north! It becomes clear why Mommy's hanging out of the sunroof wielding a bouquet of orchids like a sword and yelling at the surrounding cars to make way so that we can exit.

I'm supposed to be on the red carpet by now and somehow this dope, a professional limousine driver, has been going in the opposite direction of the theater! I realize I'm being pulled by the limo, like a balloon on a string, connected to something inside that limo by my umbilical cord which is popping out through my shirt buttons. The driver has now picked up speed and it's a very bumpy ride. We're going faster and I'm being jerked from side to side, ducking telephone wires and other hair-raising obstacles, my belly being torn. I'm fighting the pain as I pull myself toward the limo by my cord. Each time I take hold of my lifeline, I can see it's filled with such vibrant colors (and they say you can't dream in color!) all mixing and moving under the milky white skin, like a technicolor sausage. I see remnants of my past and pieces of my future flickering through the tube. I'm moments away from reaching the sunroof that will lead me inside the limo. I call out to Mommy but she can't hear me. Our driver is moving fast down Fountain Avenue now, buzzing through traffic, going into oncoming cars, horns blazing, and yanking me from side to side of the limo. I'm nearly colliding with telephone poles, holding on to my lifeline for dear life! Finally I grasp the sunroof, white knuckled, but Mommy's disappeared inside.

I pull myself into the safe embrace of the limo interior, tumbling down on top of my Aunt Rosie and Aunt Thanna. Mommy is up against the glass partition.

MOMMY, *sautéing our driver*. How'd you get on the wrong free-way you moron? What are you, fuckin' blind? Your Seeing Eye dog on strike? My Joey is up for Best Actor! You working for the competition, ya prick? He's winning that Oscar tonight!"

As Mommy is surgically giving this asshole an additional asshole, I am gnawing myself free of my umbilical cord. Then I suddenly notice something eerily familiar about this scene: sights, smells . . . The new car smell dissipates and smoke from Mommy's Chesterfields overpowers the place. We have shifted from Hollywood to Hoboken, and my sister Maryann is in the car, only she's fifteen years younger. We're now parked in front of Failla's Funeral Parlor, in Daddy's funeral limo. Six pallbearers are trying to jam a coffin through our open passenger-side door. I push the coffin back with all my strength, refusing to let it in the car. I slam our door shut and catch sight of my reflection in the door's window. I'm one of the pallbearers. My sister Maryann is crying, reenacting the events from Mommy's funeral. I remember her crying. Aunt Thanna, observing the drama while comforting my sister, is hugging Maryann while holding her false teeth in one hand and sticking a piece of Trident onto her upper palate with the other.

MARYANN, *now sobbing*. No more Mommy! *Sob, sob.* No more!

AUNT THANNA, *catching my eye, whispering to me*. It's too late now!

I open the opposite passenger door opens, and we hear the screaming crowd . . .

Exterior, red carpet. Four pair of feet run along with the three ladies in their evening gowns, huffing and puffing.

We're in front of the big glass doors of the Kodak Theatre, past the red carpet and the screaming fans. We're all sweating, running, out of breath. Mommy is next to me now, and it's grown dark, indicating the passage of time. The crew and photographers are pulling up stakes. It's a wrap, the workers are rolling up the red carpet and sweeping up the cigarette butts and plastic champagne glasses. Hollywood moves on, and this is what's left.

All the workers looked like I felt . . . miserable.

I'm trying to explain to the gatekeeper (who by the way resembles the gatekeeper from *The Wizard of Oz*) what happened and why he's gotta let me in, or I won't get my gift bag. But he's can't, he's following orders, I'm too late, and that's fuckin' that. Mommy tries sweet-talking the guy:

MOMMY. *Screaming* Douchebag!

GATEKEEPER. Look lady. . .

JOEY. Good one, Ma.

GATEKEEPER. Look Lady . . . you better. . .

MOMMY. STRONZO! Open that door!

GATEKEEPER. How many times do I . . .

And they're off!

During all this commotion his voice starts trailing off, and I can see my gatekeeper beginning to change form. He is now my fourth-grade teacher, the woman who took my reading book away from me for the year, suggesting I was a fucking flop. Then she becomes every other person or teacher who ever said to me, "You're lazy," "You're stupid," or "You can't." Now suddenly I can see that the gatekeeper is me. It's me. I'm the one who's been getting in the way of me all along. It's biblical! Joey is the gatekeeper? Why did I hold me back, keep myself from going too far? I could'a been somebody! I should have been looking out for me. Where's the fucking rule book for this shit?

By now Mommy has seen enough. She does not accept this cock and bull story.

MOMMY. Fuck this.

And we see Mary click her heels three times (just like Dorothy did) and we hear Mommy say

MOMMY. There's no place like Rome. There's no place like Rome. Let's get the fuck outta here.

We're determined, people, we're not gonna take no for an answer! "We got tickets, and they ain't scalped."

Now my dream shifts, as if I'm changing a channel, and I can hear Billy Crystal MCing, making jokes. The audience is laughing. We're crawling on our bellies in this air-conditioning duct, and our shoes are thumping on the aluminum sides, and there's dust everywhere.

We hear music, and it's getting closer and louder and another winner is announced—did they do Best Actor yet? Who is the audience applauding? Suddenly my mother gets her turquoise dress—the same one we buried her in—caught on a screw, and I hear the dress tear, and she says, "Sumanabitch," and she's coughing, because, you know, her Chesterfields play as big a part in my imaginary life as they did in real life. If this were *Mission: Impossible*, right now Mommy would be dangling on a cable like Tom Cruise, except she'd have a Chesterfield in her mouth, and it would be the ashes that trip the alarm.

We finally get to the end and I kick the vent open and we pour out, me and Mommy and Aunt Rosie and Aunt Thanna, right into the lobby, dusting ourselves off like James Bond would have done.

Now in my dream—always at this point in my dream—I'm hearing the nominations for Best Actor in a motion picture. I'm on the outside of the doors that I never get through cause, BAM!, I always wake up? I never find out. But magically my ladies are now safely seated, and Mommy's telling George Clooney what a dick the door guy was!

Over Mommy's chatter with George I hear Annette Bening over the public address system. "The Oscar for Best Actor in a motion picture goes to . . ."

And I wake up!

What gives?

—〰—

The dream begins again, yet this time, I'm still awake. I'm in the back of the house and I see the other me stage right, in a blue tux. I'm kissing my wife. I'm being called up onstage to get a trophy for Best Supporting Actor in a TV series. Wait, this isn't a dream, it's a nightmare! My brain is screaming. This can't be right. I'm supposed to win an *Oscar*! Winning an Emmy is like being the world's tallest midget; Who gives a shit? Cut! Cut! Stop the action! We're shooting the wrong scene!

It was a September evening in 2003, and we were in the Shrine Auditorium in downtown Los Angeles. This was all very real, but it still played out like a dream. I was there, but I was watching myself being there. I was standing in back, looking at myself sitting next to Nancy. We were surrounded by great character actors. Tony Shalhoub was behind me. Edie Falco was in front of me. Then there was James Gandolfini, and Michael Imperioli.

We were sitting in the lower right-hand corner of the theater, and we all figure none of us was going to win because we had such shitty seats—on the aisle, but all the way over on the side.

So we're sitting there, and all of a sudden, Shalhoub was announced—he won for lead actor in *Monk*, and, dreamlike, I watched him get up. I started to wonder whether it was a coincidence that Monk was also my father's nickname. A few minutes later, during a commercial break, we were standing in the dark and I heard somebody whisper, "Joey Pants, Joey!" And I said "Over here." I could see a dimly lit figure, I realized it was the actor Michael Chiklis. He leaned toward me and whispered in my ear, "I'm gonna hand it to you." Then he was gone.

We return to our seats to watch the big screen tribute to all the people in our industry who died that year. This is my favorite part of any award ceremony. It's always very touching to me, probably because I have a close relationship with death, having practically grown up in a funeral parlor. Mommy dragged us there every time someone in Hoboken died, because there was lots of free food. I start to choke up, partly because among those honored is Gregory Hines, a very dear and loving friend. I made *Running Scared*, one of my first important movies, with him and Billy Crystal.

When it was over, suddenly there was Michael Chiklis holding an envelope and walking to the microphone. He simply said, "And the Emmy for best performance by a supporting actor in a dramatic series goes to my friend Joey Pants." I had known I had a good chance, but I was still totally unprepared. Nancy hugged my hat falls off, I pick it up and stumbled toward the stage. On the way Tony Shalhoub congratulated me, and so did Edie Falco, Stanley Tucci and Michael Imperioli in the front row. Five or six steps later I was up on the stage hugging Michael Chiklis.

I was standing up there beside Chiklis, trying to see Nancy. I say hello to a couple of people standing there and I was holding on to Michael, and all the time my cell phone was just vibrating like crazy in the vest pocket of my tuxedo, which I had made in Italy for the occasion.

It was so bright up there. How many performers get to be on that stage with 30 million people watching? I started thanking the first person who made a difference in my life as an actor:

Florio Isabella, my stepfather.

I was flooded with gratitude and humility. I wanted to be recognized by my peers. I saw Jennifer Aniston and I see all these movie stars and TV stars. They were all lit up. Even with the lights on me I could see these people. And they were happy, they were smiling. Some had tears of joy, because they knew about my trek to get there. My trek has been their trek. Ninety percent of success is showing up, and like many of them, I've been showing up forever. No artist succeeds by talent alone, there are other forces at play. Did I win for my performance? So few do.

I had been invited tonight. I'd walked in through the front door, and still, I felt like I had sneaked in. It was good to be there, even better to win. You get to see everybody all dressed up so pretty. You get to hang with the "greats" and the "near-greats," you're part of that crew. Of course, this moment too passes like the weather, you're up, then you're down. That's the sin of Hollywood. You're never remembered for your personal best. It's always, What have you done lately, Mr Shakespeare?

But in 2003, Emmy voters gave me a trophy. She had wings like an angel that were sharp, slightly dangerous. The statuette was heavy, similar to the many trophys Daddy had won during his bowling career. Everyone kept smiling, looking at me, and I imagined that this would have some kind of benefit for me—not for my career, but an emotional benefit. It was a high. It felt good at that moment.

But then my voices started whispering negative thoughts in the back of my mind: "Big deal, it's only a Emmy. It ain't enough. You're not enough."

When I was a little boy I would watch the Academy Awards and dream about my acceptance speech. Now I can't watch any awards show, let alone the Oscars. I'm too jealous. It's like watching the woman I love marry my best friend.

When I was a kid, how could I have known about the politics of show business, all the lobbying and money that goes into winning an award? A studio can spend half a million dollars in advertising just to get a nomination, and then it's a million dollars to try to get the opportunity for a win. And all those awards shows! There are so many now, you should win just for showing up!

That's why, even as I stood there clutching my Emmy, I felt like that song: "Is That All There Is?" I had hoped for so much more. Secretly, I wanted to be greater than them all. To be a 1940's movie star. I wanted to play the best parts in the best pictures. To be the first guy through the door. Instead, until *The Fugitive* in 1992, I felt like I had built a career on scraps, waiting for five actors to turn a part down before the directors came to me. Cursed with my Neopolitan attitude: There won't be enough. Don't ask for too much, you'll only get hurt. Or if you succeed, you'll have to pay a terrible price. All the time that I was incredibly ambitious, I was also afraid of getting the success I deserved, because I was afraid to ask for it. I have centuries and centuries of Neapolitan ancestry ingrained in me.

But that night I didn't get to keep the trophy they handed me. When I left the stage, they took it right back. How's that for symbolism? A beautiful escort led me to the table loaded with gold-plated angels and assigned me one. Then I went off to do the press stuff—ten different kiosks, news media, print, foreign press.

This was Hollywood, right? The big time. And yet, I was preoccupied with this feeling inside, or the lack of. A numbness. I needed something, a drink, a pick-me-up to pop through that cloud. There were bars to the left of me, faces to the right. I got a double vodka, because I had to feel good tonight. I couldn't drink like I wanted to, because I had to work the next day. I was working on the new CBS show "The Hander," and I had a very early call. HBO had put me up at the Peninsula, a really nice hotel in Beverly Hills. And HBO let us just charge everything. My son, Marco, and some friends had dinner there the night of the Emmys, and back home in Connecticut my daughter Dani and a bunch of our friends were watching the show on television. *Access Hollywood* had sent a crew to cover our family if I won. I wondered if the fix was in, if they knew before I did.

I was working the room. All our dear friends were there. Friends from the days when we didn't have anything and we were just actors trying to make a living and make a name for ourselves. I drifted off to another party and wound up at the Peninsula again with Nancy, my darling Nancy. I love her so much, and she was so understanding that night.

She would have to be. The dark thoughts were there that night—a night of celebration and success and friendship, and being part of an industry I love, and the industry telling me I was OK. But in the next few years it would get worse. And I would pound myself for those dark thoughts. *You're not grateful for all this, shame on you! Look what you got. What's wrong with you?*

In the coming months the bright lights of the Shrine Auditorium would fade as I was drawn inexorably toward the darkest night of my soul.

—⚊⚊—

Three decades earlier, the friends I was with that night and I were all the same—just starting out in the business. Except you couldn't really call it business, because there was no money, just training. In the first seven years of my career I made no more than $1,000 a year. We weren't looking for a break. I was looking for the next tenement basement where somebody was trying to make a play happen.

When I was eighteen, I went to New York City with nothing but a New Jersey accent. I was in acting school and studying with the famous Herbert Berghof, part of my never-ending love affair with people who thought less of me, who thought I was some street urchin who couldn't speak English. I wanted his approval, but I was a kid and I was surrounded by people in their midtwenties to early thirties. I swept up around the place and worked as stage manager so I could get my lessons for free.

HB Studios was very affordable then, and is today. Herbert Berghof had worked with Max Reinhardt in Vienna, and was a charter member of the Actors Studio. He married Uta Hagen, and they ran HB Studios. I always thought HB stood for Herbert Berghof. Years later I found out that it really stood for Hagen Berghof. HB Studios was and is at 120 Bank Street in two three-story brownstones, right next to each other.

The office was on the first floor, and through a door on the right was a large rehearsal hall. They had a one-hundred-seat theater and classrooms large enough to accommodate makeshift kitchen sets. They were on rollers, as were couches and chairs, so that when we did scene studies the set could be changed in five minutes. The place was noisy: doors always slamming and people singing and piano players doing scales.

When I first met Mr. Berghof I insisted that he teach me and not put me in a beginner's class. I know from chutzpah. I loved the characters there. Like John, an effeminate guy who was probably in his late thirties, who worked as the studio secretary, setting schedules and counting the class size. He had a dog named

James Dean that was no more than four pounds. John always kept James Dean at his side in a travel bag.

Week after week I sat in Mr. Berghof's class, diligently soaking up whatever lessons I could: Listening to Herbert and the students discuss scenes the acting partners brought in. Watching the others doing scenes, taking in all the criticism Berghof leveled at them, and trying to take notes. Ron Silver was in that first class. So were Roberta Wallach, Paul Thomas, Al Sinkys. Now Ron and Al are gone. I can still remember Al's beautiful baritone voice. He was my first acting mentor and teacher, much more important to me through my developmental years at HB Studios than HB himself. Al was a complicated fellow and his demons could entertain mine. The man had enormous talent, but he epitomized the gifted actor who falls short of the brass ring. He didn't realize that show business is schmooze, or that winning is 90 percent luck and 10 percent talent. Al was 10 percent luck and 90 percent talent. Working the rooms is where it happens. Three minutes with the right director could have changed the game for Al.

I started bringing my tape recorder with me to class. I was embarrassed by my undiagnosed dyslexia. I couldn't keep up. I thought I was stupid and lazy, but I had to learn to work despite my disabilities. I sat there for four months before I found the courage to get up in front of the class and do a scene. I had gone from high school to an HB master class, and most of the actors there were old pros, with nine or ten years of working experience on me.

My entire body of work at that point was a play in high school, but I was able to start doing some scenes that were right for my emotional and geographic wheelhouse—*A Hatful of Rain*, *Lovers and Other Strangers*, *Death of a Salesman*.

Once I had a few of these under my belt, I started going from

theater to theater, saying I'd played those parts in regional theaters. So they couldn't check up on me, I found regional theaters
that had gone out of business. My résumé was filled with un-
truths. I had worked on the character in acting school, but I never
did it in a real play, never did it in a theater. I had never been inside of the theaters I listed. Even the directors didn't exist. I took
a chance that I wouldn't be found out, because I just couldn't go
in with a blank piece of paper.

In those first three years I worked five times harder than anyone else in order to be ready for a job. If somebody else worked
on a scene for class for three hours, I put in fifteen hours. mem-
orized my lines and then read off script during auditions, making the director think I'd be even better after rehearsal. I found
wannabe directors and talentless playwrights and auditioned for
plays that would never see the light of day. They were my opportunity to fall on my nose. I could practice with these guys in
a basement room of a tenement building, where they had five
kitchen chairs and a "stage" that was eight feet by ten feet, and
get the experience of acting in front of people. The experience of
going into a room filled with strangers, having prepared a character that I thought would be interesting to them.

The first scene I did in class was from *A Hatful of Rain*. I did
it with Michael Kell, who went on to act in three David Rabe original works and became a very accomplished playwright. Michael
and I were inseparable in those early years. He had wavy dark
brown hair and freckles, loved to dance, and was on a bowling
team. Michael and I rehearsed for three or four days before
bringing the scene to class with Mr. B. When we started I was
scared to death, I even felt flu-like symptoms, but then soemthing
came over me. A calm, spiritual in nature, inexplicable and powerful, like riding a wave. when the scene ended I had no cogni-

tive memory of what had occurred. I've chased that feeling for forty years, and I'll chase it the rest of my life. I've never known who I was, except in between "action" and "cut."

Mr. Berghof was a towering guy. He had ice blue eyes, and he was bald—like I would be in four short years—except for long white hair on the sides. He wore white cowboy shirts with white pearl buttons and had a big Buddha belly. He smoked all the time and had cigarette burns on his western shirts. That day I noticed him reacting differently; both Michael and I noticed. I hadn't felt his full attention on me before in rehearsal. When the scene was over I could see in Berghof's eyes that he thought there was something there, that he was surprised, impressed. I had gotten his attention, and that's all I needed to keep going back.

I had a "gift." Well, that's what they called it in acting school. I was emotionally available. I learned how to recall appropriate emotions from my life experiences; I could draw on my past for the future life of the characters I was playing. Using the "affective memory" technique, I practiced recalling specific moments from my past, and put them in my emotional toolbox for use as needed.

This is how it worked: First I'd get into a relaxed position, in a chair, with my eyes closed. Then I'd slowly re-live events I saw in my mind's eye. It was as if I was in our kitchen back in the 1960's. I could see the table, see the tablecloth, smell the tomato sauce cooking. I could see the bread on the table. By bringing up my past and using my imagination, and practicing again and again, could trigger emotions I'd felt back then and use them now. When I heard my Uncle Popeye's voice in this memory, I would experience on stage the feeling I had when I was with him. I'd use this technique only if the play didn't produce the right emotions in me. Those were the tools, the combination of being "emotionally available" and having been a bullshit artist my entire life. I enjoyed the work.

Emotions were acceptable in acting school. They are our instrument, I was in luck, because when I was growing up emotions were always acceptable in my house. You could say that we were always entitled to our feeling, especially when we had nothing else. My family was also conniving, in the sense that we were always trying to beat the system in order to get ahead, or just to survive. Everyone that lived on welfare was doing the same. Dishonesty was rewarded; I learned to lie, cheat and steal my way out of any jam. So I became incredibly comfortable in acting school. Also I was insane, so I was ideally suited to being an actor: I lied and I was highly emotional.

But remember, acting isn't feeling. Acting has nothing to do with being able to cry on demand. Acting is the magic of transcending an experience so that the *audience* has the feeling. I can be up on the stage, laughing or crying up a storm, and the audience feels nothing. What's the fucking point to that, right? So I still had a lot to learn.

—m—

The stereotype is true. Wanna hang out with actors? Go out to eat in Manhattan.

My first job was at O'Henry's Bar on Sixth Avenue in the Village. Yes sir, I've got about eight months of experience, I told the manager. I gave him a list of the restaurants I'd never seen the inside of, along with references and phone numbers. Had the manager checked up on me, he would have been chatting with several of my classmates from HB Studios, where I was studying the other kind of acting. It was such a rush to practice acting with civilians. I am the original backdoor man. The guy who can talk his way into anything, whether it's a waiting job or a party in Cannes.

If I was working on a scene in acting class, at the restaurant I would act as if I were that character. I would wait on people in character, like Billy Bibbit in *Cuckoo's Nest*. I wwo . . . wwo . . . would stutter. "The sp . . . sp . . . special of the day . . ." The diners always interrupted. "OK, we know what we want. We don't want the specials. We just want hamburgers." Did this mean my acting was good or bad?

The times were affordable; rent control was in effect. I could be an independent guy. There were lots of jobs, and if I needed a job I could get it. I would work at one restaurant, get myself fired, and then the same guy who owned that restaurant would pay me off the books at another restaurant. Once I learned the trade I could work at night and audition for plays during the day. If I got a play, I would shift my waiting hours around or just quit. Being in a play always meant three weeks of rehearsals and then twelve performances: Thursday, Friday, Saturday, and Sunday, for three weeks. Later, when I landed roles in professional plays, like my first Actors' Equity play, I would give up my job and, if it was out of town, sublet my one-bedroom apartment.

I used to see the great director Elia Kazan just walking along on the sidewalk on the Upper West Side. I loved to walk. One night I followed him for miles. It was one in the morning. I was on the other side of the street, dreaming of working with him one day. Then I saw he would be doing *The Last Tycoon*. I sent a picture and résumé to his office in the hopes that he would see me. He returned my picture and résumé in a letter saying, "Thank you for your interest. Unfortunately all the casting will be done in Los Angeles. I know how expensive these photographs are, so we are sending back your photograph. And best of luck to you." I mean, who does that? A guy at that level does something like that!

Three years into this life, three years after my escape from Hoboken, I turned twenty-one and found myself in White River Junction, Vermont, freezing my ass off for the privilege of doing a winter theater festival. It was 40 degrees below zero. It was so cold my nose hairs froze together. I was supposed to be there for four months as part of Green Mountain Rep, performing one-act plays by Henrik Ibsen and Israel Horovitz in a little ski town where all anyone wanted to do after a full day on the slopes was go straight to bed. Theater, anyone?

I'd never been on skis before. Hell, I didn't even know what a ski resort was. It was my first time outside of the New York/New Jersey area. Until then, New York City was the extent of my world beyond Hoboken and the Jersey Shore. I'd made it across the Hudson into Manhattan, where I was living in a boarding house on 90th Street.

One day I saw they were auditioning for the Vermont gig and I showed up. There I encountered what I thought was the most beautiful girl in the world. Her name was Nonie. She was from Chicago and was working as a stage manager but really wanted to act. She and I hit it off. I did fine in the audition, got the call, and headed north for my first real professional acting job. Sure, I was going to be a star in Vermont, but I was really going to be with Nonie again.

When I got there, Nonie was not—she'd taken a children's theater job in Atlanta. And now there I was alone, thrown in with a bunch of intellectuals. Not only was I the youngest guy there, I had nothing in common with the rest of them.

For starters, because of my learning disability, my days were filled with a lot of confusion, isolation, and insecurity. Lots of insecurity. You have to understand: They have trees in Vermont. Trees everywhere. Covered in snow. It's wilderness. And it's *cold*. Everyone else made friends quickly and started pairing off after rehearsal, just as I'd hoped to do with Nonie, and then it was night, and I was isolated in the loudest silence I'd ever known.

We were living on the top of a mountain in White River Junction in log cabin apartments that an Englishman named Robert O'Neil Butler, who was in love with the theater, had built on his grounds. To get up there, even in good weather, you parked halfway up the mountain by a barn and took a little four-wheel-drive jeep they left there up the steep road to the house.

Five of us decided one day to see friends in New York, so we squeezed into someone's little car and off we went. Heading back that evening we drove right into a blizzard that had settled in on White River Junction. It was the dead of night. And the jeep was still a half a mile up ahead. Straight up.

So an actress named Lillah McCarthy and I decided we would crawl up this mountain road, get the jeep and drive back down. All the way up we were slipping and falling, and we were soaked by the time we made it. Then we proceeded to argue about who would drive down. Lillah was a control freak, and I was a control freak, and the snow was falling hard.

Lillah had lived in Vermont, and she knew the road, and I grew up in Hoboken. But I'd have none of it. I was going to drive that fuckin' jeep. I was fine till I released the clutch, then all hell broke loose. The jeep began veering from one side to the other, so I jammed on the brakes. Our little jeep started fishtailing, and we started turning 360s. There were sheer dropoffs on either side of the incline—a cliff like you see in Monte Carlo, just add the freezing cold winds, ice, and snow. This was straight out of a Hitchcock movie.

Lillah was screaming at me: "Pull this fucking car over, Joey! Pull over NOW!" Goddamn! By now I was completely out of my mind. Outta of control, that's just me, but I'd also lost control of the jeep. Slamming down on the brakes had no real effect. The jeep kept going twenty-five to thirty miles per hour down the very narrow hill, turning 360s all the way. I was freaking, Lillah was freaking. We were bouncing off the snow embankments on each side. What if we broke through? Then we'd be going over the cliff doing a Princess Grace! The mountain was clearly winning, and clearly Lillah should have been driving. The problem was, I was. So Lillah was doing the next best thing: she was trying to open her door and jump out of the jeep! We were rolling twenty-five miles an hour, and she was trying to scramble out.

Hindsight being 20/20, I thought I handled it pretty good. I was reaching over the console and grabbing the door to save Lillah . . . from me! I had started laughing, hysterically. I knew there was a good chance we could die going over the cliff. Still, I was laughing as I managed to catch a tire just at the edge of a snow pile. We stopped dead in the snow pile. Dead quiet. At this point Lillah and I got out and slipped and slid the last thirty yards back to the second car. We got in with the others and all slept in the car for the night, stuffed in like circus clowns.

I was way, way out of my comfort zone up there. I was hundreds of miles from home, pursuing my dream, and somehow nearly took a header off a cliff, laughing the whole time. Was that an appropriate reaction? By the morning, however, I'd buried those feelings. Shit happens, it was over. Just a big joke. Lillah and I—well, somehow we ended up good pals and have remained so to this day.

There were emotional highs, and then there were the emotional lows. One day we were rehearsing a one-act play by Horovitz about two sewer rats, one from New York City and the other from Connecticut. It was called—surprise, surprise—*Rats*. In the play, the country rat is looking for a way to get in the city rat's rich territory. The city rat doesn't let anyone share his domain, because that keeps him powerful, but the country rat persuades the city rat to let him stay. I could have told the rat how to do it. The play is about greed and manipulation, conniving for a position. These were things I knew something about at the time, but I would soon learn much more.

I played the role of the country rat from Connecticut, which, interestingly, is where I now live. In those days, though, it may as well have been Mars. Connecticut isn't too many geographic miles from Hoboken, but it's about a million cultural miles. I couldn't relate. I couldn't understand my character, or grasp the full intention of either the director or the author. As it turns out, the country rat I played was incredibly insecure—sound familiar?—as he matched wits with the city slicker. The feelings I was conjuring up to become this character got close to those that existed in my real life. Too close. I was accessing and using emotions that were still very raw, very intense, not in the least bit ready for prime time.

I was acting in a real theater at last. Up till then, our performances at resorts were always inside these ski lodge cafeterias up atop the mountains. Months, up to my ass in snow. Working at the Stowe Theatre Guild, this was different. Two hundred seats, a real playhouse—this was regal by comparison.

I was struggling that afternoon. Our stage manager Margay was on book as we rehearsed; Lillah was directing me and my acting partner Fred. I understood what was needed for my character,

I just couldn't find it organically in me. I was trapped inside my own body, judging myself, my soul suddenly frozen with fear. *I suck! I'll never be better than average!*

I was struck still, as though I was having some out-of-body experience. I could see myself struggling with the work, and I feel my dream of escaping my past slipping away. If I couldn't prove myself as an actor playing a friggin' rat, then how would I ever fly free? I would always be tethered to my post, always be only a few blocks away from the New Jersey projects, and very far away from a life I'd been so sure my talent would place within my reach.

Now my ears are ringing, and I see my mother hitting herself. My brain is doing this to me. The chemicals. Was it something I ate? I'm thinking, *I'm not going to get my dream! I'm a hack, I suck, I can't stand being me but I'm trapped inside of me! I'm never going to shake my past.* When I thought of success as an actor, I thought I would have money, and that would buy me self-esteem and beautiful women. Now that's fading fast. *But I have something, don't I? Isn't that what the acting teachers told me? That I have talent. I have a gift!*

Kneeling onstage by now in a fetal position, I could sense my four horsemen of the apocalypse—fear, bewilderment, frustration, and despair—riding thunderously toward me. My knees aching on the wooden floor, my acting partner's feet now beside me as he made his speech. But I was completely lost. Thoughts rushing through my head, panic and fear beating my foolish dream to a pulp! I heard a knocking sound.

It was me banging my head against that stage floor. Punishing myself, my defective brain for selling me a bill of goods! Punching and scratching my face, as if I were trying to escape my human bondage. "Stop it, Joey! Stop it! Fred, do something!" Lillah cried from the audience. Fred, my actor friend who played the Manhattan rat, broke character and rushed forward to grab my arms and save me from myself. "What the hell are you doing? Stop it!"

I looked up. Fred continued to hold me down, keeping me from doing any more damage. I wanted to kill that rat fuck inside of me! But the Vermont altitude was depriving me of the extra oxygen I needed to finish the job. My thoughts took me to Florie. I was panting as he did, the emphysema that would eventually kill him robbing him of oxygen, his face turning red while he gasped for air. Lillah had rushed onstage to manage the crisis, and was doing first aid on me with my head resting on her lap, like a cornerman treating his fighter's cuts. I had done some damage raking my nails down my face, from the hairline straight to the bottom of my chin, drawing blood along the way.

Eventually, they managed to calm me down. They gave me a glass of water, and Lillah called it a night.

The next day I was back at work with this feeling of dread. I wanted to hide and avoid discussing my disastrous performance with anyone. A few fellow actors asked me how I was doing, and I covered up with the excuse that I had been trying some affective memory technique that went awry. It was never mentioned again. What could they say about the 8,000-pound albatross that hung as plain as day around my neck? Certainly I didn't dare mention it. I was already stuffing the memory deep into my subconscious.

We ignore BD when it appears. That's something I'd learned. Things happen, and then you move on. And I trusted that it was the right thing to do, because I'd learned it from a pro, my mother.

—◊—

The great skiing in Vermont that winter made it difficult for us to find our audience; apparently people had so much fun skiing during the day, they were too exhausted to go out later to see a play. A meeting was called at Butler's main house, part of a beautiful compound with two guesthouses, the apartments where we stayed (which were not yet completed), and a corral for his horses. We were standing in his post-and-beam living room with its enormous windows looking out at snowcapped mountains when OB (that was his nickname) announced that he was shutting us down, and we would use the remaining six weeks to help finish construction on the estate. Apparently this was part of our contract, but of course I hadn't read the fine print. He thought he would be directing us in banging nails! Was he nuts? We were stunned, and I looked toward Lillah, sensing that for the first time we finally agreed on something.

"But OB!" said I. "Wait a minute. I'm no carpenter!" But before I could go any further, Butler interrupted like Sydny Doolap, thinking he had us nine aces up his cheating sleeve. In his *very* British accent OB said, "You must! You see, I've written it in your contracts!" Again I protested, this time with the nonconfrontational approach, very polite as if I were speaking to a good friend, or your mother. "But OB!" I said. "You see, I misplaced the contract, somewhere up your ass!"

—◊—

I was out of there on the next Greyhound Special. "Sixty days of limitless travel, for a dollar a day . . ." Ah, when gas was cheap! After my mini nervous breakdown, I said to myself, I'm going to Disneyland! And I set out to see not just Disneyland, but the whole country. "All gone to look for America," as Simon & Garfunkel sang to us.

Everybody was restless in the early '70s. Me, I wasn't just rest-less—I was *petrified*! But when we were twelve years old, Cousin Patty and me made an adolescent vow that at age twenty-one we'd tour the country. I've always been of a mind to do what I say. So I had to do this—keep this promise to myself. I needed time to figure out who I was. Plus, I'd never been anywhere. I hadn't even been on an airplane, except once, to visit my dad when he was in Miami.

I wanted to experience life. I thought I hadn't experienced anything. I didn't give any credence to my upbringing, my fam-ily history. Also, people looked down on my New Jersey accent. Everybody at acting school was from Texas or South Carolina. I was ethnic, and we didn't have many Italian-American actors. At that time Al Pacino hadn't blossomed into a bona-fide movie star. Frank Sinatra or Jimmy Durante came the closest. We Italians were thought to be very emotional and sensual and lovable, and that was good, but I was trying to be something different. I auditioned for parts in Tennessee Williams plays, and when those roles were cast they went to others. Arthur Miller, who wrote *Death of a Salesman*, is a Jew from Brooklyn, but they usually cast young midwestern men and women to play those parts.

So I took the Greyhound and I caught up with Nonie from Vermont in Atlanta. By then I needed pocket money, so I did cleanup work as day laborer on a construction job. (Maybe OB's instincts were right after all.) I kept searching for an answer. If I didn't end up an actor, what was I going to do with my life? I went up into Canada, where so many boys my age had gone to escape the draft. I went to Wounded Knee, South Dakota, where they'd had that massacre. The conflict between Native Americans and the government was still playing out. History was unfolding before me, and I was there, perhaps because I wanted to root for the underdog. In New Orleans I stayed in a youth hostel—they were big then. I listened to blues and jazz, and three times a day went to a little restaurant off Bourbon Street to eat red beans and rice, which they eat a lot of there, especially on Fridays, when the Catholics can't eat meat. A plate was twenty-eight cents. If you wanted some sausage in it, it was fifty cents. And I'd buy a carton of eggs and boil them and keep them around. In Alabama I stayed in a five dollar a night, fleabag hotel where lots of prostitutes were coming then going.

In Daytona Beach I saw a hippie boy kill himself. He was looking for a different kind of peace, I guess. Standing on the second floor railing of his motel, he did a swan dive headfirst into the hard concrete below. It was like watching Greg Louganis on TV, diving the gold. The boy's head made this awful splitting sound, and then there was brain matter mixed with blood thick as jelly; bits of his long bleached brown hair made lighter from the Florida sun stuck to his formless skull. I wondered what could have been going on in that brain of his that he needed to quiet it forever? Now his secrets were oozing out of him. The body lay lifeless, when just moments ago he was so full of it. That was my first time seeing a dead body that was not in funeral makeup.

Back on the bus I headed north to Washington, DC, to see the spring cherry blossoms full in bloom. I especially liked the museum tour at Ford's Theater, where Lincoln was shot. Another good brain ruined! His bloodstained clothing were on display under thick bulletproof glass. Until now I hadn't made the connection between the hippie and my visit to Ford's Theater, or understood why those two experiences have stayed so vivid in my memory. I had no idea how much that boy in Daytona and Abe had in common with me.

The realization that life was too goddamned short finally hit me. We're all the same, Abraham Lincoln or a troubled hippie—we're all perishable. I did a lot of walking over those sixty days. I decided to give acting ten years; if I couldn't make it by then, I'd know I tried . . .

—⁂—

It was good to get back to New York, where accents weren't accents and I could be absorbed into my cocoon in the city. I picked up my life pretty much where I'd left it. I studied acting. I waited more tables. And I continued meeting the angels who would guide me on my road to the asylum.

I worked at O'Neal's Baloon, an upscale hamburger and beer saloon across from Lincoln Center, as maître 'd. I even got Florie my maître 'd job after I trained to wait tables. In 1973, O'Neal's was *the* place to be seen. It's where I grew up. Jim Kiernan, my buddy from HB Studios, was also working there as a waiter. He got me the job. It was a great opportunity to earn money while I was going to acting school. One of the owners, Patrick O'Neal, was a real actor, while I was trying to be one, and he always made it easy for me to come back to the job after a show closed and money ran out. The actor Michael Moriarty worked there as well; he had just come back to work at the Baloon after finishing the film *Bang the Drum Slowly*. With two big movies under his belt, he was in between jobs, but in less than a year he would win a Tony Award for his work in *Find Your Way Home*. Now he was paying his dues and waiting tables with me. Waiting tables was what actors did.

O'Neal's Baloon was on 63rd and Columbus Avenue, just across from Lincoln Center, New York City's new home of the Metropolitan Opera and the New York State Theater, which meant the Baloon was always filled with beautiful dancers flirt-ing with the young waiters, who flirted back. Patrick O'Neal and his brother Michael also owned the Ginger Man (named after a play Patrick was in) just down the street. The story I heard was that the Baloon was originally called O'Neal's Saloon, and when it opened they had the name spelled out in huge neon letters above the entrance. But it turned out that state law prohibited the use of "saloon" written on any marquee, so out with the S and up with the B, leaving "Baloon" misspelled. This made about as much sense as that old law. But it worked.

Patrick sat on the Board of Directors for the City of New York, and he had known they were going to build Lincoln Center on this spot on the Upper West Side. If you've seen *West Side Story*, that's the neighborhood where they filmed it. It was all going to be torn down. So Patrick got a thirty-year lease to the Hudson Hotel, which was directly across the street from where Lincoln Center for the Performing Arts—including the Aveey Fisher Hall, the Metro-politan Opera House, and the Library for the Performing Arts—would eventually sit.

Patrick made a fortune, and so did I—I was making fifty, sixty dollars a day. And I made a lot of lifelong friends in that place. Dick Harvey was the manager at O'Neal's Baloon in my time. He was a big guy with a handlebar mustache, who got around on a motorcycle, and I loved him very much.

I had a crush on a pretty girl who worked in the office for a long time. Her name was Gail. She wound up working in casting, and she got me work on commercials as an extra. I did a bank commercial with Tim Conway. I was just one of the people stand-ing in a line.

Almost every waiter working in the joint was gay, except

for Jim Kiernan, Billy Sandeson, Flo, and Dick Harvey, our management. I was nineteen and had never been around gay men. In high school my friends teased me and said I must be gay. It was something about the way I carried my school books— under my arm—and of course, the fact that I wanted to be an actor! Man, it's tough becoming an adult. These days, I see parallels between the fight for gay rights in our country and the struggle for equal rights for people with brain dis-ease. Being openly gay in 1970s could be harsh. But I didn't really know what gay was, and their ribbing caused me to fear my own sexual identity. I was always affectionate with men. I was close to my feelings for them, I would hug them. But did that mean I was gay?

In the end working at the Baloon with the gay men I grew to know, respect, and understand was a great education and a great relief to me. I discovered that although I loved many of these men, I didn't want to have sex with them (and likewise, they probably didn't want to fuck me either). Did that make me homophobic? Who knows? But, I must say, thanks to all those good-looking male ballet dancers I had a wonderful time with dozens of beautiful oversexed ballerinas who weren't gay either!

The fact is, I had this overwhelming desire to be with women. Ever since I was a kid I'd had a powerful sex drive. I'd wake up with my pajamas stuck to me and think, what the hell is this? When I figured out how to masturbate, I'd do it three or four times a day, if only as a way to calm myself down enough to concentrate on other things. A good portion of my teenage years was spent in the bathroom, trying to finish before my mother kicked down the door first, then bellowed, "What the hell are you doing in there!" She was the type to kick down the door and then knock. (When I made the documentary *No Kidding Me Too!*, I interviewed Wendy Richardson, a marriage/ family therapist and addiction specialist who pointed out that a lot of men who have BD develop compulsive sexual behavior. She reported that top executives at well-known companies have confessed that the compulsion interferes with their work life. "I can't focus, I can't concentrate unless I go into the bathroom and I masturbate [first]." Turns out, sex addiction is a common Deadly Symptom among people with BD.)

My growing obsession with sex would eventually get me into a lot of trouble. But at the time, it was just part of being young. I had managed to lose my virginity when I was 18, but at the time my knowledge of women was limited to Mary Fist, the only thing that would play with little Joey and the twins. Working at O'Neal's Baloon was a true coming of age experience for me in many ways—mostly in regard to women.

O'Neal's was filled with ballerinas from Lincoln Center. Pretty girls walking with their toes out and eating cottage cheese and drinking Tab soda. Maybe 80 percent of the ballet boys were gay, so that made me all the more appealing to them. And they were in a bigger hurry than me! God bless them! Most of the visiting ballet companies played for only a week or so. I remember sleeping with a girl from the Royal Danish Ballet and the Bolshoi Ballet (which was tougher, all those KGB). I even shtupped a girl from the Stuttgart Ballet. Some of the girls couldn't even speak English. Well, in 1973, neither could I!

One of my fondest memories was a date I had with destiny—an Italian beauty—and our rendezvous in the basement apartment on 86th Street I was subletting. My date was just gorgeous. She came with her friend, also pretty and a few years older, maybe twenty-seven. The friend acted as our translator. The three of us drank some wine. Then the older girl says, "Well, time for bed. I'm gonna go back to the hotel. Will you take care of my friend?"

It's time for bed all right! "Absolutely," said I.

This beauty spoke only Italian, but clearly she had determined that she was going to go, as the song goes, "All the way." Ah, the memories! I was an innocent. I was trembling, she was so pretty, her hair a short sandy blond. I remember thinking, "Thank you, God!" She felt so good in my arms. Looking deeply into my eyes, in the heat of our great passion, she said only three words, and she repeated them twice: "Please no baby, please no baby." That's the only English she knew. I fell in love!

Then, two weeks later . . .

I fell in love with a lovely Dutch girl from the Royal Danish Ballet too. We spent one week together, seeing New York City through her eyes. It was so romantic. We never consummated the relationship. Oh, to have that feeling again—the first time you meet a girl who affects your heart that way. When I had to say goodbye to her I was lovesick. Heartsick. I couldn't eat. Whenever I was lovesick I could not eat for weeks.

Everthing was a new experience, and I was lucky to find myself surrounded by people who were willing and able to help me. The O'Neals were really good to me. So was Dick, the manager, even when he had to fire me because I had made one mistake too many. He used to do this to people when he got mad.

He'd huff, sigh. "I don't want to do this," he'd say. "I gotta let you go man," Then he'd open up a drawer, get out a checkbook, and say, "How much do you need?" He'd give me five hundred bucks. "This isn't a loan," he'd say. That's the kind of people who fell into my life.

I was multitalented: I could get hired and I could get fired. I didn't have a preference. I had the experience I'd gained at O'Neal's Baloon under my belt, and if I lost one restaurant job, at that time there was always another to be had. During my years of acting school I worked as a waiter at so many restaurants: the Baloon, the Ginger Man, the Harvey Chelsea Bar, and countless others. I established important relationships with angels who had a real love of theater. I gained a real love of the work. I saw waiting tables as a way out of poverty, a way out of the projects, a way into the arms of all these beautiful ballerinas and movie actresses. I was learning about people, testing my craft, experiencing the wider world.

Part of experiencing the wider world meant experimenting with alcohol.

The first time I purposely got drunk was when I was about twenty years old. I was stage-managing a Pete Handke play at a small theater on Bank Street in the West Village. Al Sinkys was directing, and Paul Thomas was playing the lead.

On opening night there was a party at a friend's house around the corner from the theater. My pal Michael Kell was there, as were Al and Paul, and everyone was drinking red wine. The people were in their thirties and forties and here I was, just a kid. I was hanging out with these folks who were older than me at least by ten years. I liked hanging out with older theater people because I was there to learn, and I wanted to learn quick. That night I had decided that I was drinking to get drunk. Really the only reason I ever drank was to change my mood. I drank so I could be more social, so I could fit in, or I drank because it would be easier for me to have a good time. Soon enough I got into a real crying jag because I was feeling sorry for myself. I was in love with somebody, it would never work between us, and grief was just pouring out of me as fast as the red wine was flowing in.

The details of the evening grow fuzzy at this point, but eventually we wound up at the elegant apartment of one of our benefactors. Somebody said, "Just sit here," and deposited me on a chaise longue, where I promptly passed out. When I woke up the room was spinning and spinning, and eventually I began to projectile vomit. I had had nothing to eat, so I was just spewing red liquid all over myself, my clothes, and all over this lady's suede chair. Women began screaming. One lady was yelling, "My God! My God! Get him off! Get him off!" So my friends took me into the bathroom and aimed my face into the toilet. I'd vomit, they'd flush. And at one point I vomited and opened my eyes to see the cold water refilling the toilet bowl, so I started sucking up the water into my mouth. I was gargling with the toilet water to get all the particles of vomit out of my mouth.

My friends' reaction was stunned silence. Al was fascinated. As actors, we were always taught to look for telling moments and behaviors we could incorporate into our work. I remember hearing Al Sinkys saying, *My God, how brilliant. What a brilliant choice.* I was devoid of any kind of shame; it just seemed like a good idea at the time. They took my shirt off and put it in the sink and soaked it, trying to get out as much of the red wine as they could, then they gave it back to me, and we were on our way.

Having grown up in the '60s and seen what drink and drugs could do, and was already doing to some of my friends, I promised myself to stay away. There was too much evidence around me that alcohol and drugs would get in the way of my success. Even though I was drinking regularly in my twenties, it was only wine—that couldn't hurt, right? I somehow in my subconscience believed that I was allergic to alcohol, because of the way it made me feel. I'd say *I won't drink too much.* A little bit of alcohol did the trick.

It's funny about allergies! If I were allergic to frankfurters, that would be it. Frankfurters make me sick! I would avoid them, because I would know that I could have a comfortable life staying away from them. I wouldn't have to go to twelve-step meetings for frankfurters. I never drank like that. Back then I really was a cheap drunk; three or four glasses of wine, and I was gone. I got the feeling that I wanted, and I was fine and I could even stop. An alcoholic, I was told, couldn't stop. But I wasn't that kind of a drinker, so I figured I must not be an alcoholic.

Alcohol and sex became closely tied. I wanted to stop, but then I'd think, how could get a girl to sleep with me if she wasn't drinking? They wouldn't want to sleep with me sober. What a shame I thought so little of myself at that time. And this was before the real fear of any kind of disease. You saw someone that was attractive and you'd ask them. Or they'd ask you. Both alcohol and sex (and later drugs) helped me blur my reality, to anesthetize myself.

My early years in Manhattan during the '70s were a gloriously freeing time. I was a sponge just sucking up as much culture, artistry, and knowledge as I could hold. Getting a waiter job was as simple as walking down a street; unlike now, it was relatively easy for kids like me to support themselves while going to acting school. I was always being reassured that acting was something that I had an aptitude for. I was determined to establish a legacy on film, something that would remain long after I perished from the earth. But I still had a long way to go.

CHAPTER THREE

An Egomaniac with an Inferiority Complex

I n 1974, my sister, Maryann, was sixteen. I had left home a few years before, and since then, she and Mommy had been going at each other pretty good. Maryann no longer wanted to live at home. Now it seemed that Maryann was dating a poor Irish lad from West New York, New Jersey, and Mommy did not approve. He never had a chance. Maryann wanted to move out, but Mommy wouldn't have it, so Maryann threatened to quit school unless Mommy agreed to let her go. Things were not pretty on the home front, and I was at a loss for what to do.

I shared my frustration with my new best friend Jeff Silverman, an aspiring young man like myself with dreams of being an actor. He had recently returned from Vietnam and was studying on the GI Bill. We were both going to acting school under the tutelage of the fearless John Lehne. John was of the belief that if you personally had difficulty expressing certain types of emotion, then it would be difficult for the character you were playing to do so as well. He had recommended to several of his students a therapist named Ralph Ricci at a place called the Center for Emotional

Re-education, and eventually seven or eight of the sixteen members of our acting class were seeing Ricci for confrontational group therapy. Jeff suggested that Maryann and Mommy go and get a free consultation. Seeing as it was free, what could the harm be?

Mommy was anxious to find a professional who could talk some sense into Maryann—or at least, persuade her to Mommy's point of view—so an appointment was made. They took the bus in from New Jersey and went to see Ralph, and afterward they came to O'Neal's Baloon, where by now I was waiting tables, and Florie was working as the day manager.

I had just finished the lunch shift and cleared all my tables. I poured myself a cup of coffee and picked up a bacon cheeseburger platter, then headed for the six-top that we waiters used for folding napkins, eating lunch, and you know, doing the general kibitzing we did before starting or ending a shift. I could hear Mommy then see Maryann and Flo as I turned the corner.

I walked over. My mother was smoking what was probably her third cigarette. She was having a fit. Mommy was mumbling almost to herself, as if in a trance, or working out a complex algebraic equation. Maryann was eating her lunch and trying to keep a straight face.

MOMMY, *streams of smoke shooting from her nostrils.* Joey . . . Joseph! Get over here!

MOMMY, *as I sit down.* Where did your Jew-fuck friend find this shoemaker? . . . The cocksucker! . . . You know what he said to me? Therapist my ass! He said your sister's wanting to quit school is *MY* fault!

Maryann, eyes down, continued to inhale her cheeseburger.

Wow! I thought. I gotta meet, no, *have* to meet, the guy with the balls to tell my mother *that*! Tell her that she might bear some responsibility for the confusion and sadness in our unhappy home. So I went to find him.

I began group therapy in the spring of 1974, just shy of my twenty-first birthday. I remember heading down to 122 East 22nd Street, just off Second Avenue and ringing the fancy bronze intercom. A pleasant female voice greeted me and buzzed me into a converted garage that was now an office. The bronze plate on the door read THE CENTER FOR EMOTIONAL RE-EDUCATION. I opened the door slowly and entered a large room, where the receptionist took my name and asked me to please have a seat. After a few minutes a well-dressed man appeared through double padded doors, looking enthusiastic and wearing a big smile. We talked for a while in his office, and he turned out to be as charming as he was good-looking. Apparently groups met on the building's ground floor, and he lived in an apartment with his wife and two kids on the floor above. To soundproof the group room, he had had double doors and padded walls installed. The wall coverings looked like burlap, and every few feet along the walls were vertical pieces of natural wood, which if you stared at them long enough started to look like bars on a jail cell. There were no windows.

This was a confrontational form of therapy. The Center for Emotional Re-education was relatively new, and I learned years later that Ricci (who is also the father of actress Christina Ricci) never had any formal training as a therapist. No credentials whatsoever, as far as I knew. Later he started to work in tandem with a certified therapist, but in the beginning it was just him. His approach was, "Are you happy? What did you feel was lacking in your emotional upbringing?" I decided I would listen and learn. I ended up listening and learning three days a week, sometimes in thirty-hour marathons, for the next ten years!

There was a lot of screaming. On my first day, almost thirty years ago now, I remember I was sitting in one of the rigid plastic chairs arranged in a circle, and suddenly this guy next to me starts *screaming* at me. "You slimy sack of shit!! I can feel your stinking lying vibrations coming out the pores of your skin! I don't trust you!"

Oh, Jesus, I thought. *What the fuck am I in for?*

Looking back, it dawns on me that I just traded one dysfunctional family for another. Growing up, the Big Cheese at home was Mommy . . . and now for the next ten years it would be Ralph. At least Mommy fed me and did my laundry! Even so, this felt like progress.

Throughout my life, all of Mommy's love (and there was a lot of it) was expressed with one condition—things had to be done *her way*. I had to be faithful, to never love someone more than Mommy. I can still hear Mommy's voice echoing in my adolescent ears, *"Remember! You can have five wives, but you only have one mother! Joey, do you love Mommy? Do you love me more? Most of all? More than Daddy, more than Maryann? MORE THAN FLORIE?"* For an insecure twenty-two-year-old egomaniac, who was not yet a man, this was heavy shit!

Mommy always came first, and now it would be Ralph. He needed to come first. Ralph encouraged the group to let out all of our anger, all of our fear. We were to follow his lead and be as honest as we could with ourselves and everybody else. He told us it was OK to feel what we felt, and so we did—we let it all out. I remember describing my mother to the group, and working myself up into a sobbing, screaming tirade: "Fuck you. Me first! Fuck you. Me first! I'm lovable! You're lovable! Why couldn't we change? Does it have to be this way? I'm entitled to happiness. I'm lovable!" I got caught up in the spirit of it all, a lifetime's worth of anger and rage and then euphoria began to pour out of me right there on the carpet.

These two-hour "sessions" left me feeling great. All that energy and adrenaline from all that jumping around and screaming. Knowing what I do now, I realize I was feeding my imbalanced brain with the feel-good hormones, dopamine and norapenephrine. My brain, with its genetic dis-ease, craved the rush.

Over the years I had already learned to self-medicate the natural way by running, though of course I had no idea that that's what I was actually doing. All I knew was that every day when I felt restless or depressed or just hungover, I was compelled to run—for twenty-eight to thirty-two minutes, or about five miles—until an internal switch flipped and my agitation gave way to a feeling of peacefulness and centeredness. I'd started running regularly when I was in junior high, after I'd had to prove in gym class that I could run one mile, and when I realized that I could both boost my mood and control my weight with this one trick, I was hooked. Only later did I realize that there was a quantifiable biological effect of exercise: I learned when doing my documentary that taking a brisk fifteen-minute walk is the equivalent of taking 20 milligrams of Prozac.

Group was the medicine I needed to keep the monster inside asleep. It became a habit, like running. It made me feel better physically and emotionally. I realize now that I needed group to keep me from petting the dragon living inside of me. That self-destructive predator, waiting for its due date to annihilate me and everything I love. Group kept me from shoveling nourishment into him. After about six months of sessions, I was getting the hang of how it worked, and starting feeling better, hopeful even. Some members mentioned that they were seeing a change in me. *And* . . . after all that sharing and caring, I was becoming one hell of a hugger!

The group dynamic was powerful, but often Ralph's reaction was the only one that mattered. One day I received some horrible news. JJ, the first real pet I'd ever owned, given to me by the one and only Alfred Knight, had died. I was overwhelmed with sadness and hurt. Where better to share it?

Alfred Knight was Florie's business partner. Alfred was the go-to man for the Upper East Side—he could get everything you couldn't get on Madison Avenue, like Cartier and Saks. Alfred was Florie's protegé at their alma mater, the University of Atlanta Federal Penitentiary, and they stayed close friends and business associates on the outside. To the best of my knowledge that association did not cross over to Alfred's primary day job. Alfred was a pimp.

In his book *How to Win Friends and Influence People*, Dale Carnegie was right on the money when he said that the art of communication is knowing a man's name and making him feel like he's the most important guy in the room. Alfred was always very polite, a soft-spoken man, and like Florie, he always remembered everyone's name, something I could never do. Alfred was charming, handsome, and direct. Flo had mentored Alfred while in the can, and Alfred was his eager pupil. A pimp with dignity. He was the only colored man Flo trusted with his life.

Alfred Knight. He was handsome. Light skin, the color of caramel, reddish brown hair. How striking he was, sharp, smart. So much style. He was tall and slender, and when he crossed his legs you could see his cream-colored silk socks peeking out between his custom-tailored cuffed gray slacks and his shiny alligator loafers. This is almost fifty years ago and I can still remember the color of his socks!

Like Florie, Alfred had all his clothes made at Lyme's Haberdashery on 57th Street, off Park, and one flight above a Chinese restaurant. Lyme's catered to the best in fashion. In those days that meant judges, lawyers, movie stars, and wiseguys. Unlike the type of dress you found at other clothing stores, Lyme's was known for classic English fashion. Not the superfly look of pimp uniforms that were as identifiable as the Boy Scouts'. You'd find those gents all around Manhattan, particularly 11th Avenue, near where the Lincoln Tunnel crowd (this Lincoln guy's name keeps popping up!) would stop for a quickie blow job on their home. Alfred dressed more like a politician; I always thought he looked so handsome, like Jack Kennedy. In fact I have to admit in writing right now that his was the style I was after for my character in *The Sopranos*. My look was a compliment to Alfred Knight.

They were such a handsome couple, Alfred and his beautiful wife, Amanda, who was also his star client. They were the first interracial couple I'd ever seen. You didn't see black guys with white girls or vice versa at that time. I didn't know prostitutes even got married. Whenever we were over at their place, or they were over by us, Mommy would always try to corner Amanda to up and quit.

Mommy would try to liberate her: "Amanda what's the matter with you, you're a beautiful girl, you can have any man!" Amanda would just smile, or at least that's how I remember it. There was an ethereal quality to her, as if she wore a glaze that protected her. Or maybe it was drugs. I couldn't begin to wrap my head around what brought her to this, but I could tell she loved Alfred. She called him Daddy.

It's not many kids who have well-dressed pimps and ingenue prostitutes as role models. I credit Alfred and Amanda with my lifelong obsession with style and clothes.

We were still living in the projects when I met them for the first time, and the juxtaposition of the projects and this opulent prewar Riverside Drive building was jarring. The elevator to their eleventh-floor apartment was copper and there was a leather bench with copper button trim at the back of the car. I could see my reflection in the shine of the elevator operator's patent leather belt that fit handsomely around his double-breasted coat.

Upon entering their apartment for the first time, I could smell vanilla—it was Mrs. Knight. She was so beautiful and I fell instantly and permanently in love with her. I was thirteen years old and remember clear as day the rush of heat that hit my ears and the weakness I felt in my thighs. Her skin was the color of vanilla ice cream, complementing Alfred's caramel colored tone, and her eyes were piercing blue. She couldn't have been more than five or six years older than me.

Their apartment was beautiful. Everything was so tastefully done. Amanda would glide across the floor, like a seagull with a strong wind or an angel. I remember she was tiny, too, and had the figure of a ballerina. That day at their apartment Amanda wore a silk powder blue nightgown and she had a matching robe that broke at the back of her knee. The nightgown fell a little higher than the robe and she wore white fluffy slippers to match. She made such an impression on me. I have combed the planet trying to find those legs—they were perfect. But immediately my mother's look of disgust told me that what Amanda was wearing was somehow inappropriate.

My sister Maryann was with us as well, and was equally adorable in her off-white and pink polka-dotted dress. Her outfit complimented Alfred and Amanda's toy poodle, JJ. Maryann showed so much affection for this well-groomed white pup with the pink ribbon around its neck that they actually gave her the dog later that evening.

That toy poodle represented something powerful—a lifestyle that impressed me, a formative childhood crush, an important show of affection that had no conditions. Ever since then I've loved dogs. They're a great species. Dogs get it—they're sensitive to the rhythm of the universe. Is it a coincidence that *dog* spelled backwards is *God*? They can smell cancer in humans with 96 percent accuracy! They can sense a tsunami coming! They live moment to moment. When I was in my darkest days I had ten of them; now I have four.

By the time I had left home, JJ was already pretty old, but when Mommy called with the news that JJ had up and died, I was distraught. At group I started to tell everyone my dog, JJ, had died. I was sobbing, rolled up into an emotional ball; twenty-one people were in a circle and I was in the middle and then . . . nothing. They were quiet. They didn't know what to do or how to respond. Then Ralph, who had been stoic up to now, erupted with laughter. Suddenly everyone started laughing. At me!

"Joey, come on, what the fuck," he said. "It's a dog." I was crushed, and hated him just then.

But at the same time, I loved and trusted Ralph. He had become my mentor, and at that time he was what I needed. I looked at the experience as an investment in my God-given talent. But there was no god in that room—none to be found.

Right here is the fucked-up part: He was supposed to be my doctor, my therapist! And yet he had his own need to build himself a family that would never question him. He was manipulative, like Mommy, and like Mommy, he was sick! Today I realize how fuckin' nuts this is! He created this Jim Jones atmos*fear*, minus the Kool-Aid. Ralph wielded a lot of control over us, and put a spell on a lot of very powerful people.

I remember when Ralph would say "follow my lead, emulate me." I saw a part of Ralph that lived inside of me. I could identify. His group became a sort of club, like the Twelve Step Program. But in the Twelve Steps, there is no leader; the only leader is a loving God, as I understand Him. In Ricci's sessions you had to go with the emotional flow of whoever was the group leader. We were seated in a circle, but it still had a point or head and that person/persons validated the feelings.

I had an overwhelming fear that I'd end up the scum my mother thought all men were—that I'd end up her father, that fire-breathing monstrous dragon. My grandfather was an abusive drunk. The bastard part of my grandfather, that's what I worried I'd be. That my environment would make me . . . emotionally dishonest. I wanted to be a stand-up guy, not a product of my environment. In this group I was told which feelings were appropriate, as determined by Ralph Ricci. He had to give the OK, and only then would the group have permission to experience certain feelings. We all did it. It was the party line. If I didn't go along, they ostracized me. So I went along. At the time it didn't feel like dishonesty, it felt right, true!

This was all part of my truth training as an actor. At that time my feelings were fact. I knew my mother loved me, but group therapy said, at what price? It told me to know better, that she fucked up. The truth was in that pudding. It became my job to fix her. And if I didn't, I'd get my ass kicked. (Remember, I was paying money for this!) I experienced all of the emotions in that room. Somebody would tell me how to feel and I would feel it. The emotions would erupt and range from sadness to anger to vulnerability. The fact is I felt better after these sessions, and because I felt better I thought they were right.

I was getting a lot out of that group therapy. I was learning to be a different kind of person. I was learning to be a stand-up guy, to not manipulate, to tell the truth at any cost, to be painfully honest even if the truth might injure the other person.

I learned to be able to say that I wasn't the best at anything. I learned to relieve myself from this unnerving pressure of having to be great. So what if I wasn't the best actor in the world, at least I was the best looking! OK, maybe I got the best-looking thing fouled up. Maybe I wasn't the best anything. I was just Joey and that was enough. So, this form of self-acceptance was working.

I truly believe that group therapy helped me not to fuck up my first long-term relationship. Before I met my future first wife, I had not been with a woman I cared about for more than two weeks, never even ninety days. Usually by ninety days you know if it's going to work, if you're going to the next level. In my relationships with women, the moment they showed affection for me, I lost interest. I became cold. That had to do with intimacy. Group therapy enabled me to have the appropriate emotional expression I needed, to be vulnerable and open. When I started to fuck things up, I would go to group therapy in the same way I'd go to acting class—I was getting feedback and judging my actions.

I learned a lot from those sessions about how to deal with other people and how to understand and express my emotions, but I can't say I ever came to a true understanding or acceptance of what was wrong with me.

I've always felt that I was different, and there have also been times throughout my life when I have felt that there was something wrong with me, but I just didn't know what it was. I didn't know how many others felt the same emptiness inside, the hole that I tried to fill with therapy, counseling, money, drugs, *any-thing* to regulate myself, to tame the beast. It wasn't just me, you know. Other people noticed that I was different as well. Some people would just out-and-out call me crazy. Or they would say things like, "You're one of a kind," or "Joey's just Joey," or "They broke the mold with you, Joey." For years, I thought people were complimenting me when they said things like that. I had no idea that they were seeing so clearly what I could not see, what it would take me years to finally see.

—⁂—

The whole therapy process played very well into the type of training I was getting as an actor. I started group therapy at twenty-one, and I was in group therapy until I was thirty-one. I studied acting for a good fifteen years. I was a student of human nature. I wanted to be an actor, specifically, not a hyphen, like an actor-producer-director. In John Lehne's class we used to do these exercises—you don't have to be an actor to do them—based on just watching people, like on the subway. You find a person of interest, then based on their behavior you give them a whole life story. And it doesn't matter if you're right or wrong. Then you go into class and create that character. As a young man I spent a lot of time reading, or let's say learning to read, the works of the Russian acting teacher, Constantin Stanislavski. His first and second books, *An Actor Prepares* and *Building a Character*, explain how to approach the rigors of acting by studying life. His method suggests sitting in a quiet peaceful area and reading the play through the first time without any interruptions. These were teachings for people who didn't have ADHD with a manageable pinch of OCD. I would jump out of my own skin. I couldn't concentrate. Thoughts that were just the noise of the day, or the voices of thoughts, ran wildly through my mind. Then I would get frustrated and mad at myself, all this energy would build up until I'd be running around the block or on the track field when I was still living at home. Back then I was ashamed that I couldn't do as the book suggested.

Thanks to my acting coach, John Lehne, I found my own method of working, the only method that has worked for me. John knew about my dyslexia, my reading handicap, that I couldn't write fast enough or clearly enough to keep up with the sessions and read my own handwriting afterward. The moment you put a pencil in my hand, I'd freeze! I would tense up over my past traumas in school, over my mom's frustration with me studying. Right now it's all coming back: even as I write this I'm getting stomach cramps. Anyway, I'm a visual learner, so in order for me to learn something I've got to see it or hear it. So at John's suggestion I began recording my work sessions with him (remember, we did not have video yet). Then at home, on my time, or in my dressing room, I could break down all the work we did and start writing notes at my own speed, noting the moderations, beats, intentions, behaviors. Later on as recorders became smaller, I learned to bring mine everywhere, into everything: my doctor's appointments, deal offers with my work, even when I bought my first brand-new Toyota Celica convertible. I recorded the deal so the car dealer couldn't change his tune later. I found my brain could only retain 70 percent of a conversation, so this way I played everything back at home, stop and go, writing at my pace and making my notes into my book. It's how it works for me.

—m—

One day at scene study in HB's class, I remember being blown away by a pretty little girl who had just finished her work on a scene. She was really good, confident and commanding! I mean, for a kid her age! Her name was Roberta. Little did I know that she, Michael Kell, and I would become friends for life. Or how important she and her family would be to me. They became incredibly dear and would also prove to be very important connections; they were some of the angels who would guide me through the wilderness that is the struggling actor's lot in life. Her parents were Eli Wallach and Anne Jackson.

Roberta was two years younger than me. I was nineteen then, and having only recently lost my virginity, I was still awkward around the other girls in class, most of whom were easily seven years older than me and already out of college. I am reminded of how shy I really was. Friends reading these words today will say, "Get the fuck out! Not Joey!" But it's true. I was shy. I built this outgoing Joey character from scratch. A little of Florie with a pinch of Daddy mixed with some of the tough guys I grew up around for spice. And though I would have resented the thought in 1972, a lot of my persona came from my mom . . . dear old Mommy.

When we first met I had a secret crush on Roberta. She was cute but I was two years older. I even went to see Roberta in her high school production of *Anything Goes*. Afterward Michael and I were invited to meet her parents . . . *to have dinner . . . at their house*! I was petrified. I mean, her mom and dad were famous actors! I was a kid, fresh out of high school, living in the city for the first time, and at this point I'd done only four or five backroom productions. And the fact is, I had never been to dinner at a friend's house, never mind a friend with famous parents. Both Michael and I were scared shitless.

We showed up at 6:30 *sharp*. That's when we met Roberta's brother, Peter, and her sister, Katherine. I liked Peter right off; we were the same age. We too became friends, and over the years

Peter and I remained close. Many years later, I finally got to act with Roberta when she guest starred on an episode of *The Sopranos,* and when Peter directed me in an animated feature with his father, Eli and I were finally costars.

Eli and Anne were famous for their elaborate New Year's Day parties. Everyone in the theater, all the dignitaries of New York, would be there—everyone from Dustin Hoffman to Tennessee Williams. I remember the first time Michael and I were invited for the New Year's Day party. We showed up at the front door, dressed to the nines. I knocked, a little nervous: Annie opened the door and we shouted, *Happy New Year!* Anne, looking a bit surprised, let us in. "Oh, hi boys . . . Come—come in." I was surprised to see her wearing Levi's and a V-neck sweater, and wondered if we were totally overdressed. Anne looked a little bewildered. "The kids didn't mention that you guys were coming. Um . . . Roberta and Katherine are out running errands. But come in, would you like some coffee? We just made some."

As we moseyed to the kitchen, Michael looked at me as if to say, *Did we mess up?* I saw Nellie their housekeeper cleaning and setting up for the party. Again the thought crossed our minds: Did we fuck up? Annie, pouring coffee, asked, "Did Roberta know you guys were coming?" I was in the alcove between the kitchen and dining room, fumbling as I tried to extract the invite from my inside pocket to see what kind of blunder we'd made, but then I was distracted by a wall of spectacular photographs. Photographs of Eli with Clint Eastwood in *The Good, the Bad and the Ugly*. Eli with Carroll Baker and Karl Malden directed by Elia Kazan in *Baby Doll*. Photos of *The Misfits*. At that moment, thirty years of legendary films were represented on that wall. I said to myself, *If my career ever takes off like Eli, I will have a photographic memory of my life hanging on my wall . . .* and I'd be so grateful for it.

When the doorbell rang a second time, I was shaken out of my trance, and I looked down at the invite in my hand. The invitation read "Please Join us for a Happy New Year Brunch," but the date read Sunday the 2nd! This was Saturday the 1st! I could hear Roberta just back with her siblings, Peter and Katherine. At the door I could hear Eli say, "What the hell!" as more guests started to arrive. Eli was laughing, yelling out to Peter, who was also laughing . . . my pal Michael was laughing so hard he had to wipe a tear from his eye. Then like something out of *A Christmas Carol*, I swear, Eli and Peter had to run down to Zabar's to get a dozen bagels and lox for the small group of friends who like us couldn't read the damn invite.

New Year's Day party, take two: On Sunday the 2nd, we knocked again, and this time Eli opened the door. I was nineteen and Michael was twenty-five, but Eli was looking at us like we were fifteen. I think he was concerned that these kids staring at him would ruin his party. "Oh, boys, come on in. You can go into Roberta and Katherine's room." Meaning, don't come into the adult party. Then he changed his mind. The day before we may have proven ourselves to be idiots, but at least we were well-behaved idiots, so he said, "Oh well, just come on in." So there we were, flies on the wall.

As we edged our way into the living room I came face-to-face with Maureen Stapleton who was holding court in the middle of a very funny story. She had everyone laughing. She played all the parts and could take you into the reality she was imagining. Maureen was incredibly realistic, in the moment, and the stories she told were brilliant, tragic, gut-wrenching, and funny. She reached out there through the character she embodied. Later I went to see Maureen in *The Gingerbread Lady*. Then I second-acted it (meaning I snuck in during act break) three or four times. I became a bit of a fixture around the Wallach house that first summer. We were invited to Eli and Anne's big house in East Hampton. I had never been to East Hampton. I only knew the Jersey Shore. In fact, I'd never even been to Long Island. Michael and I took the train out for the weekend, carrying mozzarella cheese I'd picked up at Fiore's in Hoboken because I was going to make lasagna for everyone.

I get there and holy shit, Joseph Heller is there. And Peter Maas, and Murray Schisgal, Kurt Vonnegut, Jules Feiffer. They were all gathered on the sun porch having cocktails. Great Gatsby living in the Hamptons.

At this point, and for the next seven years, my humble career consisted of waiting tables and going to acting school three times a week, and doing the plays. I came from the Hoboken slums, the projects, but through the Wallachs' generosity I landed in this white wicker world. Artists, writers, all these creative types. I was out of my element, but luckily I had the natural ability to make people believe what I said was mine; to take somebody else's words and make them mine. I could learn to fit in here.

—◊◊◊—

Whether he intended to or not, Eli became our mentor.

Michael and I wanted to pick Eli's brain because he was one of the original members of the Actors Studio and had worked with Elia Kazan. Theater still had such a presence in the '70s. You made your name in the theater, and then you went to Hollywood. This great man, already accomplished in 1973 with *The Good, the Bad and the Ugly*, was something of a hero to me. His career was the kind I wanted, that I thought attainable. I looked up to him and his wife. Eli told us stories about his career. During

World War II he was a hospital administrator. After the war he used the GI Bill to go the Neighborhood Playhouse acting school where he studied with Sandy Meisner and got into the Actors Studio. He struggled along the way, to be sure. At one point early on, he thought about throwing his acting career away and applying for another administration job at a hospital. Then one of his first breaks came along.

"But, Eli," Michael asked him, "don't you look at those struggling days as somewhat romantic?" Eli glared. "Are you crazy? They were miserable. I was filled with jealousy and rage to see actors I knew couldn't shine my shoes get the jobs that belonged to me." Eli has never been happy unless he's working. In 2010, at age ninety-five, he was honored by the governors of the Academy of Motion Picture Arts and Sciences for his lifetime achievements. "How you doing?" I asked him recently. "Two pictures I'm in—two! I just did . . . what's his name, you know, um, the Michael Douglas thing was the first one, and, uh, and, uh, you know."

This little guy with a cane still loves to go out. I so envied that ability when I first met him. He just never got depressed. That's not part of him. Even today I can't get out of the house some days. I cancel everything, I isolate. I want to go out, but then . . . I wind up staying home, talking myself out of going. Sometimes it's really hard to have fun.

The Wallachs' encouragement meant a great deal to me back then. There's a photograph of Eli lying on his bed with an enormous crocheted black and pink blanket my mother made for Eli and Anne as a Christmas present. It was the only way she knew to say thanks to them for looking out for me. They were blown away and have that blanket to this day.

—◊—

By 1972 I had become an Equity actor—meaning I was a union man—with a part in the very successful off-Broadway play *One Flew over the Cuckoo's Nest*. This was the play's northeast college tour, therefore it was waaaay off Broadway. I played Billy Bibbit, a young patient who lives in constant fear of his mother. Nurse Ratched uses this to her advantage in the asylum, and takes on the role of his substitute mother. Billy was like a little boy, a virgin with a chronic stutter, particularly when Nurse Ratched was in the ward. Then the main character? R. P. McMurphy decides to make a break for it, and sneaks in some of his girls, with booze, and they do a bit of the in and out. When Nurse Ratched finds out that Billy has consummated the relationship with his girl, she plays the mommy card, saying "I'm ashamed!" And Billy, in a real crowd-pleasing moment, replies defiantly, "I'm not!" Then she threatens to tell his mother. She knew exactly where to stick the knife. So exit Billy stage left—he breaks down and cuts his throat.

This part was a big break for me. Remember, I was the kid who never made it out of remedial English class. By the time I got to high school in Hoboken and Cliffside Park, the general consensus was that I'd grow up to be a failure. But that became the fuel that drove me. I was going to prove my doubters wrong, and this was a big step in that direction.

Billy was the complete opposite of me. He was so afraid of his mother. He wanted to be a good boy, to please. He wanted everyone to love him. In the play, McMurphy, our reluctant hero, couldn't understand why the guys just took Nurse Ratched's shit. He was faking insanity. Like me, he had to be alone, do it alone, and never ask for help. The only difference was, I was faking *san-*

ity. Forty years later I interviewed Dr. Dean Brooks, who at that time ran the hospital where they filmed the movie. He insisted on getting them to shoot there. He wanted to give the patients an opportunity to work on the movie. That was the deal: if he let them film there, some patients would be extras, and some would work with the camera crew. It was from that experience that a good portion of them left and went back out into society. Ken Kesey, who wrote the novel on which the movie was based, had figured it out. The lunatics are running the insane asylums. I suppose I did so well in that role because I could relate to having an overbearing mother figure, to being a crazy person, to living with crazy people.

When I was a kid, "asylum" meant prison, only worse. When I was six or seven, just after Maryann and I started getting really out of hand, I started throwing fits in order to ensure I got what I wanted. I believe this had a lot to do with my baby sister Maryann joining our family and knocking me out of the box as the only child.

My cousin, our family historian, will attest that I was a spoiled brat! Absolutely relentless. Daddy always caved to my demands, but Mommy would get on the phone . . .

MOMMY, *dialing the phone as if making an appointment for the beauty parlor while seven-year-old JP is throwing a conniption, screaming because he doesn't want to put his school clothes on.* You get dressed right now and go to school or I'm calling the nuthouse you little sumanabitch!"

Mind you, I'd never been there, but I was deathly afraid of the local asylum.

JOEY. No, no, Mommy, NO! I hate it there! I ain't going! I ain't going!

MOMMY. Hello. Can I please have the phone number for the Snake Pit? Yes, that's right, the insane asylum. Yes, I'll wait.

It was Acting 101. Around the same time I discovered there was no Santa, I found out there was never anybody on the phone.

MOMMY, *her hand over the receiver, and in a hushed, agitated voice.* Stop it, Joseph!

JOEY *ignores her request and beats up his school clothes on the kitchen floor.*

MOMMY. Pick it up! Are you gonna stop? (*Into phone.*) Can you please hold a second, I gotta get a pencil . . . 201 . . . yes, OL9-4272.

And she's writing this shit on the wall, next to the phone. As Mommy starts dialing, we see Joey has stopped beating up his clothes.

JOEY. Please don't call the nuthouse!

Mommy holds up her hand to Joey as if to say, "Don't interrupt me while I'm talking."

MOMMY. Hello? Hello? Is this the nuthouse? I need help with a crazy kid.

JOEY. The men in the white jackets!

MOMMY, *turning.* Yes, to get you, Joey! And when they get here . . .

JOEY. I'll be good! I promise, I promise!

MOMMY, *back into the receiver.* Can you please send a car to 202 Monroe?

JOEY. No! No! I'll go to school right now!

MOMMY. But they're coming now!

JOEY, *as he runs to the front door still buttoning his shirt.* Tell them I went to school and that I won't do this anymore!

The apartment door slams closed behind Joey. As we see Mommy hanging up phone, we hear a faint voice coming from the receiver.

OPERATOR. At the tone the time will be 8:09 a.m. and nine seconds . . . *beep.*

She saved these performances for my worst fits, and sometimes she'd be begging them to come and get *her*. I was terrorized at the time, but like everything else, I eventually got wise to Mommy's nuthouse routine, and the calling-the-orphanage routine. I was already living in a nuthouse. I could have had a better chance in the Snake Pit! Olivia De Havilland came out all right! My first visit to an actual asylum was research for when I played Billy Bibbit. I was eager to get it right so I contacted the administration, and they were more than happy to show me around. I spent two days there. Then I realized I shouldn't have been so scared! That place was a picnic compared to living with my mother!

In my early years of acting, playing those characters was the only time I knew who I was. When I was playing somebody else, I felt like me. Acting? Therapy? Is there a difference?

—m—

In 1973 I won a role in a play called *Winnie's Noodle Surprise* at a small off-off-Broadway theater. I was doing the play with a wonderfully beautiful actress, Violet Dunn, and our costar (I wish I could remember her name—she was from the Yiddish theater and she was getting the audience every night). Violet was in her seventies at the time. In her younger years she had performed on Broadway, a real Broadway star. Her character Winnie is an old lady who can't get by on her Social Security checks. She can't pay the rent, and all she can afford to eat is cat food. So she decides to make it a point with the mayor. How to get the mayor's attention? I played a delivery boy who shows up at her door one day, and she proceeds to drug me. She cooks up something she calls "noodle surprise" and laces it with sleeping pills. So I have some and I'm drugged. When I wake up, I'm tied up and being held for ransom. As the story progresses, I become her ally, and in the end, the mayor comes and saves the day.

During the first act Violet drugged my character, knocked me out, and tied me up in her wheelchair. In the next scene Violet sets her plan. This scene was a riot, and our audiences were hysterical every night, wild with laughing. Meanwhile I had to be out cold, center stage, for twelve minutes while they're having all this fun. Not easy to do.

On opening night I opened an eyelid and looked out into the audience, and there in the front row was the most beautiful creature I'd ever seen. I was keeping up with the script, but all I could see was this beautiful girl with a big, big smile and long dark hair. She was Eurasian, Chinese-German. Quite stunning.

After the play, we all went out for drinks and to a party uptown. At the party I learned this girl's name was Morgan. I talked to her for a few minutes, but she didn't want to talk to me. I was working the room, meeting girls and trying to hook up, but nothing was working. Maybe the ballet wasn't in town. Later, the party was ending, she was still there, and she started talking to me. I was hoping it was late enough for her to lower her standards.

I talked her into going downtown for breakfast, my treat. I didn't have any money, so I took her to a place called the Little Flower where my acting classmates and friends Lauren White and Aleta Reason worked. I knew I could get a free breakfast out of Aleta. I figured I could also borrow five bucks from her, which I did.

After a full breakfast and some meaningful conversation, we walked back to my place at 107 Sullivan. I was going to grab ten bucks for her cab ride home since she lived on the East Side in the 30s. Now we were on the sidewalk in front of my building. I kissed her goodbye, then she says, "Joe, you know I'd really like to stay, but I'm not into having sex tonight. Could I just sleep over?"

I started hearing bells and whistles! "Well shit yes, Morgan, yeah! Tripping over my words, I said, "OK . . . let's go."

—∽—

We were divorced eleven years later.

In the meantime, I had a career to build. Even though I was getting extra work and the occasional theater job, I felt like I just wasn't getting anywhere in New York. I would get close to significant parts, but wouldn't get them.I learned I had the natural instinct to get in the door, being a Hoboken hustler by trade. But you couldn't always get past the kids at the front door. I dedicated two days of the week just to banging on doors and following up with phone calls, trying to charm my way into a meeting—the theory that the squeaky wheel gets the grease.

I didn't know anybody, and I didn't have any connections, but you make your own destiny. I worked harder than anyone else and did whatever it took to get the job. I believed that only success would make me happy, and boy, I wanted to be happy. I wanted to fill up the empty, gasping hole in my chest. To do that I used the good parts of me—my quick wit, sense of humor, humility—and I used the bad parts—my deceptiveness and the dark influences of my past.

—∽—

I recently spoke to a group of 350 people in Texas. During the question-and-answer session, a woman in the audience asked, "Well, what would have happened if you'd not made it?" Just thinking about that, I started sobbing uncontrollably in front of those people. It was very similar to the feeling I had in Vermont when I had what I understand was an honest to God nervous breakdown. It's the feeling of dying. It's the feeling of death. That "why am I even here?" feeling.

I have always believed that God helps those who help them-selves. In the early days of my career, I had to remind myself that if I only had two months' rent left in the bank, I had to find an-other job. I had to go out there and make an audition happen for myself. Hound those agents. Get in that audition room no mat-ter what. Get that opportunity.

I remember that quote in *Patton*, when Patton says: "I've al-ways felt that I was destined for some great achievement, what I don't know. The last great opportunity of a lifetime—an entire world at war, and I'm left out of it? God will not permit this to happen! I will be allowed to fulfill my destiny! His will be done." That was me. Me and Patton.

I hustled jobs, I hustled people, I hustled people I knew to hustle people I didn't. I had enough natural instinct to realize that at these casting groups the kids in the front were doing all the work. You know, the assistants, and aides to the assistants. They were the ones stuffing the envelopes, they were reviewing the submissions of actors, they could make or break you for a particular part.

Here's how it worked: I landed my first meeting with an agent, Peter Witt, because of Anne Jackson. He represented her, and she convinced him to meet with me. Kathleen Letterie worked as an assistant there. I became friends with her and invited her to come and see me in a play at the New Dramatist. After that she started submitting me for parts without Witt knowing.

When I was still in New York, Kathleen submitted me for *Dog Day Afternoon*. They brought me in based on my looks, and I read with Al Pacino. It went well enough and, lo and behold, I got a call back. Peter Witt's number two, Clifford Stevens, was like, "Oh, who? Oh boy! Here we go. This guy's getting call backs." It was my first real nibble of serious heavyweight interest.

I began to have regular meetings with Clifford Stevens. He guided me. "This is what you have to do. Build up a résumé and get more experience in this industry," he suggested. "And this is what I'm gonna do. I'm gonna keep an eye on you, because Annie and Eli Wallach have said that you are not without talent. And so what you gotta do is get auditions with the Theatre Communications Group and you gotta go out there and do more theater. And continue your studies." "But," I said, "but how? How am I gonna get through that door without your help? I mean, can you take the risk of sending me out there and call them and tell them you're calling for me?" They call this "hip pocketing" in the industry these days. I was able to bully him into getting me some auditions.

Then into my life came Annette Handley, an agent for Leo Bookman. We became friends; she came to see me do *Cuckoo's Nest*. She wanted to represent me, because she was interested in me as an actor. She introduced me to Leo and she became my agent. She was so good, she eventually broke off and started Berkus, Cosay, Handley, and Stein. Berkus and Cosay later formed United Talent. Annette started going to group therapy, and Ralph was very impressed with her. He had ambitions beyond listening to people scream, so he had scraped together some money and invested with the talent agent Harry Ufland, and they were going to California. Ralph offered Annette a job as an agent if she would move out there. When Ralph got to L.A., he started running group therapy but maintained a group in New York as well. Sort of bipolar bicoastal. Then Ralph started working on me. "If you'll come out to L.A., I'll introduce you to Harry," Ralph said. That's all he said. He didn't promise me anything else. Just that he'd provide a meeting for me.

By this time Annette was already out there and my acting

teacher John Lehne had gone out a year earlier, and that made me feel safe about going. This was the show biz exodus circa 1970s. Morgan and I were living together on Sullivan Street in SOHO. Morgan was waiting tables too, and we started raising money to get to L.A. by working as many shifts as we could. My mother borrowed money from my father's girlfriend to pay for two one-way tickets, so we left New York and joined the swelling westward migration of actors, agents, and therapists.

—m—

There is nothing like going through the front door having been vouched for, having a big name validating you and your work. Your résumé is different when it says UTA, CAA, or ICM on it; you have that endorsement helping you. When you go in the room to audition, you have five minutes to win that part, so you need all the help you can get. When I arrived in California in 1976, I was riding the momentum of the creative partnership between Ralph Ricci and Harry Ufland, who had just formed their own agency. Ralph was Ufland's business partner; he was manager of accounts for the agency and chief therapist. Harry had just splintered off from an enormous agency, and now was a boutique agent. At the time the Ufland Agency represented people like Harvey Keitel, Bob De Niro, Martin Scorsese, Louis Miles, Yaphet Kotto—he represented what was probably the finest, most diverse list of actors, directors, producers, and writers. Harry Ufland's name on my résumé really made all the difference in the world. The casting directors saw me, they were glad to see me, and the rest was all up to me. Harry had taken me on because I was in Ralph's group therapy, but I started booking jobs and justifying their decision. I was at the right place at the right time. I was focused on my hopes, the possibility of success, and the opportunity to make it.

Here's my secret: my game plan was . . . I didn't have one. There was no plan B; failure was not an option. I didn't know how I would execute it. I just knew success was gonna happen if I broke my ass and took every opportunity and knocked my opponents out of the way. I had nothing to fall back on. Moving to Manhattan had been just the first step. The move to L.A. was my real escape from the Hoboken of my childhood, the formative years I spent in poverty and despair. I was now on a plane with Morgan, the only girl I had ever been able stay with for longer than two weeks, headed to Hollywood, the place I'd been dreaming of for most of my life.

When Morgan and I arrived in L.A., it was raining. It *never* rains in L.A. We stayed with Annette and her boyfriend, Chip. Annette and Morgan were already good friends. Same went for me and Annette.

My first day there, at 9:30 on a Monday morning, I went off to the office on Canon Drive and met with Harry Ufland and Ralph. We sat down for a brief meeting about my background—we went over my résumé, chatted a bit, and that was it.

"We're going to represent you, let's go to work," Harry said.

Ralph stood up and went into Annette's office. "Drop everything off your desk, Annette," he said. "Start setting up meetings."

And by twelve that afternoon I had five meetings. Was I dreaming? This was unbelievable.

But then, at the end of the day, Annette called me to say that she had just been fired. She said she was leaving the office and would see me at her house at dinner. Just my luck. I had five meetings set up, and my agent gets fired. Welcome to Hollywood.

CHAPTER FOUR

Let the Shame—Begin!

In 1977, I was twenty-five years old. I could see the Hollywood sign from the porch of our apartment on Stanley Avenue. I had been in L.A. for only a few months, I hadn't landed a part yet, and the money Morgan and I had managed to save was just about gone. So I was waiting tables in Hollywood, but I was there. I was living in Los Angeles, my future in front of me. *Fear* was the gasoline driving me toward the possibility of my success. My only obstacle was that every actor in Hollywood wanted the same fuckin' thing! And that included Morgan. Morgan was also an actress, a pretty good one too—plus she was very pretty, she wasn't afraid of hard work, and she was smart. A real go-getter. We had prepared a scene that she could perform for an audition, because back in those days, the only way for young actors to show their abilities was to do auditions with monologues and scene partners. If you're starting out today the only question asked is, "Do you have a reel?"

Through her own tenacity, Morgan had gotten an audition

for Eddie Foy III, grandson of the legendary comedian Eddie Foy. His grandpa was the creator of the family vaudeville act Eddie Foy and the the Seven Little Foys, which was a national institution back in the 1920s and '30s. Eddie III was now head of casting at ABC. Morgan brought a scene from acting class from a play called *The Girl on the Via Flaminia*. It was set in Rome during World War II, about an impoverished Italian girl struggling to survive. So we did the scene. It was Morgan's scene, and I was her scene partner, and at the end Eddie says, "Listen, that was great kids, thanks. Joe, what about you? Do you have an agent?" I said, "Yeah, my agent is Harry Ufland." And the next thing I knew, I was auditioning for the well-known casting director Harriet Helberg, and soon I had landed my first television part. I won a role in the pilot of a comedy called *McNamara's Band*. That's how my career started in Hollywood; I managed to be at the right place at the right time.

I was paid the whopping sum of $12,000, and just like that I quit my waiter job and was out of the restaurant business . . . for the moment. My last customers were John Travolta and Olivia Newton-John. They sat at my table and handed me my last check. The following day I was just about seven blocks east of the restaurant at Paramount, where they were shooting *Grease*.

—◊◊◊—

After my television debut in the pilot of *McNamara's Band*, I landed a series regular role in Rob Reiner's mid-season replacement, *Free Country*. Reiner then tapped me to costar with him in James Burrows' television movie, *More Than Friends*, which would ultimately become the genesis for the feature film, *When Harry Met Sally*. This led to the part of Angelo Maggio—a role originated by fellow Hobokenite Frank Sinatra—in NBC's miniseries adaptation of James Jones's *From Here to Eternity*. Angelo Maggio and his buddy, Robert E. Lee Prewitt (Steve Railsback) are soldiers on a weekend pass. While at the New Congress Club, their local whorehouse, Maggio is drunk and provoked into a personal brawl by Sergeant Fatso Judson (Peter Boyle), a sadistic bastard who is also in charge of the army stockade (a.k.a. jail). The fight is broken up by Staff Sergeant Warden (William Devane). Maggio gets six months in the army stockade after going AWOL. He tries faking insanity to get out of the army, only to be beaten so badly by Fatso Judson that he goes insane and dies trying to escape.

From Here to Eternity was my first important role in Hollywood. Yes, it was television, but it was a *miniseries*, which meant it was more than halfway toward movie form. Natalie Wood and Kim Basinger rounded out the principal cast.

Winning this role was more than serendipitous. For the 1953 movie version, Eli Wallach was offered the role of Angelo Maggio first, but he turned it down to do a play. Frank Sinatra took it instead, and would go on to win an Oscar for the performance that revived his career. There were so many ties to my past and present—for me, winning the role of Angelo seemed like a stroke of fate.

We were shooting *From Here to Eternity* on the Warner lot. In 1978 it was called the Burbank Studio and shared the space with the Columbia studios. Buzz Kulik was directing. I had been an extra on another movie that Buzz directed called *Shamus*, starring Burt Reynolds. No doubt Mr. Kulik never even noticed me— I was one of two hundred poolroom extras. But being an extra was always an education. It hadn't taken me long to figure out that the longer I was invisible as an extra, the longer I could get paid and observe the principal stars as they worked in front of the cameras. Once you were established in a film, meaning recognizable in a scene, they couldn't use you anymore as an extra. So I'd try to go two or three days without being established, so that I could grab that much more work and experience. After I was cast in the part of Angelo Maggio a meeting was arranged for me to come in to talk to the director about the work ahead of us—character, place, background—which is usually the drill on important projects. I loved working with Kulik, and the crew adored him, which I've since learned is always very telling. His office was in a two-story horseshoe shaped building, just off the New York Street back lot and right under the Warner Bros. water tower. His office had a front yard big enough for the tech adviser to exercise his military muscle and train those of us doing the marching. You know, right face, left face, et cetera.

I arrived for my appointment and waited outside his office. When Buzz's door opened, I got up to greet him, and realized he wasn't alone. Standing next to him was Natalie Wood. She smiled, said hello and we shook hands, and I remember noticing she had a forceful grip. Here I was, meeting Natalie Wood! It was almost like an out-of-body experience. I was actually going to be working on a really good part in a project that might make a difference in my career. I was humbled by what she'd accomplished, and I aspired to be as savvy as she.

Natalie had *it*. Whatever *it* was that made movie stars movie stars. Was it me, or did the room seemed brighter? Was sunlight flooding the office?

She had just finished a fitting and was discussing it with Buzz. She was still in costume, wearing prewar silk stockings with the seam and a simple white dress, simple and smart, the hem resting just at her knee. Her dark brown hair brushed her shoulders. Standing there in her white three-inch leather sandals, she barely reached my nose, but she had a commanding presence. Her smile was authentic, genuine. She put me at ease.

I was seeing my past clearer knowing that Natalie Wood was real, authentic! Not a phony bone in her body. She said we should get together, said her goodbyes, and was gone.

As I'm telling this story today, I'm realizing that what struck me about Natalie Wood back in 1965 was her ability to connect with an audience—we see our own emotional vulnerability in stars like her. I saw my pain in her. In *West Side Story*, Maria had just arrived to this new country, America. She felt different, she *was* different. I could relate to that. Leaving friends behind, having to make new ones, going to a new school—I knew that loneliness and fear too. By sixteen I had passed through six different schools in four different towns, never knowing if this time we were going to stick. I was always the outsider. I didn't want to let anyone in, and feeling like I never belonged hung over me like a cloud.I think that's why shoplifting or sneaking into a party created such a wild rush of adrenaline for me—I was *getting in*! But then afterward there was always the crash, and I'd be stuck with that same old feeling inside that at any moment somebody's going to tap me on the shoulder, demanding to see my ticket.

I loved *West Side Story* because I identified with it so closely. Cousin Patty and I took every opportunity we had to see it. We would cut school and watch the movie over and over again easily twenty times. We played hooky and went to the Fabian Theatre in Hoboken, then ran over to Journal Square and stayed the entire day. We'd watch one matinee after an other and into the evening.

I fell so deeply in love with Natalie Wood's character that I made myself sick. The only one to fix me was Maria. I was over-whelmed with dread and fear, feeling like I was gonna die. I'd cry, the crying gave me stomach cramps, and the cramps made me cry. I was twelve years old and in such pain my mother didn't think I'd see thirteen! I'm not kidding! I was in love with *Maria!*

I can't remember what brought this episode on, but Mommy wasn't taking any chances. She brought in the big guns: Dopey Gus's sister Aunt Zitzi was going to do the *maluccio*. They took up a vigil, lighting candles and chanting over the heart-wrenching screams. Madonna! I felt lost and alone. Mommy sat while my great aunt repeated her old Napolitano prayers, trying to reel the devil from my soul, and I was screaming to high heaven. "I WANT MY MARIA! . . . I GOTTA HAVE MY MARIA, MOMMY! I GOTTA, MA."

James Brown had nothing on me when it came to scream-ing. I adored Natalie Wood in that movie. It was the universal themes that got me: territory, honor, love, trust. As a kid I could relate to those themes. We had an influx of Puerto Ricans mi-grating into our neighborhood. The Puerto Rican immigration pushed us one rung upward on the food chain. The Germans hated the Irish, the Irish hated the Guineas, and now we hated the Puerto Ricans. And that left our African-American neighbors for everyone to hate.

West Side Story had a profound impact on all the kids in our community. In it the gangs danced through the Upper West Side rubble where the Lincoln Center would eventually stand. Hobo-ken too was gentrifying; we would imitate the gang fights in our own rubble as city planners tore down an entire block between 6th and 4th Streets and Grand and Clinton, making way for more federally funded housing for the elderly. I even had my own Maria prototype, a beautiful Puerto Rican girl in my seventh-grade class named Wanda. Kids actually started dressing like kids in the movie. Buckles, belts, chinos, Converse sneakers.

I'd never seen or read Shakespeare's *Romeo and Juliet,* so a few years later, when I saw the Franco Zeffirelli's version of the tale, I thought, Wait a minute, this Italian guy just ripped off *West Side Story*! I was very naïve in those days. Who's Shakespeare? What is *Romeo and Juliet*? Forget it! *West Side Story* was the center of my universe and determined my destiny: I was going to be in the movies.

The day I met Natalie's husband, Robert Wagner (whom everybody called RJ) I was out in the courtyard of the Burbank Studio practicing military maneuvers with our technical adviser, a retired commander. The Commander was relentlessly drilling me and my costar Steve Railsback. Steve was playing the central character in the James Jones novel, Robert E. Lee Prewitt, my best friend in the story (and who became a good friend in life). For hours each day we grabbed our rifles and learned right shoulder, arm, left shoulder, arm, company halt, attention. We were in the middle of maneuvers when an amazingly well-dressed fellow—striped shirt, light blue ascot—approached me. At fifteen paces I spotted him. It was Robert Wagner . . . who had decided to conduct an improvisational exercise.

RJ, *whom I later learned was just wrapping up a his own World War II epic called* Pearl. Atten hut!

We snap to attention.

RJ. Are you Joe Pantoliano?

JP, *still at attention.* Yes. Sir!

RJ. Am I to understand you saw *West Side Story* twenty times?

JP. Yes, sir . . . twenty-one times . . . I did, sir . . .

RJ. Well?

JP. Well? Sir?

RJ. How'd you like it?

JP, *realizing by now I was being teased.* I like *West Side Story* very much sir . . . but . . .

RJ. But what, soldier!

JP. I LOVE NATALIE WOOD.

RJ, *laughing.* You better treat my wife nice, young man. All right.

JP. Yes, sir . . . No worries there, sir. And . . . It's an honor to meet you too, sir.

RJ, *without breaking character.* As you were.

Then he walked off. Steve and I did one of those slow turns toward each other, as if to say, did that just happen? Then we turned back to the Commander, who had witnessed the whole episode.

DC, *big smile, laughing.* At ease.

—m—

Morgan and I had set up house on Stanley Avenue, on the second floor of a four-unit prewar building. It had a fireplace, a balcony, and best of all, it was cheap. We had no lease, just paid first and last month's rent, $185 dollars a month. Our experience wasn't like the current generation's now that everything is out of reach. Morgan picked out a complete set of second-hand furniture, even the TV, for next to nothing. I was getting closer to the dream. Having been in L.A. for only thirteen months, I was already getting results. Taking up Ralph Ricci's invitation had proved to be a good bet. I often think how things might have gone if I had stayed behind. I had wanted to make it in NYC, on Broadway, like my acting heroes of the past. If I could make it there!—*then anywhere*—as the song goes. But this much was certain: Ralph Ricci had made me an offer I couldn't refuse. He was my benefactor. I'll always be grateful.

Work started up on *Eternity,* and it was intense, I loved it! Filming was exciting. Like the first time I had sex—it was familiar, like I'd been there before. Everything was all right. That's the feeling I needed, and it filled me up. I chased it my whole life. I swear working every day was and is a joy. Acting is a collaborative gig, and despite all the creative arguing, the blowing-off steam, or generally being a crybaby and complaining because you know your idea is better than someone else's, that's what we do. Well, I do, for sure. We complain, either that we're working too hard or hardly working. I still get grumpy, tired from the grind—but I love every minute of it. It's my favorite drug.

We were working fourteen to eighteen hours a day between San Pedro and the Warner Bros. lot. Morgan would get up at 5 a.m. to make coffee, then she'd wake me at 5:30, we'd have breakfast, she'd give me a kiss and a pat on my fanny, then go back to sleep. After a long day on set I'd come home, shower, eat, then get in bed and prepare for the next day, breaking down my script. I also found time to go to group therapy three times each week, and I was still in acting class with John Lehne. He had coached me on my *Eternity* screen test, then the whole process, every moment. Moment by moment, executing each scene. My look, my character—understanding how we were alike and unalike. I found my footing, built the foundation of my career while working in New York, but I learned my craft under John Lehne's guidance in Hollywood. Burbank to be exact. I spent twelve years training under him. He was my teacher and he handed me the key to the door of my creative soul. Rest in peace, John.

—m—

Natalie and RJ were my first angels in Hollywood. RJ called me "Pan-tiliono." In 1977 he was somewhere in his mid-forties, and Natalie in her thirties. My God, they were beautiful. Everything about RJ was stylish, especially his hair. It's always the fuckin' hair. I would have been a major movie star if only my hair didn't come out of a box!

I had been fitted for my first hairpiece for *McNamara's Band* the year before. I was just twenty-five years old. Since then I've kept all my hairpieces except one, which I gave away as a gift. (I gave the hairpiece from my role as Guido the Killer Pimp in *Risky Business* to the billionaire Ron Burkle, in thanks for his many favors—after all, what else can you give a billionaire?) After each role I've always lovingly put the character's name on the box and put the hairpiece in my attic in memory of the character I built. In a lot of ways there are pieces of me in those hairpieces. As an actor you take these characters with you; they're always a part of you and you are a part of them.

I had to get fitted for a hairpiece for *Eternity*. We did hair tests with Ben Lane over at the Warner Bros. makeup department, which was one of the last such departments. They became obsolete with the end of the contract player, when so much less was being done on the lot. I went in and tried on some wigs, we took pictures. Then Ben pulled out old wig boxes from the '30s, '40s, and '50s, their handwritten labels yellowed with age. Pinned to the lace underbelly of the hairpieces were two names from the old Warner Bros. contract players: Humphrey Bogart and Walter Brennan. Ben carefully placed Bogie's hairpiece on my head, and I looked at my reflection in the mirror. I couldn't believe it. I had Bogart's wig on! My head was anointed! HOLY SHIT!

Being superstitious, I took this as a good omen. I loved those two actors. We took Polaroids. Then they sent me to Bob

Roberts, the hairpiece maker on Robinson Street. I was going in for my appointment, and the guy that owned the place was walking Jimmy Stewart out. Jimmy wore a floppy rain hat and held his hairpiece box under his arm. I had to stop for a moment to take it all in. Just walking down street I was seeing movie stars everywhere. All those stars had a huge effect on me as young boy dreaming of being in the movies.

As I was getting fitted for my own wig, RJ's assistant, an Englishwoman named Liz, called. She announced she was calling on Natalie and RJ's behalf and they wanted to invite me and my girlfriend to dinner.

The Wagners' home was on Canon Drive, three blocks up from the township of Beverly Hills. Beverly Hills is in essence a little village, not unlike Hoboken in that respect. The Wagners' was a New England–esque white clapboard house with navy blue shutters, adorned with night jasmine and rosebushes. Unlike most celebrity homes, it was only twenty-five yards from the sidewalk, with no fence or gate protecting it from curious stargazers.

I drove up at the appointed hour and hesitated. At that time, in 1978, we were driving a '69 Opel Kadett station wagon with 70,000 miles on it that we bought for six hundred bucks. It seemed totally out of place—this was a car that even the help wouldn't be caught dead in. So I parked it several houses up from theirs, out of sight and completely out of mind.

Morgan and I walked up the brick driveway, past their dark green sedan, up to their front porch. I pressed the pearl key of the copper intercom beside the brown lacquered front door. A man's voice over the intercom barked out a command—"HELLO!" We answered overlapping each other: "Hi! It's Morgan and Joey!" We stumbled over ourselves with nervous laughter, waiting for the intercom to tell us to come in. Instead the large door swung open

and revealed RJ Wagner himself, who greeted us both with a big
smile and Morgan with a warm hug. His V-neck sweater lay over
his fresh white shirt, opened at the collar, with a blue paisley silk
scarf. RJ led the way into his home, which was handsomely appointed in warm tones of brown and green.

Passing through the living room I could hear the sound of
laughter filling the next room. We had just missed the punch line
to the story being told by RJ's and Natalie's lifelong friend, the
writer-director Tom Mankiewicz. I liked Tom instantly. He was
a tall, slender man, his thin blond hair neatly combed over the
thinner hair beneath it. His right hand almost always cradled
the end of a half-lit cigarette, and he had a raspy voice only
cigarettes could produce. Tom, the son of the director Joseph,
and nephew to Herman, had written *Superman* and two Bond
screenplays.

Natalie was sitting on a child's wooden rockinghorse, feeding her youngest, Courtney, who was in a high chair. She got up
to greet us, hugging both Morgan and me while making sure not
to get any crumbs on us.

Their older kids joined us at table, and we stayed up talking long after they were sent to bed. We talked about where I
came from and where Morgan came from. I got to know about
their lives. They were married twice, first when they were just
kids. Then they split up. Then they got married again and had
Courtney together. Their other kids, Katie and Natasha, are from
their other marriages.

There was something so wonderfully vulnerable about Natalie and RJ. They were so candid with us, so down to earth. Their
kids came first, and they cared about the same things ordinary
mortals did, like where their kids went to school. They opened
up their lives to us. We found that we could confide in them as

they shared their experiences in their own lives. They were interested in hearing about what my parents did, where Morgan came from. Both Natalie and Morgan were originally from San Francisco. They suggested we call my mom, and as I listened to them on the phone, I realized that we're all the same. We all try to make a human connection. And yet it was kind of amazing to me that such a thing could happen here. This lovely family had decided to let us in. I told them I'd seen *West Side Story* eighteen or nineteen times, but my cousin Patty De Riso had seen it twenty-five times. So, at midnight, at their house, we called up Patty in Long Island, and his wife, Gina, answered the phone. Tom Mankiewicz, Morgan, RJ, Natalie, and I were all on an extension.

GINA, *waking from a sound sleep.* Hello?

NATALIE WOOD, *in her best Marilyn whisper.* Is Pat there?

She was giggling, but she made it work . . .

GINA. Who the fuck is this?

NATALIE WOOD. It's Natalie, his girlfriend. Who's this?

GINA. This is his wife.

NATALIE. Oh, Pat didn't tell me he had a wife. Can I talk to him?

GINA, *yelling.* PAT!

By now we were screaming laughing. Then I get on the phone.

JOEY: *Gina?*

GINA. Joe was that really—Are you with Natalie?

JOEY. Yeah, it's Natalie Wood.

GINA. *laughing.* No way! You're hot shit. Are you kidding me?

Then Natalie got on the phone again and talked to Patty. Then RJ got on the phone.

RJ. Pat? RJ Wagner. What's this I hear, that you've been obsessing over my wife's movies?

I could hear cousin Pat laughing.

RJ. You weren't playing, were you Pat? You've got to stay away from my wife. I like guns.

Pat and Gina never forgot that call. We were all blown away by their playfulness on the phone.

Hollywood and celebrity, they've become everything in our culture. We treat celebrities like they do people with royal bloodlines in England. But the Wagners didn't act like royalty, and that's one of the many things that made them special to me. Natalie Wood was a movie star from the time she was six, in *Miracle on 34th Street*. I grew up watching Robert Wagner on TV in the '60s. I wanted to dress like him and wished I had hair like him. Personality is the gold standard that separates the dukes from the kings. (I guess that makes me the court jester?) In revealing ourselves to each other we ended up becoming friends.

I will always be grateful for their genuine kindness to us, a young couple just starting out. I trusted them with my fears and confusion about the business we all loved so much, and they shared stories about their own down times. From them I learned how to be available to the young actors who have asked this veteran ham for guidance.

With less than two years clocked in Hollywood I couldn't compete financially with their level of generosity. We didn't have much to offer, but they continued to reach out to us. Natalie and her girls even babysat our baby, Marco. We often went out to dinner with RJ and Natalie, and they also came to our apartment once on Stanley Avenue. The only thing new in our house was a red wood picnic table with benches that we used as a dining room table. The Wagners came over and sat at our picnic table with Annette Handly, and friends Harry and Lee Columby. When they came the whole block was ablaze because RJ and Natalie were in our apartment. I hadn't been able to keep my mouth shut, which had caused the mini riot. They were wonderful people. And RJ, forget about it.I loved that man. He's been in my life ever since.

I was learning that Hoboken and Hollywood had a lot in common. If you made a friend in my neighborhood, you vouched for that person, you introduced him to your friends, you took responsibility for him; the Wagners were doing the same for me. They introduced me to this elite community. They let us into their lives, and we got to know their family and close friends. That included Mark Crowley, who was once Natalie's personal assistant, and went on to write *The Boys in the Band* and produce the first two seasons of *Hart to Hart*. Mark was a gentleman, very smart, thoughtful, and kind. He and Natalie were inseparable. He had helped to devolop *Hart to Hart* with RJ and Tom Mankiewicz. Tom must have been a red-haired freckle-faced kid; what was originally vibrant red hair was now sandy red mixed with patches of gray. I remember his fingernails were always stained yellow from nicotine.

Maybe RJ and Natalie felt some obligation to give back to us because of the kindness, generosity and mentoring they had received when they were first starting out. RJ told me stories of the angels in his life—Spencer Tracy was a mentor to RJ, as were David Niven, Sinatra, and Gregory Peck. But RJ was so very likable. Throughout their house they had photos of all these great movie stars, 8 x 10 professional pictures in beautiful sterling silver frames that were signed personally to RJ or Natalie or both of them. They had a real respect for film history and the people who created it.

Another example of their generosity: I was trying to get in on a movie that was being cast, and my agent could not get the meeting with the director, Paul Mazursky. I asked Natalie if she might call him for me. Natalie picked up the phone, and within minutes I had an appointment.

Mazursky greeted me and as we sat down he said jokingly, "You have an important friend." When I heard that, I realized that this was a courtesy meeting. He had already cast the part. Well, at least I met him, I thought, and I thanked him for seeing me. My thinking was, OK, maybe not this time, but maybe the next one. RJ and Natalie introduced me to everybody. Directors, actors, screenwriters, everybody. The director John Irwin was staying at their guesthouse while he was doing a movie in L.A. We went out to dinner and got to know each other. At the end of the evening I spotted former governor Ronald Reagan and his wife Nancy having dinner alone and whispered the news to our table. RJ looked up and hollered, "Hey Ronnie! Try the veal, it's the best in the city!" Then he grabbed me by the wrist and we marched over to meet the future president of the United States. I met their pal Gregory Peck when he was doing his morning workout at their house one day. I said to myself, there's Gregory Peck bench pressing. All these actors who were in the TV set I wanted to be in as a kid. The makers of film history. And they were kind to me, giving away to me what was given to them.

—◊—

Before *Eternity* I had never seen the inside of a star's camper. My experience of dressing rooms from the theater was shared spaces located next to basement boiler rooms. The first time I visited Natalie's trailer I was awestruck. I took the long step off the ground onto the steel double stair that folded out from beneath the trailer door, and when the door opened I was greeted by Ed Butterworth, Natalie's makeup man; her hair dresser; assistant Liz; and her dresser. The interior of the dressing room was surprisingly modest, and I heard Natalie in the back bedroom shout out, "Hi, Joey . . . I'll be right out." In return I shouted back, "OK . . . Take your time, Nat." After a few moments Natalie, wearing an oversize men's shirt on loan from wardrobe, I'm sure, to protect her hero costume for her scene after lunch. "Hey JOEYYY! . . ."

The forty-five-foot motor homes, back in 1978, were unbelievably beautiful. If you had a motor home it meant you were important. Agents would negotiate them into the deal, and of course I hadn't negotiated anything. So when Natalie finished shooting her parts in *From Here to Eternity*, it was on my first day of work, and she insisted that they provide me with a motor home—her motor home! So I graduated up.

—∽—

RJ and Natalie invited us out on their yacht. This was a really, really big boat, a sixty-footer called *Splendor* after Natalie's movie *Splendor in the Grass*. It was magnificent. And the kitchen, oh man! It was bigger than my mother's! And this one floated! When they invited us I brought mozzarella in from Fiore's in Hoboken, also peppers, and onions, and Italian olives, and all the Italian bread I could carry.

They gave us a cruise on the *Splendor* as a wedding present, and, of course, they came with us. On the first morning in I came up with my morning coffee and I saw RJ fishing.

RJ. Joey, do me a favor and hold on to this rod.

RJ goes below. So I am holding his fishing pole—this is not like what you use for stickball in Hoboken—and there are two guys zooming around us in a little boat. There were about fifteen to twenty different yachts anchored out in the bay, maybe twenty-five yards apart from each other. Finally these guys motor up to me while RJ is still below.

COP 1. Hey, good morning.

ME. Hey, good morning. (I'm thinking, this must be how sailors talk.)

COP 1. How you doing?

ME. Fine.

COP. Catch anything yet?

ME. Nope, not yet. (Not used to chatting with fishing caps, I was clueless.)

COP. Do you have a license to fish?

ME. Um, a license to fish?—R Jaaaaaaay! (*No answer.*) RJ! RJ! (*Screaming.*) You got any licenses to fish?

RJ, *comes on deck.* Oh yeah. We've got tons of licenses. Don't worry.

He ducks back inside and comes back with a old cigar box, and he's pulling out all this stuff—keys, floaters, and about seven or eight licenses—that were all expired! Every last one of them. So this boat cop had to give me a ticket.

RJ. Well, let me pay for it. Give me that ticket.

ME. No, it's my ticket. It's mine.

COP, *handing it to me.* And no more fishing.

I wanted that ticket. I'd never broken the law for fishing off a sixty-foot yacht on the Hudson in Hoboken.

On our last evening we were going out to have dinner, the dress-up kind. I wore my white linen suit, and I was looking really good. To get to the island we'd used a rubber dinghy, which was lashed to the back of the yacht. To get on their dinghy, you stepped on a mahogany plank, which was about four feet wide, and then stepped into the dinghy. Well, I was the last guy. I had not practiced this enough growing up in Hoboken. I put my foot on the dinghy, and inertia took its course. As the dinghy began moving away from the *Splendor*, my legs began to scissor.

I'm standing with my left foot on the Splendor and my right on the dinghy. My legs spreading wider and wider, opening until I— with my Panama hat, white linens, my suede shoes, wallet, everything—went right in the ice cold water.

Cut to a few years later: I was preparing for some last minute Thanksgiving shopping when the phone rang in my kitchen. "Pantoliano? It's RJ Wagner. What are you doing for lunch?" He was shooting *Hart to Hart* at the Santa Monica Airport, just a few miles from my home in Venice.

I drove out to the airport. The Santa Ana winds were blowing, and as I entered RJ's motor home, the wind nearly blew the door off its hinges. RJ was there with his costar Stefanie Powers. I was friendly with Stefanie, having worked twice with her on *Hart to Hart.* We had lunch, and I remember sitting beside Stefanie and across from RJ, showing them the latest baby pictures of my son Marco. I was walking RJ back to set when he mentioned that Natalie and he would be spending the upcoming Thanksgiving weekend on their boat in Catalina with Chris Walken. Did we want to come to Sunday brunch that weekend, either on *The Splendor* or somewhere near us in Venice?

RJ never called to confirm that brunch. When I heard of Natalie's death Sunday morning, my thoughts instantly went back to my honeymoon weekend and that mahogany plank that extended out from the rear of *The Splendor.* I'll always wonder if Natalie slipped into the icy water as she went for the dingy, just as I had.

—∞—

Before *Eternity* aired, they had a premiere, which was unusual for television—it was a big screening at the MGM studio's Cary Grant

Theater. The show ran about three and a half hours without the commercials. During a break, there was a dinner, and Mickey Rudin came up and introduced himself to me. He was Sinatra's attorney.

"I've represented your predecessor for the past thirty years," he said.

"What's a predecessor?" I said. I didn't know that word.

"Frank Sinatra."

"Oh."

"Frank has asked me to take a look at you."

"What do you think?"

"I think you did a pretty good job."

"Thanks very much. Tell Frank I'm Captain Pete's grandson." Frank knew all about my grandfather, because his father worked under Grampa Pete as a fireman too.

The morning after the *Eternity* screening I got a call. It was RJ and Natalie.

RJ. Good morning, JP! Listen, you were incredible—

NW, *interrupting.* Hello, hello? Oh Joey—embrace these times. They only happen once! That feeling like—

JP. Like I'm floating? (*Now they were both speaking.*)

RJ, *laughing like I found the secret word.* YES! Never take it for granted.

NW. Yes. These feelings, that newness—cherish them. You only get one dance, Joseph. This is a wonderful time. Enjoy it. If you need advice, anything you need to talk about, let us know. (*Then at the same time.*)

NW. I love you Joey.

RJ. I love ya kid. Enjoy it.

When the reviews came out, they were mixed. Some great, some murdered me. The *New York Times* said Sinatra's got nothing to worry about from Joe Pantoliano. Then others said I was a revelation.

As the Wagners suggested, I did enjoy it. I was excited and the phone rang a lot around that time. But the good feelings didn't last.

—∞—

In those early Hollywood years I was gradually accumulating the success that I thought would make me whole. Even so I'd get a movie like *Eternity*, and start worrying that I'd get killed before I had a chance to finish the movie. My voices would continue to reassure me: *Cheer up, the worst is yet to come.* I went to group therapy, yes, but I was ashamed to talk about what was really going on in my head, and the less I talked about it the more prevalent it became.

I lived with an excruciating feeling of raw vulnerability. In my training as an actor we were encouraged to be vulnerable, to show our feelings, to let them out. Well, that was good for my work, bad for my life.

Actually, my first couple of years in New York it worked to my advantage; once I had sex with a young lady in my acting class and in the heat of passion I was flooded by sadness and started to cry. She thought I was swell, and girls like to talk, so she told some of the girls how sensitive I was, and soon I was fucking up a storm. Every third girl in acting class wanted to have a go with me. Sensitive, my ass! The truth is I was scared to death about being vulnerable with any woman.

This feeling of vulnerability was overwhelming me. When I had nothing professionally, I was driven by the fear that I would never get anywhere. Then when I started having some success came the fear of losing it. It was crippling, this secret feeling that

I had no right to any success, but at the same time desperately needed it.

—— ∽ ——

By December of 1978, it had been only twenty months since I'd arrived in Hollywood and by all accounts I was having the best professional year of my life! I could not help feeling indebted to Ralph for it. It was Ralph's suggestion that I move to L.A.; he'd offered me only his guarantee that if I showed I would get a sit-down with agent Harry Ufland. Ralph had made it clear that the buck would stop there, with Harry. If Harry didn't see any future for me, so be it. But he did, and their investment in my talent continued to grow.

Soon after the success of the *From Here to Eternity* miniseries in 1979, NBC decided to make it a television series. They wanted me to come back and be a series regular even though my Maggio was killed. Oh boy, they were throwing money at me. My agent Harry suggested we see how much I could get. They offered me $20,000 per episode and $150,000 for a pay or play (meaning I'd get paid whether they made it or not) movie of the week. So for fourteen weeks of work, they were offering $350,000.

We turned them down.

I wanted to be in the movies, and hoped appearing in *From Here to Eternity* was one hell of an opener. In 1979 there was still a stigma about doing TV; it might hurt your status. Movies were what I wanted, where I had the most to say, and I was young enough to hold out. So I went to back to work waiting tables. In New York this might be a sign of strength—*His standards are so high, he's waiting tables rather than taking that part*—but in Hollywood it was a sign that you were circling the drain. People thought I was nuts. (Little did they know . . .) The irony is, both

Kim Basinger and Barbara Hershey said yes, and it didn't hurt them any.

I called on my old friend Matty Giadarno, who knew my mom and dad back when we lived on Seventh and Adams in Hoboken. Matty *was* Matteo's Restaurant, which was a very big hit in L.A. Matty was one of Frank Sinatra's old neighborhood buddies, and Frank had invested in his restaurant. Matty made big money from day one! He had one small problem . . . *Matty liked the ponies.*

The story I heard was that Matty was in Las Vegas when Sinatra was performing there. After the shows, everybody would wait to catch a glimpse of Frank, and one day Matty was waiting with them. He was all disheveled and smelly and hadn't slept or eaten. Then Frank comes out."Hey, Frank! Hey, Frank!" Matty shouted.

Frank sees him and walks over. "What the hell happened to you?"

"Oh, I got no money. I sold my car. I'm living in these clothes."

So Frank gives him a thousand and says, "Go get yourself straightened out."

Matty goes right to the tables and blows it all. And the next night he's waiting for Frank again.

"I told you to get something to eat and someplace to sleep," Frank tells him. "Get yourself some clothes." And Frank hands him another thousand dollars. So Matty is following the Pantoliano business model to a tee.

Now it's the third night, same thing. So Frank says, "Fuck you. Get in the car." And Frank drives him to Hollywood.

Matty opened Matteo's in 1961, when Kennedy was the fair-haired boy. Sinatra would have after-hours parties there and invite Kennedy. Maybe because of Frank's influence, it became the place to be. Every movie star in the world went to Matteo's.

Everybody loved being there; it was Matty's living room, and all his friends were there. Red Buttons, Dabney Coleman, Rock Hudson, George Raft, Milton Berle, and all the stars of that time. So I went to Matty's and asked for a job, and he gave me one for two days a week.

That place was filled with characters like Clarky, who grew up with Matty, and lived upstairs and worked there taking book. The celebrities loved to place bets and play the numbers, and Clarky would call in bets to the boss in Hoboken. Clarky looked like a stable bum—he never took a bath, but he always had a wad of cash on him. Five, ten thousand for running book. Clarky got his name back in Hoboken because he had elephant ears that reminded his friends of Clark Gable. Clarky ran numbers out of there till he moved back to his old job in Hoboken. Sooner or later we all wound up back there.

A lot of waiters and cooks working at Matteo's were degenerate gamblers like Matty. It was a dis–ease they too couldn't stop. There was Fat Tilio, a waiter by trade who lost more than Matty ever did—a great waiter, but the customers could barely understand the evening specials through his thick Mexican accent. He'd be working all night at the restaurant then all day at Hollywood Park, then back to work at Matteo's to pick up more cash tips to spend on track tips.

You have to realize that customers went there less for the food and more for the show. It was Matty's lovable personality that drove the place. At any restaurant you need a star, the guy in the front who sets the tone. His brother Mikey was a close second by a nose. The best that Hoboken had to offer. Matty had rheumatoid arthritis so he couldn't move his upper body, as if he had no neck. He'd turn his head from his waist. So he'd be standing there in the middle of the room, shouting, "Mikey, Mikey come here. All right, give 'em table four, give 'em table four." Then he'd see his pal George Raft, with whom he'd just lost money on the ponies, and want cheer him up. "Hey Tilio, Tilio, get over here! Go ahead, piss on George Raft's leg, bring him some luck." George Raft would laugh. Matty was loud and he would say whatever came to his mind. He treated everyone the same. He would lean over to a beautiful woman, as though to speak in confidence, and say, "Hello. I'd like to give you a fuck right here." She'd think he was incredibly charming.

There are tons of restaurants people can go to, but they went to Matteo's to see Matty. People often came to the restaurant to see him explode on somebody. They always deserved it too. One Saturday night the place was packed. Rock Hudson was at my table, and Ethel Merman, Gregory Peck, and Frank Sinatra were in the house. Matty had menus under his arm and was running around putting out the Sunday fires. A lady named Mrs. Johnson was on line with a reservation for a party of four. They were waiting for a table and getting antsy. "Lady, please," Matty says. "Have a drink on me! We're trying."

He tells me to put a check on my table 14. "But Matty," I said, "they just got their coffee." Don't you hate it when you've just spent three hundred bucks for dinner, then as soon as you get dessert they slam the check down on ya, giving you the bum's rush? Well, somebody like Matty told them to, that's why.

About ten minutes later my table opened up and Matty started looking for the party of four. "Mrs. Johnson? Mrs. Johnson? Party of four?"

She was nowhere to be found.

"Johnson!" he announced dramatically, and everyone in the place turned around and stared. "Where da fuck she go! Where's Johnson?" His brother Mikey announced that she up and left.

MATTY. Mutha fucka, do you believe this bitch! (*Now Matty's interrupting Rock Hudson's dinner and asking loudly.*) Rock! Sometimes you gotta wait, no? If I tell you you've gotta wait fifteen minutes, you're gonna be mad at me? You're gonna break my balls? You understand I'm trying to do the right thing here?

ROCK HUDSON, *agreeing, laughing and clapping, and wiping tears out of his eyes.*

MATTY, *throwing the menus up in the air.* That mutha fuckin' bitch.

It was like they were doing a bit on *The Carol Burnett Show*. It was hysterical. People were laughing and clapping, enjoying the show. That's why people went there, for the human drama. Matty was one in a million! What a character. And believe me, Johnson never came back!

Working at Matteo's meant guaranteed fun, along with a steady cash flow. Matty would give me a six top and deuce—two booths and table that fit six. Matty would always give me the high rollers, and BAM! They'd drop a couple hundred dollars on the table for a glass of wine and a plate of pasta, and they'd always tip a hundred bucks. I was making two or three hundred dollars a night. That's all I needed.

By the time I started working at Matty's my TV debut in *From Here to Eternity* was just starting its three-week run on TV. I hardly did a great job on the miniseries—I mean, Frank Sinatra became an Oscar winner in the role, I became a celebrity waiter. My customers couldn't believe I was their waiter at Matteo's—people wanted me to sign their menus.

And when the old timers came in, I got the same reaction. One evening Fernando Lamas was having dinner with his wife, Esther Williams. He couldn't believe it when he saw me.

FERNANDO, *as I'm serving their meal.* You can't fool me! You are *marvahlous*! I'm telling you, so wonderful! Why are you here? You doing research for a movie, yes?

(He nudges Esther.) You see, Estah? *(Estah eating, not inter-*

ested.) You see? This—this is a real actah. He cares. He's doing research!

JP, *smiling and trying not to attract attention.* No sir, thanks, but I'm just in between jobs.

The more I try to straighten this guy out, the more he thinks I'm ribbing him. Now he's laughing and saying,

FERNANDO. No, I know you. You are *marvahlous*! It's impossible. It's impossible. You're doing research.

—◊◊◊—

One Sunday night, Matteo's busiest night, my first customers were Lucille Ball and three other gentlemen: husband number two, Gary Morton, NBC's Fred Silverman, and Mickey Rudin, my predecessor's lawyer. He was doing Johnny Carson's new contract with Fred Silverman over a glass of wine and Matty's World Famous Chicken Beckerman. I approached the table, handed out menus, and said hello to Mickey and Fred, who were very surprised to see me. Mickey then introduced me to Lucy: "This is the actor Joey Pantoliano. He played Frank's part in the remake of *Here to Eternity*." Lucy looked up from her drink, cigarette tightly in her teeth, then she hands me her empty glass and says "Hey, Maggio! Get me another double vodka and soda." *She* wasn't impressed! Silverman and Rudin were eyeing me carefully as I made my exit. They must have been thinking, what is this kid, nuts?

I got one of the other waiters to take my table. It was uncomfortable. Later I was in the back near the bathrooms adding up a check when Rudin walked by.

Rudin said, "You know who I'm dining with tonight, right?" "Yeah," I replied, sounding impressed.

He said, "Fred wants to offer you the opportunity to reconsider the series."

I was humbled, but I'd made up my mind already. "No—no thanks."

So I turned down the $350,000—twice. Instead I was a living on tips.

Finally, the straw that broke my mother fuckin' back. About two weeks after I turned down the series for the second time, a low-level television casting director approached me at the restaurant.

"Joey, what happened? I had big money that you were gonna be a big star."

Oh boy, I thought, *what a douche bag. Fuck you twice! Please!*

I called my agent to mention the incident, and to his credit, he said, "Look, What's it gonna take to carry you through, say the next three months until you get your next job? What's it cost you to live?" Well, I said, about $2,000 a month. So he said, "Fine. We'll advance you six thousand. Quit waiting tables."

So there I went. I didn't like borrowing money, but I did. Morgan was doing clerical work for a real estate office, and I was going to acting school and started working for a messaging service.

They were good times. Morgan was very loving to me. She still got up with me every morning and and made me coffee and some toast and wished me off to work. Twelve months later, I got *The Idolmaker*, my first movie after *Eternity*. We shot at Matteo's for a week!

—m—

Morgan and I had by this time scraped up enough cash to get married.

On March 31, 1979, we held the ceremony and reception at the American Legion Hall on Highland Avenue, right below the Hollywood Bowl. It's a beautiful Art Deco building that still stands. I rented the hall, with its long Art Deco bar, for $300, a fraction of its usual cost. We had also arranged with the Legionnaires to host our rehearsal dinner the evening before the wedding, and we asked thirty friends to help decorate. So you could say we paid $300 for two nights! A real bargain! Everyone chipped in what they could. One friend, Kenny Marino, had a flower license, and we bought the orchids wholesale. We paid about $500 for everything, including my suit and Morgan's vintage dress. Our cash flow being anemic, I told everyone that we were registered at the Bank of America. As far as gifts were concerned, money was always the right size and the right color.

We were married by the minister of the Church of Christ. My mother, father, his girlfriend, Betty, my sister—somehow we all squished together for an amazing picture of the entire group, something like 275 people. The boxer Billy Devine, RJ, and Natalie were there. My mother was so proud of the fact that Natalie Wood was there, that all these movie stars were at my wedding.

Natalie and RJ came with their kids Courtney and Natasha, and gave us that honeymoon on *The Splendor*, as well as a loving cup in silver and gold. It was engraved: TO MORGAN AND JOEY, MARCH 31, 1979. LOVE, RJ AND NATALIE.

We had put our wedding guest list together at just about the same time my agent-therapist relationship was eroding.

The Saturday before the wedding, March 24, 1979, started out normal enough. I was in the habit of going to the early group therapy session, at 10:30 a.m. That morning I was working around my fear, my anxiety about my creative and financial future, my commitment of marriage, my fears of being powerless at age twenty-seven. The unknown was exciting, and scary. Saturday morning sessions would run as long as three hours. Ralph was leading the group at Barrington and Olympic Boulevard, and nothing seemed to be wrong or out of place.

So it was way out in left field when Ralph, in the last few minutes of the group's session, just blurted out, "So is Annette Handley still coming to the wedding?" Silence. Then he demanded, after all he'd done for me, that I uninvite her. It was a move that had everything to do with control and power. I would expect this from my family—when you're putting a wedding list together you're sure to run into problems when you find out Uncle Mario is not talking to Aunt Louise. But from your therapist? When they were interviewing agents for the job in Los Angeles, it was I who introduced Ralph and Annette. We stayed with her when we first arrived in Los Angeles. I know that there was bad blood spilt over Harry and Ralph's decision to fire Annette, but that had been almost two years earlier, and by all accounts, everyone was doing just fine. Annette had fulfilled her ambition to become a literary representative. Her new company was thriving, and we continued to stay very close even when she later moved back to New York City.

With only fifteen minutes left to the session I thought I was about to make the quick getaway. I needed to participate in a play reading being conducted by the veteran actor Rudy Bond. Instead I was dragged over the smoldering coals of ego-driven pride and conceit as the group members took their cue, each one of them taking their individual pounds of flesh: Why I was being selfish and uncaring? How dare I this and that? I got my ass kicked by everyone.

Finally, three hours later, I stood up and just said, "No." I wasn't going to buckle under. "She's going to be there, Ralph," I said. "And we'd love you to be there too, but it's our wedding." I was uncomfortable, confused and angry. The lines between agent and therapist had been blurred. It was inappropriate for my therapist to enlist the other group members to argue about agency matters during a session. Ralph had totally set me up, and then and there, I made a conscious decision. My days with Ralph and that agency were numbered. In the end, Ralph and Annette were both there, and everybody had a good time. But by then the cracks in my relationship with Ralph had started to show, and it would eventually crumble.

—m—

Around this time I was haunted by a recurring dream, which made such an impression on me that I remember it to this day.

The dream was always the same: I'm in the apartment on Stanley Avenue in L.A. and it's three a.m. My wife is sleeping next to me quietly when I smell something burning and I sense light on my closed eyelids. I'm afraid to open them, but I do and I see a bright light in the hallway, shining against our open bedroom door. As I get up to see, I hear a roar and a rumbling and shaking, like an earthquake. Morgan screams, and I can hear the plaster and the wood splintering as I realize this is no earthquake. An enormous smoky creature is breaking through the doorway. It's a dragon, a fire-breathing dragon, and one that would give all the Japanese a run for their money. He's breathing fire, spitting it out toward me. His head is fifteen feet tall and thirty feet wide. He's tearing into our closet and he's tearing out bits of my clothing and my hairpieces, my wigs, and chewing them up. Somehow I grab the fire poker from my imaginary fireplace. Jump on his head, off of his nose, and I'm trying to stab him in the eyes while being thrown around. It was like being on that mechanical bronco that John Travolta rode in *Urban Cowboy*—which I'd probably seen recently. I start screaming, "You can't have her. I won't let you make me break up with Morgan! I won't leave her!"

I realize now that my dragon represented some of the darker

parts of my life. The shame I felt for even having the thought that I might leave Morgan was that I was getting somewhere, the thought that I could have something, or someone, better. In a way the dragon was also an easy out; I could blame him for all of my self-centeredness, my ego-driven desires.

On the set of *Eternity* there was a girl, an extra, who was very pretty and we were talking and sizing each other up on stage 7. On that stage you would go through a padded door and then there was a red light that would tell you if they were rolling and you'd need to wait until the red light was off before you could make an entrance or an exit. I happened to wind up in that little room with this brunette. Just forty feet away the light was flickering red and all you could hear was the sound of the bulb clicking on and off, on and off. I took her and we kissed, I felt the heat rising to my neck, wicked and exhilarating. I had been twenty-two years old when I met Morgan. I wanted it all, right now. That's when I started accumulating secrets.

CHAPTER FIVE

The Hunchback of Hoboken

Brooklyn, New York; Red Hook, to be exact. July 1980: day forty-eight of fifty-six during the filming of *The Idolmaker*—a big day for me. Both my dad and Florie had come to see me on set, the first time both of my father figures had been able to watch a movie being made and watch me living out my dream as an actor. I was so excited, so proud. I had finally arrived.

Time: 12:45 p.m. "Cut! Print!" our director, Taylor Hackford, yelled out to the script supervisor. Hackford was tall and movie-star handsome. He was standing beside the A camera, watching the acting. Taylor continued bellowing in director-speak: "If the gate's good on A and B cameras we move in for coverage." With that I could hear our first assistant director, his walkie-talkie stuck to the side of his mouth like a malignant tumor: "That's a broom on the master, if the gate's good, this will be the last setup before we break for lunch . . ."

Next we heard: "The gate's good . . ."

Then, pandemonium! The film crew invaded the neighborhood like Normandy. All the departments were repeating the AD's commands.

"Background reset, first positions," said the AD.

Someone else yelled, "Second team flying in!"

Pieces of moments, actions . . . put them all together and they equal a movie. In our case, a damn good one. The second assistant camera yelled "Camera reload . . ." Sixty crew members, different departments, each with one action and purpose . . . wardrobe, set dressers, hair and makeup taking Polaroids. Photo memories. Evidence to match what would have to be repeated in the next setup.

The prop master took photos of a half-eaten tuna fish sandwich. Wardrobe took a shot of the lead, Ray Sharkey, and me on the escalator, while the assistants took pictures of the extras in front of and behind us. Attention to details, that's where God lives, and believe me, you need God when you're making movies, because it's a miracle every time they turn out good. The bulbs are popping, their owners yelling, "Flashing!" An alert, meaning there's nothing to worry about, we're just taking a pictures! The crew knows to do this so Electric doesn't think they blew a fuse, or 50,000 volts of electricity that the gaffer might not be able to account for.

TAYLOR, *gesturing with a wink and smile.* JP you need another sandwich?

JP. Nope, no thanks, boss I'm good . . . Anything, just please, no more tuna fish sandwiches!

Everyone cracks up.

It seemed like a good idea at the time . . . Earlier that morning, I had been eating tuna sandwiches in a scene that we shot over and over again. In this particular scene I was eating while

Ray Sharkey and I were riding down a long escalator to the street below.

After seven takes I stopped swallowing and began spitting the chewed food into a bucket each time after Taylor yelled cut. But by then it was too late. I had ingested one too many tuna fish sandwiches. Just as Daddy and Florie had finally arrived at their first-ever movie set, so proud of their son Joey acting in an MGM movie, just like that other Monroe Street kid, little Frankie Sinatra, the contents of my stomach started to boil, and I felt queasy. Daddy sat in my chair, his last name on the back. Meanwhile, at Ray Sharkey's insistence, Florie rested in Ray's chair.

But before I could impress Daddy and Florie with any acting, they watched me throw up all over Ray Sharkey's Beatle boots. Not one of my greatest moments, and I still wonder what those two important men in my life were thinking as they saw me heave-ho in Brooklyn. Maybe they chalked it up to nerves; some great actors were known to throw up before going onstage. But not me. The irony is that the scene never made it to the final cut.

"Ladies and germs, this will be the last setup after lunch."

Right after the first AD yelled lunch, everybody scrambled. Wardrobe was rinsing sprinkles of vomit off my snakeskin pants as I introduced Daddy and Florie to the actors Gene Kirkwood, Howard Koch, and Peter Gallagher.

We walked back to my trailer, Daddy and I moving slower than usual because of Florie. I noticed how his emphysema was taking its toll. This once stunning, immaculately dressed man was now crippled by disease, beaten by time and by the crimes and sins of his past.

I had wanted to make my motor home perfect for their visit. This was the second time I had rated high enough to qualify for a forty-footer. Set dressing provided some flowers. Earlier I had sent my driver to pick up some Italian pastries and iced cappuccinos. He thought I was crazy; nobody had ever sent him out for coffee before. You have to understand that each trailer, which held a dressing room, kitchen, and bedroom, was assigned to a particular artist during these twelve- to fourteen-hour days, and trailers were to be maintained, cleaned, and driven to the desired location by a teamster. Those were union rules, not Joey Pants's rules. But we were in Red Hook, a tough neighborhood in Brooklyn, and in 1980 transportation and Teamsters were an intimidating prospect. The driver was more likely to tell the artist where to go, not the other way around.

We walked a few steps up the trailer and eased Florie onto the couch, because for him the short climb was like running the 100-yard dash. He was huffing and puffing as he looked around the trailer. Both he and Daddy commented on how big even the kitchen was, and marveled at the electric blender planted right into the end of the counter. I walked Daddy back to my bedroom to show him how much room I had there too, and in doing so found my driver out cold on my bed, asleep. My well-thought-out plan had just gone awry. Thinking I could get the driver to exit gracefully, I said, "Hey Merv, look, we broke for lunch and we're gonna eat now." Without even opening his eyes, Merv replied, "That's all right Joe, youse won't bother me," and dozed right back off. So much for status.

Daddy and Florie were long gone by the end of the day, and as I left the set I was still buoyed by the idea that both Daddy and Florie had been at my side all day.

I returned to the apartment I was subletting during shooting. I called my answering service, wrote down my messages in the order of importance, and called up my wife. She answered the phone, we chitchatted and I told her about Daddy and Flo . . . and the Teamster. Morgan sounded nervous and excited, and finally she interrupted to tell me, in a voice that said she wasn't sure how I'd take the news, that she was pregnant.

A baby! Wow. We'd been married less than a year, five months to be exact. I was both happy and confused. "What do you wanna do?" I asked her. Was I really ready for this? Was she? Were we? We decided we'd sleep on it.

Morgan and I had been together for three years and married for less than one, and there was no denying that cracks were developing in the foundation of our marriage. My drinking had become an issue, and had already resulted in one DUI. The warmth of our early years together was definitely cooling, and we had begun quarreling on a regular basis. That night I went out to dinner and ran into playwright and friend, John Ford Noonan, a bear of a man, known for his unusual mind. John was always an arresting figure with his dark brown beard, long hair, Oshkosh overalls, and his signature mismatched Converse sneakers, the left one red, the right one green. John also wore a red bandana, which made him look like a jolly pirate.

When I told him my news, John was instantly energized, and began telling me the joys of fatherhood and about the daughter who had come into his life three years earlier. We went down to the South Street Seaport to visit the set, which was still active because they were shooting nights. We stayed out drinking for hours, talking about our fathers. Later, doing a line of coke in the stall of a dingy men's room somewhere on the East River, I knew I wanted to have this baby.

—⁂—

Crescent City California, four months later.

I was starring number one on the call sheet for the first time, in a horror movie, *The Final Terror*.

The first-time director, Andy Davis, held in his hand an Arriflex 35 mm camera while he sat in the passenger side of a pickup truck. Driving back to the motel where the cast and crew were staying, Andy had five hundred feet of film left in the camera, and we improvised our way home while we still had some light. Andy would tell me to scratch my cheek, park the car, look at the alarm clock on the dashboard, wind it up and exit the car. "Cut! Print! That's a wrap!" yelled this exuberant man with a big smile, holding the love of his life, a movie camera. This was the first of four movies I would do with Andy. Joe Roth was producing and among the cast were such unknowns as Daryl Hannah, Akosua Busia, Rachel Ward, Mark Metcalf—kids, really. I was the one having a baby, but I wasn't behaving like a responsible adult. Most nights I was drinking, trying to keep that dragon in my psyche under control, but I was failing. Even so I wanted to do the right thing by my wife, Morgan, whom I loved. She chose me as her husband, and I knew she deserved better.

I was lost in the lush green wilderness, deep in the California redwoods, tree trunks so wide you could drive a pickup through the enormous holes carved into the center of a few of them, and I wasn't happy. But more than that, I became confused by this uneasiness that had taken over me. It affected my daily routine. I had no appetite, and I was running now every day, overcome by the conversations that occupied my head. I was ashamed, pretending to be someone else—I started to lead a double life.

I had developed a habit—well, you could call it an urge even—that when things were going good, I went out of my way to foul them up! By now my seven deadlies were in full force—all my symptoms had become addictions—I ate too much (or not at all), drank too much, shopped too much. Even sex—everything I did was to alter my state of mind, to satisfy the urge that stemmed from my dis-ease. And being away from home had its toll on me.

I knew my marriage was on a fault line and that I was at the core of the fault. My wife still loved me, but I was a coward. I wanted my cake, sneaking around stuffing my brain with anything that would keep me insulated from those thoughts. Betraying the love of my life. I live with these sins and I am still so sorry. Fighting my demons was a constant struggle. By early September we were back home on Stanley Avenue. Morgan continued to work for the commercial real estate broker; I did messenger work and odd jobs as a carpenter's assistant (again with the hammer!).

That fall I was offered a job in San Francisco, Morgan's hometown. So we were off to Alcatraz, where I was doing a four-hour prison break miniseries, and where we were able to visit family and friends. We also made new friends, like Tony Ponzini, one of the actors in the show. We were living on Fisherman's Wharf during the three weeks of location shooting on the Rock. By now Morgan was showing. One evening Tony and his wife, Sharon, who lived in L.A., mentioned the wonderful benefits of the Venice Beach lifestyle. It so happened that the small house across the street from theirs on Venezia Avenue was coming up for rent! It had an extra bedroom for our new baby. The price for the house was $500 a month, almost three times what we were paying on Stanley Avenue, but my angels continued watching over me. By now I was able to repay debts I owed the Wagners, who had helped us out a few months earlier, and the IRS, and

I'd even bought my first new car—that 1980 Toyota Celica (on time, of course—fifty-eight more payments, and it was mine!). So we decided to move to 343 Venezia Avenue. When we returned to L.A., Morgan started prenatal yoga and Lamaze classes, and I began to practice yoga a little myself. I was trying to manage my drinking. Abstinence seemed to be the only surefire way to control it. For the next twenty years I lived as a conscious alcoholic, going three months without a drink, then a series of slips, then twelve months sober, but always going back, motivated by what I now recognize was depression.

Christmas had come, and this would be the first time we'd spend the holiday on the West Coast. The baby's due date was around the corner so we practiced breathing and had fire drills, pretending that our baby was coming. The morning of January 10, 6:45 a.m., Morgan gave me a gentle tap on the shoulder. "Joey, it's time." Her bags already packed, she had calmly taken a shower before waking me. I jumped into action. While I brushed my teeth I yelled out excitedly—to no one in particular, except maybe myself—"This is GREAT honey! I'm wide awake! This is gonna be a piece of cake. I had a good night's sleep."

Marco Dominic Pantoliano was born on January 11, 1981, at 1:41 a.m.; twenty-two inches long, nine pounds, four ounces. His amazing mother, so healthy and strong, delivered him without the aid of an epidural! She and Marco were home by early evening the same day.

On the way to the hospital I had glanced out of the corner of my eye and saw a street sign called Marco Place. Suddenly I thought, if it's a boy, the name Marco could work. Morgan had already picked Tayo if it was a boy and Neva if it was a girl. But when our baby boy was born, the name Marco just felt right. So Morgan and I welcomed our son, Marco, into the world. Our Little Marco Man, our only son, named after a street sign. You can't get more romantic than that!

The year that followed was a roller-coaster ride. After appearing in *The Idolmaker* I was running errands for a producer for $5 an hour off the books. I was still in acting school and still collecting unemployment, and Morgan was still working at the real estate office.

Around the end of November my agent called about the film *Monsignor*, directed by Frank Perry and produced by Frank Yablans, and I had the opportunity to audition for Perry to play Christopher Reeve's sidekick. I didn't get it, and instead I was offered the role of a dying GI, appearing in only one scene. It was a small part, sure, but as a consolation, I got to die in Superman's arms. In Rome! Ah, viva Roma, the land of Michelangelo, Fellini, Visconti, and Sophia Loren. So many great movies had been made in Rome. This would be my first trip to Europe and it would mean that Marco would celebrate his first birthday in Italy, the country of his forefathers.

—m—

On December 31, 1981, we were hosting our annual New Year's Eve bash at our little house in Venice Beach. I always worked myself into a tizzy. I sensed that somehow a great New Year's Eve celebration would be an optimistic guarantee that God would provide for me in the coming year. Always setting myself up for some great night that never came. I was looking for perfection in the New Year, starting with this perfect night when I was a kid, I remember all the fun we had. My whole family would gather to celebrate with a feast, either at my Aunt Tilly's house or ours. I'd get all dressed up, as would Mommy and the rest, everybody decked out head to toe.

At the stroke of midnight, Mommy would grab a broom and sweep out the old year, making room for a better and more prosperous one to come. Then Mommy and the other ladies in our building (all the Italians) would all bang pots and pans to welcome in the New Year. But by the end of the night my uncles would be shitfaced, and those pots and pans would be tested on the tops of their heads.

For me as a little kid, New Year's Eve was always magical— or that's the way I chose to remember it! But as an adult, I could never reproduce those great times no matter how hard I tried.

True to form, this New Year's Eve would end disastrously. It would turn out to be the last I celebrated with Morgan. That year Morgan had planned a small, intimate party, not the blowout we usually had. Morgan was up most nights with Marco. To tell you the truth, I was barely there to help. My head was so far up my ass I just couldn't or wouldn't carry my load. Morgan imagined having ten to fifteen good friends over for dinner at our small two-bedroom house. But earlier in the day, one of the friends I had invited called to say another good friend from New York was unexpectedly in town. Could he bring him? Morgan and I agreed.

The food and company was great, but it wasn't the kind of party I usually looked forward to. Then just after 11 p.m., an hour before the bell rang, my bell rang. Outside a car full of clowns had pulled up, and I was so happy to see them pouring out of their little clown car and straight through our front door. Soon there would be a three-ring circus. With me as ring master! Our "plus one" had come along with another six guests in tow. The clowns carried flowers and bottles of champagne to soften the blow.

Morgan was sitting in her favorite rocking chair listening to Nat King Cole when they arrived. My Morgan, looking so beautiful with her long hair and motherly glow. Rocking between our

Christmas tree and fireplace so pretty they glowed, and nursing our new son for all the clowns to see.

"Shhhhh! You'll wake him!" she said as they trooped in. Her face, which had been serene a moment before, now had a look of panic. As I welcomed the crowd she shot me the look I had come to know so well, that look of disappointment.

The party was no longer what Morgan had planned, but *I* wanted to go with the flow. I wanted to go go go! I rationalized that we had only forty-five minutes until Happy New Year, and Italian hospitality was in my blood, as were the seven glasses of Guinea red that I had ingested along with some recreational blow. "Honey," I said. "Come on!" I liked big parties—much easier for me to hide, and harder to hit the moving target. But I knew she wasn't going to let go. As I poured more drinks, I could see Morgan felt hurt and betrayed. She assumed that I had agreed to let the clowns show up. She thought that I had gone behind her back and said sure, the more the merrier. Technically that wasn't true, but in the moment it seemed like a great idea! Act first, never think of the consequences! She asked "Why did you do this?" visibly upset. The poor kid had tears in her eyes from this latest betrayal, Marco crying in her arms.

Now I'd been caught off guard too. But I was drunk enough to argue. "Look, honey, they're already here. They're our friends— well, some of them are—besides, it's 11:15 p.m., and they didn't come empty-handed."

She wanted me to kick them out and wouldn't take no for an answer. We both knew she would be the one nursing the baby at 4 a.m., while I was nursing a hangover!

"I don't care," she said. "They have to leave, Joey. They came uninvited, and this is not that kind of party. There were other people I would have invited if we were going to have a big party.

We left good friends off the list. And who will clean up and feed the baby? You?"

I didn't care that she was right! But I grabbed my NYC pal and hid my embarrassment. I explained that the drugs could stay, but they had to go. Understandably, he did not take the news well. The boisterous crowd left faster than they came in. They were pissed and would remain so for years to come. I had thrown them out of my house less than twenty-five minutes before midnight. They ended up ringing in the New Year at a Mexican bar down on Venice Boulevard. The only people in the place who could speak English, they watched the Times Square ball drop on a black-and-white TV above a Cuervo Christmas tree, surrounded by a bunch of cholos shooting their guns in the air. *Feliz año nuevo!*

I'm not pretending to be an angel. At the time of that party, I was irresponsible and self-centered, and I wanted to be everybody's friend. Ironically, our quiet party ended in a screaming match with punches thrown! Not between me and Morgan, but between two of our invited guests. People do crazy things when they let the genie out of the bottle! Then life went on. The next morning we simply packed our bags for Rome.

Isn't it funny how I unconsciously worked to repeat the familiar misery at home? My Italian uncles and my father drinking until they got sick, ending the evening in fights, then making up the following morning! The big *aha!* is, that behavior wasn't really Italian! It wasn't even normal! Before I was able to look at all of this LIFE, and learn to separate my culture from my crazy, I thought that it was. I can look at my past now and smile knowing that I don't have to bring my familiar misery to my children. I knew then that my marriage was ending, and that next New Year's Eve, if there was another woman in my life, that it would end poorly too.

—∾—

As they say in the rooms, "Being humble doesn't mean you stop thinking about yourself. It means that you start thinking about yourself—LESS."

One night's work in Italia stretched into a Roman holiday. We had five weeks in Italy to eat and drink all the good Guinea red we could, all over the boot. I came to the conclusion that there were two types of people in the world: Italians, and those that wished they could be! What a way to start the New Year! This was way better than being a fireman, which is what Daddy wanted me to be. And here was my own son, experiencing life Italian style. Dear God, had my dreams begun to come true? How astonishing! But a real blessing turned into a curse as my drinking increased. I was always counting those calories. As I drank, more food had to be sacrificed—bringing a new meaning to the expression, having to "eat and run." I'd force myself to run the extra miles the following morning to burn off calories but also to flick that switch, to calm my restlessness. I still had no idea that I was depressed. The concept never occurred to me! I was only drinking wine, how the hell could that hurt me?

Frank Perry shot my scenes in just one night. The World War II uniform that I wore was pulled out of a pile of reusable uniforms. A week later I had the crabs—nasty—but nothing could bring me down. We went on to Florence and walked everywhere. Then one afternoon while walking on the Ponte Vecchio we bought Mommy a beautiful necklace—it had a porcelain figurine of the Virgin Mary engraved in gold.

In less than two weeks, my mother would be taking it to her grave.

On the last day of January, we headed back from Italy and went straight to Jersey for my cousin Roseanne's wedding. We had all been looking forward to Roseanne's wedding, and no one was disappointed. It was a great time. My mother and I had the last dance that evening. We were all in a good mood.

The following morning we were in the senior citizens' building where she and Florie were living. They had a small one-bedroom apartment, and Morgan and the baby were still sleeping in their bedroom. I was in the kitchen with Mommy and my uncle Pete, my mother's brother, who had come up to visit. He hadn't been at the wedding the night before because he was on the other side of family, the Centrella side. Mommy poured more coffee as she and Pete continued talking, enjoying each other's stories, Mommy sharing gossip about the night before. But Mommy was under one of her spells.

By now my sister, Maryann, had shown up, and she was changing the baby while Morgan showered. Mommy had a couple of bullets for Maryann's boyfriend (He was Irish! Need I say more?), and started amusing herself by embracing the stereotype. She was generalizing male behavior, saying we were all alike—"weak-minded sumanabitches" acting like *ubriachi* (Italian for drunks). At first it was a comedy routine, showing off for Morgan who by now was brushing out her damp hair. But she wouldn't let up! Finally I said, "Ma, what is it with you? I don't understand. Why do you hate men so much?" She took a drag of her cigarette, and as she exhaled she said defiantly, "Let me tell you something! The best man in the world ain't good enough for the worst whore!" My wife, who was sitting next to me, feeding our son, who had just a couple of weeks earlier celebrated his first birthday, announced she wanted to go home. I too had had enough. Florie drove us to Newark airport, we dropped Morgan and baby Marco off, and I took a bus to Manhattan.

I had been asked to stay in the city in order to meet the director of the movie *Eddie and the Cruisers*. I was staying with my old friend Michael Kell.

Michael was the one who took Florie's distraught call the next morning. When Michael gave me the news of my mother's death, I laughed. I couldn't believe it. To my way of thinking, she was invincible. She couldn't die. She was faking again, just wanting attention! It was all an act, the five strokes, the operation, even that bypass that damaged her vocal cords, making her sound in the last two years of her life more like Louis Armstrong than Ma.

In a few hours I'd be crying. Then laughing. Experiencing a gamut of feelings. Alternating between my masks of comedy and tragedy as easily as I changed hats.

CHAPTER SIX

If It Ain't One Thing, It's Your Mother!

O n that third day of February, 1982, I walked into Failla's funeral parlor, shaking off the bitter cold. I wanted to talk with my mother. Jack, the funeral director, said it would be fine if I wanted to be alone. I knelt before my mother's casket, thinking maybe now she would have her eternal peace.

We had argued two nights before. We had done this so many times, but now even in my emotional stupor I realized this one we couldn't patch up. Time had run out.

Looking at her I was struck by my mother's unnaturally rosy cheeks, her makeup way overdone! I grew up hearing the gossip of my elders—their words echoed through those faint whispers stored in the caverns of my mind. "She looks so alive." "Like she's sleeping." "They got her smile perfect." Horseshit. Our culture dictates we deny death, we mask the inevitable truth by dressing up our dead. It's grotesque! We say, "Till death do us part!" We will all part! What's the big deal, what are we so afraid of? Caressing my mother's cold dead hands, the web of rosary beads that she rarely used in life now entangled in her palms, I realized she was empty. Her soulless body had no answers for me. Our Mary was finally at peace. God forgive her.

I had been convinced my mother was invulnerable to death. And in a way I was right; my mother lives inside me, inside my children. I know this because I see her in them all the time, in these stories and memories that I've shared with all of you. She is the best part of me. She is part of my own immortality, the DNA that will live long after I'm gone. Mommy's heart will beat with a rhythm that will shape the hearts and souls of my children and grandchildren, those unborn.

After my mother's death, the fabric of my life started to fray. Her death exacerbated a fear in me that time was running out. I wanted to embrace life while it was still inside me; I wanted to be free so I wouldn't have to do what anybody wanted me to do.

By now, I was a constant disappointment to Morgan, and pretty soon there was nothing left but anger. We were two people who had lost their trust and faith in each other.

The more successful I became, the more I wanted to run away. As I started finding better parts, we started saving some money, but when success found me, I drank more. To fit in and to stay up. I thought the drink was working for me.

I remember Morgan waking me up in the middle of one night because I was peeing on my nightstand, hitting the lamp and the phone and phonebooks below. I was sleepwalking and thought I was in the bathroom. The next morning I looked at the telephone books and saw they were five times their ordinary size, having expanded from the moisture. At that point both of us knew I had a problem.

Growing up, I knew that drugs and alcohol might get in the way of my success, so I couldn't afford to use or drink. I tried marijuana in school but didn't like it. It made me paranoid. It made me feel like everybody was watching me. I felt out of control. I went to see *2001: A Space Odyssey* at the Fairview Cinema, where all the guys were taking mescaline, because they said the only way to see this movie was to be high on mescaline. I took a tab of mescaline and immediately had a panic attack. I went into the bathroom and shoved my hand down my throat and vomited it out. Not least of all I was afraid of what Florie would do if he found out.

The first time I tried cocaine I was at twenty-four. That first time, I even paid for it. I went in on half a gram while on location in Florida. I was shooting *The Mean Season* with Kurt Russell, Mariel Hemingway, and Andy Garcia. As you can imagine, it was all over the place in those days, especially at work. Cocaine helped me stay up; it gave me energy. I only used cocaine when it was around, and it never really became a problem, partly because I never liked to pay for it. Coke was expensive— no, exorbitant.

My problem was alcohol and my favorite was wine. I loved drinking wine. But I was always concerned about calories, and I was told that if I drank vodka, I could get twice as much of the high. So I added vodka on the rocks to my medications. I would drink, have a great time, and then wake up with a hangover, and then I'd go out and run it off. And usually I'd stop drinking for two days after that. If I drank too much, I would say, "Oh my God, I'm never going to do this again." I thought I had everybody fooled.

Sex was an addiction too. There were girls around, approaching me. It's like being an alcoholic and everywhere you go a waiter is coming up to you with a martini. I'd impulsively act out. My brain is like the primitive brain, the one that acts only on instinct. The whole prefrontal cortex, the rational one, my thinking doesn't go there. It goes to the old, primitive brain and then kind of works its way around. By the time temptation gets to the higher brain it's too late. I've already done it.

I've done everything I can to keep my daughters from falling victim to the same addictions. When my Melody was thirteen, my wife Nancy and I sat down with her—just as we just did later with Isabella and Daniella—and offered her this opportunity. That

1. if she were able to abstain from drinking and drugging and
2. not have sex (and blow jobs counted!)

until she was twenty-one years old, I would

(a) buy her a brand-new car and
(b) give her $10,000 cash.

The total: $50,000 in grand prizes! Now, every thirteen-year-old is going to take that bet. Melody took the bet and kept her word until she was about sixteen years old, when she wanted to renegotiate. She said it wasn't fair and how could she possibly make it to twenty-one? To which I answered, "Hey! I never made this bet to lose." You see, Nancy and I thought if we could keep Melody from being sexually active until she was seventeen or eighteen, great. Which is exactly what happened. Right before Melanie's high school graduation she sat me down to say that she was going to lose the bet, that she had determined that the boy who was in her life at that time, with whom she felt completely comfortable and was very much in love, was going to be the boy. Well, now I was humbled and honored that Melody felt comfortable enough to have this conversation with her dad. But what about the younger girls? How would we get Daniella to make the bet? Nancy and I worked it out with Melody to pretend that she

was still a virgin until she was twenty years old, and then an-
nounce that she had lost the bet and succumbed to her womanly
needs.

I made the same bet with my middle daughter, Daniella,
and she was determined to beat her sister! But then she was almost nineteen and still a virgin, and I was freaking out because
I was afraid that I messed up this kid's mind and she was going
to be frigid or something. So right before Daniella's nineteenth
birthday, I told her that she should have sex—that there must
be a boy in her life that she liked enough to have sex. I couldn't
afford to pay her, I told her. So the bet was off with Daniella but
we had to pretend that it was on for Isabella . . .

—m—

Back in the 1980s, work was my real mistress, the only thing I really
cared about. It kept me full, created the illusion that I belonged and
I didn't have to think. For that I was extremely grateful.

Filming *Eddie and the Cruisers* would occupy my winter of
1982.

Now, I'm not bragging, but I can say with more than a little confidence that I have had good working relationships with
the majority of the directors I've worked with over the years—
and that's eighty-plus films. But I'd have to say, Martin Davidson
was not one of them. I already told you where my head was at,
and in all fairness, he never got me because I didn't get him.

Filming was a miserable experience, and so were our hotel
accommodations. We were housed on the Jersey side of the Walt
Whitman Bridge, which separated us from Philly, in the infa-
mous Rickshaw Inn. The Rickshaw was the preferred assasina-
tion spot for guests visiting ladies under the bridge and staying
forty-five minutes or less, and it fit my dark mood perfectly. It was

difficult working on a movie where on any given night it seemed everyone was getting good use of the hotel beds—except me. I was searching for some magic elixir that could remedy my unhappiness. I was toxic. I was celibate (though not for lack of trying). Morgan's visits felt strained, awkward. I'd run out of boardwalk, and those March winds froze whatever love I had for myself and for her. I couldn't feel anything.

I was no longer a husband, but still desperately wanted to be a father. Every evening I'd think, my drinking isn't the problem. It's the solution! But then the hangovers, the getting sick each morning—that was killing me. Why did I do that? Never again! I'd say. Then I'd be out again and again. I was either drinking or promising not to drink, obsessing: *I can't drink, I can't drink.* No peace of mind, ever. Looking back, I can see now I was so sad and confused over losing my mother. My relationship with You Know Who was never resolved. But at the time I didn't want to feel those emotions. I didn't want to have to think or deal or reflect on my life or my mom's death. Running, drinking. Drinking, running. My MO was to just shut my eyes, put my head down, and keep on going.

If anything, I was more comfortable feeling anger. Why did she do it to herself, smoking all those cigarettes? Almost out of spite, I picked up smoking again myself. A big part of my pain was that I couldn't help my mother. I couldn't fix her, I couldn't save her, I didn't understand that she was sick. That I was sick. In the end my marriage to Morgan went kaput. I was the saboteur who broke a ten-year run. I carried with me a lot of feelings of shame and resentment knowing the primary role I'd played in the implosion of my marriage.

I started working on *Risky Business* in August of 1982. Morgan and I had officially separated by then. I'd found an apartment that would work temporarily. Thank God I had this job, I thought. Work was the answer. That's all that mattered. I'd be happy when I got to Chicago. I had liked working there in the past and I still had friends there.

Risky Business was one of the movies that defined the 1980s. It was a huge hit for Warner Bros., but it began as a low-budget film with no big stars. We were staying in the suburbs of Chicago, and each morning during filming I would get up early and go for a run. I was running five times a week, three to five miles at a time, and while I knew how very important it was to my well-being, I didn't quite understand how much.

One morning after a run I jumped in the pool, and when I came up there was a beautiful girl with startling blue eyes, Rebecca De Mornay. She was twenty-two years old and very likable, both confident and totally down to earth. I liked her right away. We talked and found out more about each other. Later we went to rehearsal together, and that's where I first met Tom Cruise.

I took a run with Tom after rehearsal, and I realized he was as likable as he was ambitious. He was all personality, yet very respectful. In my entire career there were only two actors who told me they were going to be big stars—Ben Stiller and Tom Cruise. I would never say something like that, especially not at that age. Guys like Tom become movie stars because they transcend. They enable us to get a glimpse of ourselves in them.

Risky Business defined the '80s, but did I think Tom Cruise was going to become a big movie star after this? No. And not off that movie. I thought the film would be OK, it would come, then go. But a monster hit? (A good many of the hit movies I've done have been with Warner Bros., actually. *Risky Business* was my first big movie ever; the next would be *Running Scared*, then *The Goonies*, *Midnight Run*, *La Bamba*, *Empire of the Sun*, *The Fugitive*, *Bad Boys*

1 and *2*, *The Matrix*, *Daredevil*, *Memento*. The Warner execs called me their good luck charm.) Meanwhile my personal life was out of control, and I knew it. By the end of 1983 I tried to quit drinking for good. My thinking was that I had to get in control, and that I could stop drinking with will power. I asked my friend Kathleen, who knew something about AA, and she took me to my first meeting. It scared me. By now I had left group therapy, and I was afraid of trying something else. I went to more meetings. But I could not comprehend the idea that I would never drink again. I thought I could do it on my own. My pride and ego were all tangled up. I wanted to be distracted. That was easy. I was single for the first time in ten years.

—◊—

But at this point, all of us in *Risky Business* were still just beginning our careers. We were housed in honey wagons, dressing rooms carved out of the bed of an eighteen-wheeler. The higher your number on the call sheet, the better your chance of a good place on the honey wagon. As they say, there are no small parts, only small dressing rooms.

We proud Screen Actors Guild members walked up the folding steel accordion stairs and opened the doors to our palaces. On each door was a plastic star—that would mean movie star. Your character's name was written using a Magic Marker, making it easier to wipe off the smudged remnants of names that came before yours. Your fan club wouldn't want to see you in this shit hole; the pathetically small sink opposite the toilet, a dressing table and a desk. And a cream-colored plastic folding chair. Filling out your palace was a brown foam rubber cot for you to dream starry dreams. If you were lucky the air-conditioning actually works and keeps you from melting like the MGM witch.

It was glamour, baby! Hardened San Quentin murderers would have run gladly to the comfort of the gas chamber to avoid our cozy quarters. Charlie Manson had more room than we actors.

There were a lot of really beautiful women in Chicago, but now that I had my freedom, I didn't know what to do.

The cast was friendly, and the atmosphere lively. Paul Brickman, the director and writer, was lovable, talented, and knew what he wanted in each of those brilliant characters. Working on this movie just felt good. Anytime I'm working in front of a camera it's a gift. The best remedy for depression that I know. For me, it's always the most rewarding part.

I had difficulty being by myself; having any kind of quiet time made me really uncomfortable. Drinking made it easier to hang out and participate in the fun. Chicago was a convention town, and these people knew how to party. Saturdays there would always be plans, and I would go. One night Tom and I went in to Chicago to see Sean Penn, because he was doing a movie, and we had dinner at a Chinese restaurant on Michigan Avenue. It felt good to be in another city doing what I wanted to be doing with my life and seeing that these kids had dreams too, and the dreams were coming true. I wanted more of that.

Where one ends up in the showbiz food chain is a crapshoot, and no actor can fully take responsibility for how his or her career pans out. There are so many forces at work. For me, these last thirty years have been a blessing of highs and lows. Somebody once said, shit happens while you're making other plans! I have had my share of ups and downs and I got what I deserved. I've made a living as a working actor. This means that I'm always looking for the next miracle. I'm optimistic. I keep hoping to get lucky one more time. Staying lucky and making my own luck is the name of this game. I'm not complaining, mind you. My God has blessed me with the gift of gab, and the energy to be persistent, to find opportunities. Doing good parts in good pictures that are winners. Just one out of every five will keep me in the game!

It was much easier to get ahead when I was motivated by hunger. Anything was better than what I had growing up, but after I had some wins and grew accustomed to some level of success, I found it harder to go for the neck. I've been lucky enough to work with some of the best. My work has taken me to places I could never dream of. I have worked and travelled all over the world— this is what I know, and I hold it close.

All of these blessings have no value unless I have someone to share it with. My relationships are what I hold dear, deep inside of me. So I'm as good as the best thing I've ever done. My life is a series of uncontrollable events. I don't know what comes next, but it will be my next lesson.

Come to think of it, working has never been my problem. It's living that I'm not good at.

—m—

Risky Business didn't have a big premiere. Or if it did, I didn't know about it. But the movie spoke to the culture, a history of our time, and it exploded at the box office. Guido the Killer Pimp put me on the map. My dream was starting to take shape—and so was my nose! I was thin in those days, and to my mind my nose was a big problem. My nose was to blame; it was the reason I kept getting cast playing the heavy. So I went to a plastic surgeon after that movie and said:

JP. Doc! I broke my nose. You've got to make my nose smaller.

DOC. Joe, I can fix your broken nose, but it's a good nose. If I make it smaller it will lose its character.

JP. Doc. Wherever you see character—I want you to cut it off!

But the nose job didn't help. From then on I just played bad guys with smaller noses.

—∽—

In the spring of '83 I was all settled, living in my new apartment on Electric Avenue, only five blocks from where Marco still lived. Just like that song: We gotta rock on through Electric Avenue! Number 1514, to be exact. I would live there the next four years, until just past my thirty-fifth birthday

Once again, I tried to stop drinking.

But once again I just could not imagine dating and not drinking. Or put another way: what girl in her right mind would want to sleep with me if she wasn't under the influence? You would have thought that all my recent good fortune would have done something for my low self-esteem. But no dice and still no clue. I had some short-lived, pretend relationships. You know, with the unavailable type. None of them lasted longer than two or three months. I was floating down the long river of denial. So if you know me at all by now, you know that from my standpoint, life was fuckin' good! I was just fine! I didn't want no stinking relationship—that wasn't the answer!

It took a lot of work to keep people out. With my first failed marriage under my belt, I kept my weekends with my son Marco close to my chest. I loved having him around. I continued hunting for the next job, racing and trying to fill that void.

—∽—

I've had the same relationship with eight different women over the past forty years. Every time I transferred unresolved behaviors, repeated the same actions, packed the same emotional baggage. Set myself up for failure. Acted out the same web of confusion that I saw played out in my early life. Never understanding how I gave birth to my Seven Deadlies or realizing that they were my coping devices.

There is no one to blame. I was constantly asking for reassurance while my first wife was tending to the needs of the real baby in our house. For me, too much was never enough! I was lonely in a crowded room.

I've come to understand that when I was on location for long stints, I would repeat my habit of looking for companionship with the same young women. They'd be, say, between twenty-four and twenty-seven, with issues that mirrored mine. Maybe they drank a little too much, or their fathers did. I'd create an opportunity to father them, to mentor them, to fuck them. Sex was the most important thing, but the rest of the time I would try to mold them into my own likeness. They'd be my prodigies I would be so proud, they would become extensions of me. But eventually it would end badly. I couldn't save them, just like I couldn't save my mother. These bright women would be fascinated at first. Then I'd provoke them into arguments with me. I'd encourage them to show their feelings, that they should get angry, challenge me—repeating this familiar aggravation, like my mother did. I'd even do it with my assistants, encouraging them to yell at me. I thought I was just encouraging an open and honest relationship. I thought everyone was getting something that they needed.

I met Patti on the set of the TV series *Simon & Simon.* By then I had already done the hit series *Hart to Hart, Mr. Roberts, Trapper John, M.D., Hardcastle and McCormick,* and *Robert Kennedy: His Life and Times.*

This young lady was tall—I figured maybe five nine, over six feet in heels. The first time I saw her she was crossing the street

My high school graduation photo. Same bow tie I wore while waiting tables in New York City. It still sits in my nightstand, to remind me of how lucky I have been, and there it stays if ever my luck runs out. *(Courtesy of Joe Pantoliano)*

Florie's mug-shot.
From the secret files of the FBI, covering Mafioso activity throughout these United States in the 1960s.

With Roberta Wallach and Michael Kell, Christmas in New York, late 70's.
(Courtesy of Patti Arpaia)

The group photo of my first wedding. A guarantee that
I will at least sell 300 books.
(Courtesy of Morgan Kellock)

With my mother at the wedding. She was a goddess in a really bad mood. *(Courtesy of Morgan and Tom Kellock)*

Hollywood meets Hoboken: RJ, Natalie, Natasha, and little Courtney. *(Courtesy of Morgan and Tom Kellock)*

Marco Dominic Pantoliano meet Dominic Monk Pantoliano.
(Courtesy of Joe Pantoliano)

Had lunch with Steven Spielberg on the set of his movie, *1941*. He promised we would work together. The man doesn't forget anything. Two years later while filming *The Goonies* on location in Oregon, he says, "I kept my promise, didn't I?" The man is a saint.
(Courtesy of Joe Pantoliano)

Patty and I squeezed a four-week vacation into one night in Tokyo,
then off to Shanghai, China, with one hell of a headache.
(Courtesy of Patti Arpaia)

"Hey Nancy,
you're blocking
my close up . . ."
*(Courtesy of
Giànni Bozzacchi)*

Opening of
Frankie and Johnny
on Broadway.
*(Courtesy of
Joe Pantoliano)*

Daddy Pants with Daniella and Isabella, Hollywood's next movie goddesses,
in Sinatra Park, Hoboken NJ. Marlon Brando shot *On The Waterfront* here.
A lot has changed.
(Courtesy of Joe Pantoliano)

When I grow up, I want to be the man that my dog Bogie thinks I am.
(Courtesy of Joe Pantoliano)

Me in Iraq. We are as sick as our secrets. Emotional intimacy, that is the key.
(Courtesy of Joe Pantoliano)

Roberta and Eli Wallach.
(Courtesy of Peter Wallach)

My daughter
Melody Han and
my grandson Brayden
(Giuseppe) Lee Han.
(Courtesy of Sang Lee Han)

with a group of thirty or thirty-five people, some carrying airline suitcases on rollers, beach bags, and folded beach chairs that they planned to use in their holding area until they were needed. But this girl was different! She stood out. She was carrying a garment bag folded over her arm. Her black skirt revealed her beautiful legs. I am a leg man, and this brunette had me standing at attention. She was a very pretty girl. At seventy yards away she seemed somewhat unattainable, but I would have to try.

We were on location the day we met. The company was out in Westchester County at a gas station that had to get blown up that day. Patti was an extra on the show—at the time she was trying to get a better understanding of the business and to build her Rolodex. I managed to find a way to introduce myself.

Patti and I went to dinner and a movie, and soon we were dating. It turned out that we were a little too much alike. Patti was Italian Hungarian to my Neapolitan, and I brought out the Gypsy in her. We understood each other. We both had big personalities that matched our equally big tempers. And at that time, twenty-five years ago, God help you if you crossed either of us! I had only been separated from Morgan for six months, if that. In the beginning of our relationship, I told Patti that I had had trouble with monogamy in the past. This did not go over well. She explained that if I wanted to see other people, then what was good for the goose was good for her, and I better not fuckin' cross her. During our five-plus years together, we'd be on, then off, then on. I had given her reason not to trust me, and she knew how to get even. In the end I choose to believe we were never unfaithful. At my age, it doesn't really matter!

The thing is, I've been lucky enough to have had exceptional women in my life. As with all the women I've been with, both of us had to have the last word. I had to get the last jab. So Patti and I were always fighting like cats and dogs, always over the same bone. Of course this is no reflection on Patti. I was the undefeated Italian stallion. She was the reigning champion from Chicago. At that time we were both very young and addicted to winning at all costs. Oh, they were knock-down, drag-out fights, just like the ones Mommy used to start! They helped me; I felt so alive. The tension between us was always exhilarating—in both good and bad ways. Somehow every woman that I have ever loved has gotten to the boiling point with me and given me her best shot on the nose.

—∽—

January 31, 1986.

Patti and I had checked in to a one-bedroom suite at the Mayflower Hotel in New York. Pop went the bottle of champagne, the TV playing in the background. Dan Rather wished all a happy New Year. This would be our third New Year's Eve together, and of course the preceding two had ended poorly.

We made our first New Year's resolution of the evening over a bottle of Dom Pérignon, its cork liberated and ricocheting off the parlor walls. It began as a joke: "I Joey/Patti do promise not to start anything stupid"—"Or mean!" Patti interjected, as if we were doing our grocery list of last-minute odd and ends—that would start a fight. Not this year! Amen, *sie Gott Zunt* . . . I hadn't had much to drink, and I was feeling optimistic. Patti and I, alone at the Mayflower Hotel, made this private wish, clicked our champagne glasses and went out for a night on the town.

3:15 a.m., the Columbus Bar

Success! Patti and Joey made it! Through an entire evening eating and dancing and singing!

It was well past midnight and all the carriages had turned back into pumpkins. Patti and I were going to walk the few blocks back to the Mayflower. It was unseasonably warm for the first day of the New Year. Patti wanted to pick up some food for the hotel, so we entered a deli on the northeast corner of 70th and Columbus. It was closing in on four in the morning, but this was New York, and people were coming in and out. Patti went off to a different part of the store to get a sandwich while Michael Kell and I stood at the salad bar, reminiscing in the afterglow of an evening to remember. We had run into Peter Weller and Julie Budd and Ben Stiller and his dad, Jerry; friends that we were happy to see, and they us. Michael and I were laughing and smiling from ear to ear and still looking good after six hours of hard drinking. I was telling Michael about my excitement over being cast in Spielberg's new feature film, *Empire of the Sun*, with a very young Christian Bale. In three short weeks we would be in China, actually working in Communist China, in Shanghai.

Then, all of a sudden, out of nowhere, and with nobody else in the deli, a Big 10 linebacker with a size 20 neck, all muscle and a crew cut to boot, gets in between me and Michael, and with a swipe of his arm pushes Michael out of the way to get to the salad bar. I look at Michael like *what the fuck?* Michael says loudly, "Excuse me, what the fuck was that?"

Of course, Patti remembers this differently . . .

PATTI. *Joey was talking to Michael at the salad bar and in a loud voice says something derogatory to me, in the vein of "For Christ's sake, make up your mind! This is not the Palm!" across the store without breaking stride talking with Michael. I think it took the guy by surprise. He asked if I was with Joey. The rest is history, or at least one version of history.*

Anyway, in MY version, after he shoves Michael the guy turns to him, very threatening, and says in a low voice à la Alec Baldwin, "You were in my way." I'm wondering if this is a joke. Do I know this guy? I say, "Michael, is this guy a friend of yours? Are you guys fucking with me? Is this for my amusement?" Now the linebacker turns to me and says, "Shut up before I tear your head off and shove it up your ass!" To which I reply, "You gotta be kidding. Tell me you're fucking kidding!"

All the time I was thinking, OK, there's the linebacker. Michael's five nine, I'm five ten, together we weigh about three hundred pounds, so we got him beat by maybe ten. After all, he started this, and we can finish it.

I was steaming. This was the ADHD in action, this was fight or flight, this was my mental dis-ease, the hunter in me telling me that it was time to make my move. There was no reasoning, there was no conversation about what action I was about to take, no thought of the consequences that might occur if I was to lash out at this fella. For example, a calmer mind would consider why this young man wanted to cause trouble for me. Maybe he had a gun or knife, or maybe he was looking for me to strike him so he could sue me for everything I own. But that's not the way my brain worked in 1987, especially after seven glasses of red wine, two glasses of champagne and maybe two vodkas. All I was hearing was the voice in my head saying *Tell me you're kidding me because if you're not, you cocksucker, I will knock your teeth down your motherfucking throat!* And the linebacker was just staring at me. He was looking at me like I was the smallest piece of shit on bottom of his right shoe and that my words had no effect on him. Now he was in slow motion saying, "You don't scare m—" and before he could finish I wound up, I'd picked a spot like a red laser dot on the tip of his nose. I rounded up with all my weight and I went in and—

I don't recall where Patti was at that point because it happened so fast, and I don't know if anybody else was in the store.

PATTI. *I was beside the linebacker in line. Like Joey recounts in his version of this story, he had been drinking and back in those days was sometimes oblivious to his surroundings.*

Well, it was just me and this guy. All the goodwill I'd accumulated through the course of the evening; the love, kisses, hugs I had with my family and friends, all of it went out the window because of the spontaneous nature of my imbalanced brain. I was really dressed up that night. I was wearing an Armani suit, a cashmere coat, Valentino cashmere lined gloves, and a $3,000 hairpiece that Ziggy made for me. Ziggy, who made wigs for the best. Because after all, I was on my way. *If my mother could only see me now.* I hit him, but because of the fucking gloves, my fist just grazed off. He retaliated with a barrage of left hooks into my solar plexus. I hugged him like he was my best friend to get inside so the blows would stop. Michael was on him and out of nowhere the two male Korean owners come over with machetes saying, "No fighting, no fighting," and grab us as this guy is punching me. They throw us out onto Columbus Avenue. Falling out of there we knocked over a display of oranges and apples, and they rolled down the street. Now we were on the street and I was hunkered down with my hands over my head and I could see my feet and I could see this guy's feet pointed toward me as he pounded me with lefts and rights on my back and the top of my head. I was giving cover so he couldn't get to my face. Patti was screaming at me, "Watch your nose, Joey! Protect your nose!" (I had had the nose job about a year earlier.)

All of a sudden the guy stops hitting me, and I'm thinking, *Why?* Because I can still see his feet, he's still there. I feel the top of my head and realize he's scalped me! Well, in his mind he thinks he just punched the hair off my head. I'm panicking as I see my $3,000 hairpiece tossed in the air, floating past the apples and oranges headed north on Columbus Avenue. I might be mistaken for a coward, but I run north to be chivalrous enough to save my hairpiece, which I promptly stuff into my coat pocket.

Now I realize that this guy had a friend who was pounding the shit out of Michael Kell while this guy was beating me up. Earlier in the evening, Michael had shown me one of two pair of Botticelli shoes he'd bought himself that Christmas, and now I saw my oldest and dearest friend hugging one of those shoes, protecting it like a child. Suddenly the sound of the police sirens woke all of us out of this trance. Michael darted away, grabbed a banana and apple from the mess of fruit sprawled out on the street, stuffed them in his pocket, and we jumped into a cab. As we sped away, the linebacker was still yelling expletives at me and I at him. Last I saw them they were running west on 70th Street toward Central Park.

I'm sitting in the cab and I got to tell you, I laughed so hard. It felt sooooooooooo right—even when I knew it was all wrong. By now Michael and Patti were laughing too. I was starting to see a pattern, some kind of theme. I laughed! This big full warm teary-eyed laugh born out of the pit of my heart, so real. I laugh at danger. It happens a lot, like the cliff-hanger with my friend Lillah up in Vermont? There was a feeling that overcame me and it felt so right! So familiar. I felt alive.

Patti and I traveled the world together. When I was in *Empire of the Sun*, Patti and I were in Europe for about five or six months. Filming took place in Shanghai, London, Spain, and other European locations, so she and I planned a ten-week European tour starting in Paris, then going to Florence and Venice. On the flight

back to Spain, we had some extra time to spend in the Milan airport, so we decided to do some shopping. At the time I was on a
strict diet, a purely liquid diet, because I had to look like I was in
a concentration camp. So I was constantly hungry, in more ways
than one.

I found I was always finding things that I had to have but
couldn't afford. I was making $75,000 for the entire shoot, and
I had to save. But even so I decided to swing by the airport shop,
and I was stopped in my tracks by a wallet that I absolutely didn't
need yet was utterly compelled to possess. I collect wallets—they
were always something I never had growing up—so I spent a long
while fixated on this particular wallet, doing the mental math to
figure out how I could acquire it. Remember, shopping is one of
my seven little deadlies. I've since developed coping mecha-
nisms, like leaving my wallet home when I go shopping, and not
owning credit cards, and taking advantage of the thirty-day return
policy. I became a collector—that started with wallets, actually,
then over the years as money became more available, cowboy
boots, pocket knives, watches, even pens. Stuff that I thought
would define who I was. To anyone else it's junk.

Anyway, at that Milan airport in 1987, I stared at this wallet
as if in a trance. I can still see the detail even now. The texture, the
embossed logo, even the red, green, and yellow leather piping.
On another day I might have considered shoplifting it, but at that
point in time, stealing the wallet didn't occur to me. Instead I was
most heavily concerned with what we would have to sacrifice in
order for me to have this wallet that I one hundred percent did
not need. Weighing the price against our current travel budget,
hotel fees, and everything else.

Some forty-five-odd minutes must have gone by, as I was absorbed in my task. Never once did it even occur to me to wonder

where Patti was, or how much time had passed. Eventually she walked up to me, looking very upset, suspicious. "What?" I said. "I'll tell you later," she said. "OK," I said, smiling—but she wasn't smiling back. Then I notice this guy a few feet away, and he's watching me like a hawk! Apparently this house dick thought I had done something wrong, but had no clue what that might have been. Turns out some security guards had approached Patti and taken her into a back room were she was patted down, and they emptied all of her handheld luggage.

Patti. They took my cameras apart, looked through makeup. Asked questions along the lines of: where you going, why so long, who are you with, how long have you known him. I had to wait a while for them to get a female in the room with me. It was a long while. It seemed that the two of us always got the extra once-over and dragged out of line. At the time, Joey and I chalked it up to people having seen Joey play bad guys, which gave them a weird vibe when seeing him in person. Subconsciously they may have recognized him but couldn't place him, they just had a strong feeling of mistrust in this guy. And now, this is the kicker, I looked suspicious by association. I felt Joey was oblivious and wondered how he could be standing there for that long, not watching my back. I felt the security people were wrongfully suspicious, but at the same time, I was desperately hoping that Joey wasn't doing something sketchy or that there wasn't a legitimate problem with the passports and visas.

Back in grade school when my kleptomaniac compulsion was in full bloom, stealing a wallet would surely have crossed my mind. As kids we were rewarded with a pat on the back if we had the balls to take something, like groceries or school supplies. By the time I made it to high school, it was clothes. In the neighborhood everyone—my mother especially—only traded in SWAG, items that "fell off the back of a truck." Whenever we could we got a five-finger discount. The clothes on our backs she never bought retail. SWAG was always on sale.

When we were living in the projects it was necessary to have a rep. At recess we'd brag about what we clipped, compare notes. Our values were haywire. So many kids wound up in reform school or lost an arm or a leg on the train tracks when they tried to break into shipping containers. Because they wanted to fit in, be accepted, earn respect. I was known as a quick hand artist, though I mostly fabricated that image by embellishing my stories. *"Wow! Pantoliano, that was smooth. I can't believe you got away with it . . ."*

Or if we didn't steal something, we'd play finder's keepers. Once I found a credit card and I went halvesies with a friend. We took the credit card to a famous men's clothing store in Manhattan and created a story, like an acting exercise, pretending that I was getting married and needed nice clothes. The guy's name on the card was something like Neil Rosenmeier. The salesmen called me Mr. Rosenmeier, Yes, Mr. Rosenmeier, the whole time. They asked me all about the big day, about my fiancée, and pushed me to buy a tux when all I wanted to buy was shirts. We got away with a couple of dress shirts. The suit I left behind for alterations. They're still waiting for Mr. Rosenmeier to pick up that tux. But it wasn't about the clothes, it was the rush, the feeling of the unexpected. Old habits die hard. In my twenties I was out one night at a bar called Jimmy Ray's, and I needed a paper, so I went next door to a little newsstand. I gave this guy a five-dollar bill and waited for him to make change, only he made the wrong change; he gives me change for a dollar. His bad, he owes me four dollars. We got into a big argument. He's sure I gave him $1 and I'm sure I gave him $5. He couldn't prove it, I couldn't prove it, but back then four bucks was a lot of money to the both of us. I wasn't lying to him. Finally, he gave me $4. We actually became friends. We'd sit and have drinks together at Jimmy Ray's. Well, a couple of months go by, we're all hanging out at the bar, and I'm feeling no pain. The bar is three deep and there's some drunk, a guy I didn't know who was being a real dick, and sloppy with his money. I'm thinking he's trying to impress my girlfriend, throwing money around like there's no tomorrow, leaving it on the bar. Talking, when he should be listening. I lifted five dollars off the bar and bought him a round.

When Patti and I lived in Shanghai for the filming of *Empire of the Sun*, my kleptomania was in remission. I was making money and blessed with a good future. I couldn't afford to screw it up. China was amazing, and everything was practically free there anyway. What you could do with twenty dollars in 1987 was not to be believed; it was like Monopoly money. We would get a driver with a new Volvo, driving us everywhere, all day, for six dollars. I had silk shirts made—one yard of silk per shirt—and the finished shirt wasn't any more than three dollars. I had brought some designer shirts with me and had the tailor knock them off in different sizes. I brought forty of them back for Christmas presents.

The exchange rate only fed my shopping compulsion—we were always looking for things to buy. We went into a store for the Chinese nationals, which had a fur department. The salesman holds up a fur coat, big smile, and he says, "You like? Dor!—dat's quality!" I thinking? "What's he saying, dove? Door?" He's stroking it like it's mink, and finally I get it. He's saying, "Dog." I realized, no WONDER I'd never seen a stray dog or a stray cat roaming around there!

Shooting moved on to Spain, and we did, too. The party continued. Some friends introduced me to La Ina, which is a dry sherry, and it went down like water. The fact is, drinking took away my intention to do the right thing. I didn't get in trouble every time I drank, but every time I did get into trouble I was drunk, and I couldn't see this. In Spain they would have these sherry festivals with rides and games, like the San Gennaro in New York. In Jevez de la Frontera where we were, men and women dressed in beautiful gowns, all these bright pastel colors, a carnival atmosphere. There were men dressed in Spanish matador suits and wearing sombreros.

One afternoon I was enjoying tapas while sampling the different sherries with the tasting cup I wore on my neck like an ornament—this was the custom. There were bronze statues on display in front of the hotel, and I sat there admiring these magnificent statues, epic scenes of men and their horses fighting bulls. They were just there with all the other artwork, there for anyone to touch, or even take, as far as I could tell. Nobody was looking, so I clipped one. This was a ten-pound, two-foot-high work of art. Shame on me—what was I thinking? I walked up and carried it away like a bowling ball. I walked the twenty feet back down to the outdoor bar, and placed it beside me on the table. At the time I had no idea that it had a price tag of over five thousand dollars. It was my trophy! After a while a young man approached me, a pained look on his face, and sat on the vacant chair beside me. "Señor," he said. "What are we doing here? Are you going to pay for that?" I said, "Of course!" Until I found out how much it cost. My humiliation spoke before I could. I gave it back. And somehow, I didn't get arrested.

It seemed like I was always acting out back then. Patti and I had the most impossible fights ever—so bad they were funny, really. We would ignite the worst in each other. The fights always seemed to happen under the influence of alcohol. Near the hotel in Spain there was an amusement park that had little racing cars that worked on timers. I challenged Patti to a race. I put my coins in the machine first, and then put hers in, so naturally my car ran out of time and stopped first, and hers stopped shortly after. My car was closest to the finish line, but she thought that she had won, since hers ran longer. We ended up fighting the entire way home, and when we got back to the hotel, she was still so pissed she tried to hit me.

PATTI. *I was pissed but became enraged when you flung my purse off the bed onto that tile floor. Here we are in a foreign country and I have no chance of replacing the compacts of powder and blush you destroyed. That, and you ditched me in a foreign country.*

This is just the way I choose to remember it. So I ran out on the veranda and hid behind a curtain, holding my breath only to hear her yelling, "Where are you, you muthafucka?" She was so furious she smashed a lamp. Since everything in Spain is decorated with tiles, the sound in our one-bedroom suite was just horrendous. Finally I gave up hiding behind the curtain, and hurried out to the casino for the rest of the night. The next morning I picked up all the pieces of shattered lamp and hid the bits of broken glass in the flowerbeds on the property so the management wouldn't find it and charge us extra. That day was a Sunday, so people were checking out, and as they left, I stole a lamp from another unit to replace the one in ours. You can take the kid out of Hoboken . . .

Eventually I asked Patti to marry me.

I gave her a diamond ring even though our experiment in monogamy had already failed—she had a list of boys she was seeing, and I had a list of girls. I was addicted. At that time I depended on her to play out my reassurance that she would love me and take me back. I was unconsciously mirroring the relationship my mother and father had.

It is important to remind the reader that this story happened twenty years ago, when I was really nuts! I drove poor

Patti to a place that was out of character for her. We are not the same people today. Patti is happily married, and we remain good friends.

—m—

My relationship with Patti blew up one night while her parents were visiting. A dinner party had been arranged for her mom and dad, who were visiting from Chicago. We invited our friends Nick and Shelly, Peter Weller and his girlfriend, Nancy, who was adorable. After dinner, and a lot of red wine, everyone fell into different parts of the house. Some ended up watching a movie in my bedroom. Marco and Shelly were sitting on the floor while Nancy and I were talking, holding hands and lying on my bed. Nancy was saying how happy she was for Patti and me, that we were back together and getting married. Just then, Patti walked in with her mother in tow and saw Nancy and me talking. The rest, as they say, is history. My ex-fiancée and her mom interpreted the situation as a romantic moment, one thing led to another, and soon a rip-roaring, drag out fight had the whole house shaking. I didn't mean to hurt anyone, least of all Patti or her mom, but somehow I'd done it again.

PATTI. *She was lying on top of your chest with one leg over yours. Marco was in the room watching TV on the floor with Shelly, way below the bed, and my mom and I walked in. In fact it was my mom who said, "Where's Joey?" and we came to look for you. It had been a while since you had made an appearance. I was shocked that she had to see this. A Midwest mom does not want to see her daughter's fiancé lying on the bed with some girl leaning on his chest. I was shocked, embarrassed, and I said, "Get up!" Your response was, and I quote, "This is my house, and if you don't like it, you can leave." A rather horrible situation since my mom and dad were sleeping there.*

The argument escalated until Patti struck me, breaking my glasses and scratching my nose. All I could see was red. I've seen that color no more that five times in my life. The color that sends people to prison, breaks up marriages, squeezes the toothpaste out of the tube making a terrible mess! We all have that boiling point. The voice in my head was saying, "Don't hit her in the mouth. Don't hit her in the mouth." I'm still ashamed that I did this, but I punched her in the chest. I wanted to kill her, make her evaporate and go away.

"All right!" I screamed, "I want you out! I want you out of my life!"

With that, Patti took the engagement ring and threw it away like she was throwing to home plate. And I left. I grabbed Marco and we wound up staying in a hotel that night. I went back there the next day. The house was clean, and Patti was gone.

Are you making a list of the deadly symptoms at work in my life?

—m—

In 1987, I got a call from my father and he was sobbing—it hurt too much to speak. "Florie's dead, Joey."

The last thing Florie said was, "Monk, I'm dying, I'll see you later, pal." He died in my dad's arms. How amazing was that? I always thought my mother was the glue in our family. That Florie and Daddy would be done with each other after my ma died. But that was not the case. My father started to take care of Florie when he was in the late stages of emphysema.

In the end Florie's lungs no longer worked, and he fell into unconsciousness, suffocated, and died. Cigarettes killed my entire family—my mother, Florie, and then Monk.

Sometime in November of 1987, a few months after taking care of Florie's things, my father called me and said that his left arm was all swollen. When he touched his skin it felt like a crin-kled balloon. I told him to get to the doctor. The doctor later called me and said my father, who had started smoking again in his seventies, now had all the signs of inoperable lung cancer. Un-treated, cancer spreads and cuts off the blood supply. Body parts without circulation swell up. The doctor said he didn't have long.

I was working on *Midnight Run* at the time, and had four weeks off before I would be needed back in Los Angeles. I called my cousin Bobby to ask if I could stay at his vacant apartment while he was vacationing in Florida. Money was tight at the time. I thought I'd spend some time with my father, that this would be a great opportunity to reconnect with him. And I could learn all the family secrets.

Daddy was at the cancer ward at St. Mary's with a private room and a TV set, and it seemed every time I was there, *Jake and the Fatman* was playing. He would be staring listlessly at Jake and Fatman, as if he had already decided to start disconnecting from this world. The doctor had put him on chemo but told him the cancer was inoperable and that all he had to hope for was decent quality of life.

So we would sit on the couch together, both of us pretty much checked out. Patti and I were apart at the time, and Mor-gan was already remarried. I was dating a young lady, she was an actress-model. I really liked this girl and she liked me, but I was just a zombie, and I didn't know it.

My girlfriend's mother was also being treated for cancer, and she had commented that marijuana could help counteract the nausea caused by chemo. I talked to my sister, Maryann, and we saw no harm trying it on the Monk. We had to show him how to smoke a joint, how to hold the smoke in. We were having a hard time explaining. So we brought in an expert, my cousin Beaver! But Beaver was not good at sharing. In theory he was helping my father learn how to smoke pot while I was on the lookout for the four-hundred-pound nurse who was always huffing and puffing her way down the hallway. She wasn't hard to spot. She was always stopping to lean on something so she wouldn't fall down. But she managed to surprise us anyway, and came into my father's hospital room with a bottle of Windex.

"You know this is a hospital. You can't be smoking grass in here!"

I promised Daddy would never do that again. But after he was released he did, and it did seem to help.

When my father passed away, he was laid out at Failla's, where he used to work and where Mommy had been laid out just a few years before. I was amazed by the number of friends that showed up for my father's funeral. They came and they stayed too, which spoke volumes about my father as a man. The older you get, the fewer people come to your wake. I've always loved a good wake because people are their most vulnerable. They're more reflective; their need for laughter is greater.

Toward the end of the day my cousin Roseanne approached me. I was in the front next to the casket with my sister, still greeting people.

"Come here, you gotta meet somebody," Roseanne said. The look in her eye made it clear that the somebody was an attractive female.

"I can't do that."

"Come on, she's gorgeous."

I looked down at my father and said, "What do you think? You'd do the same?" So I did. Here's to you, Pop.

CHAPTER SEVEN

The Monkey Was Off My Back, But the Circus Was Still in Town

Somebody help me! I've lost my smile and I can't find it anywhere!

Patti and I had broken up, this time for good.

The only positive outcome of dissolving a love affair is the fifteen pounds you tend to lose. I was lonely as hell but hey, my clothes fit! Another thing I had to lose: the tattoo on my ass. We'd both gotten one, a supposedly permanent expression of commitment and love: I had PATTI on mine, she had JOEY on hers. Hers also had a little butterfly, mine an orchid. I chose this orchid, remembering that a Gypsy woman from Hoboken once told me that I should always have orchids near me. That way my mother's spirit could always be near from heaven. Wishful thinking?

A year or so later, after Patti and I had made amends and buried the hatchet (fortunately not in each other's heads), I found out that Patti had covered JOEY with an additional butterfly. I had covered PATTI with a leaf. Amazingly, it turned out that we had this done on the very same night, but in different tattoo parlors!

—⚊⚊—

After we split I spent three months licking my wounds, and I was finally determined to make a fresh start. My first night out playing the field, at the China Club in L.A., I ran into my friend Samantha. She took one look at me and said, "You've got that 'I got married' look."

"Oh, no, I broke up with Patti," I said.

"Well, that's not going to last." She was laughing at me.

"No, for real this time. I'm over it and moving on and ready to start dating."

"What are you looking for this time?"

"Beautiful, tall, and nice."

"That's a tall order," she said. "Wait, I know someone, but I think she's too nice—and she has a little girl."

Fine with me, I said, so Samantha agreed to set it up with her friend Nancy Sheppard.

Nancy agreed to meet me, but not for a date, just a quick bite with me, Samantha, and her husband. I made a reservation at Il Forno, a restaurant owned by my friends Joseph and Dominico on Ocean Park Boulevard in Santa Monica. I was the first to arrive, a few minutes before 7:30. I chose a table in the back where I'd be able to see the front door. Women were coming in, some nice looking, some not. Finally in comes this five ten red-haired beauty, I mean, a knockout. I can still envision what she wore that night: leotard top, dark brown stretch pants with knee-high suede boots and a long black silk men's shirt, a gold chain belt worn around her waist over the shirt. Nancy's skin was and still is opaque porcelain, the whitest I'd ever seen. (We go through about four hundred dollars in sunblock each summer 'cause all my girls have Nancy's skin . . . but I digress.)

I'm thinking, I wish she were my date! Why can't she be my date . . . Shit, she's walking straight toward the back of the room! Then she smiled at me, and her piercing sky blue eyes had me at my knees, shaking. Shit, that is my date! Fuck . . . Now what . . . This is my date . . . Well, this will be my last date, 'cause this chick will never go out with me again.

Samantha and her husband, Danny, finally showed at least a half hour late. Nancy explains this better . . .

NANCY. *Sam had warned me on the phone that Joe was bald. That didn't bother me. I didn't care. Some of my best friends are bald—*

JOEY. *Let's pause and review the bidding. I was thirty-eight years old at the time we met.*

NANCY. *This was not exactly anybody's first date. So Joe's sitting there with his hat on backward and his hand on his head. It's a nervous habit he has. I didn't know that then. And what comes out of his mouth is this: "I just broke up with my fiancée." It was like an anvil landed on the table. Oh great! I thought. I'm a rebound!*

She sat down anyway. This had to be quick, she said, because she needed to go somewhere, meaning that if she didn't like me she could get out of it gracefully. The dinner was nice and light and friendly, and turns out Nancy actually was going somewhere, to the China Club to see friends. She invited me along, but I declined and we gave each other a kiss and a hug in the parking lot behind the restaurant, where we said our goodbyes.

As I was getting into my car, I was reminiscing. In the pursuit of happiness I've had both meaningful and meaningless sex in parking lots a lot like this one. Ah, those were the days. But Nancy didn't seem like that kind of girl. She wasn't the type of girl I usually dated. I had never dated a redhead, for one thing. Patti and Morgan were exotic-looking ladies. Nancy is also the only woman in my history who doesn't have that "destroy" button—even when pushed, she's never cruel—which is what my mother, Morgan, and Patti had in common with me, that potential for cruelty. Nancy was freckles and just as sweet as pie. Nancy grew up in Mount Dora, Florida, and I think part of her nurturing quality comes from her southern roots. It's really a beautiful thing. That southern hospitality, it's genuine. I come from hunger, and for the longest time I thought her kindness was an act! No one is that nice! It's hard for me to believe, twenty years later, that the second shoe still hasn't fallen!

We had made plans to get together again, and a few months later we went to Tommy Tang's for dinner. Afterward I leaned into the window of her white Volkswagen Jetta to kiss her good-bye, and she kissed me back. Twenty years later I'm still trying to figure out why! We started dating but didn't consummate the relationship for three months.

Eventually we had been seeing each other long enough and had become serious enough that we believed it was time for our kids to meet. Her Melody was four years old and my Marco was eight. We went to the Rose Café for breakfast, and while we were eating, Nancy's glasses fell and broke. Afterward, we piled into my white ragtop Toyota Celica convertible and I drove to a repair shop. I jumped out.

When I came back Nancy had a funny look on her face. When we had a moment alone, she was smiling. "You're shameless!" she said. "I can't believe you would do that—put your son up to this."

"I have no idea what you're talking about," I said.

"When you went into the store, Marco turned to me and said, 'Nancy, do you love my dad?' "

"What did you answer?" This was something I had to hear.

NANCY. Well, I don't know, Marco. I just met your dad.

MARCO. Do you like my dad?

NANCY. Yes, I like him very much.

MARCO. Have you slept with my dad?

NANCY. No, I haven't.

MARCO. Are you going to sleep with my dad? Are you going to sleep with him tonight?

Well, after I was able to convince Nancy I had nothing to do with Marco's grilling, Nancy and I laughed. Later at my house, the kids were playing, and Nancy and I were in my bedroom—on the same bed where I had been holding hands with the other Nancy seven months earlier. I kissed this Nancy and said, "You know, it would mean a lot to Marco if you'd fuck me."

This is the Joey mouth with no editor at work in the brain.

It is a great mystery of the universe that Nancy puts up with this.

—⚏—

Now I'm sprawled on my couch. I've just been interrupted from a great afternoon nap. With my eyes partially closed, I'm listening to a man's voice that's very familiar, but I can't place it. Then I realize I usually hear him talk over the theme song from *The Tonight Show*. I know that voice! It's Ed McMahon. Heeeerrrre's Johnny! My left eye opens just a crack . . . just enough to evaluate whether this is a dream or a bad reaction to my ADHD meds. I can feel the crushed-velvet fabric of my couch under my freshly shaved skull, soft and cool, and see its gorgeous purple color in the glare of the large Zenith nineteen-inch color TV which I got for a steal (literally . . . while I was shooting *Eddie and the Cruisers* it fell off a truck and landed in its final resting place, our East Hampton beach house).

I open my eyes fully and there's Ed McMahon, but he's thirty years younger. Theeerrrre's Johnny Carson! Now I know I'm dreaming, because he's been dead for ten years. He's wearing his Carnac the Magnificent hat. As he's taking it off he says—

JOHNNY CARSON. You've seen and read about our next guest. She was really riding high before she met him. A successful actress and model, Nancy Sheppard for unknown reasons fell head over heels in love with Joey Pants. She has just been presented the Congressional Medal of Honor by President Lincoln, for staying married to Joey for more than fifteen years. She has also received two Purple Hearts and a lifetime supply of Paul Mitchell hair products.

Nancy comes out wearing an angelic white silk negligee and fishnet stockings. As she walks to the set with her runway model stride, a brightly lit halo hovers over her. The audience gives her a standing ovation. Dean Martin stands up from the chair and kisses her hand and she takes a seat on the couch next to George Gobel.

JOHNNY. Nancy, you could have had anybody.

DEAN MARTIN. She coulda had me!

The audience laughs.

JOHNNY. Care to tell us how this happened?

NANCY. It was actually a blind date.

DEAN MARTIN. Well, that explains it!

NANCY. I showed up at the restaurant in a ponytail and no

makeup. I see this bald wonder at a table in the back, and I sit down.

GEORGE GOBEL. I've made mistakes too.

NANCY. And the next thing you know, we're dating. But before things went too far I said, "Listen, I kind of like you, but before I really like you, here's the deal: Number one, I was married before to a guy who stole all my money, so if we ever get married we'll have a prenup.

Number two, if we ever think about having sex you have to have an AIDS test, I have to have an AIDS test, and we have to make sure everything's kosher. And number three, if you're sleeping with other people, you have to tell me about that, because then in essence I'm sleeping with them, and I have a kid and I'm a mom and I can't take that chance.

DEAN MARTIN. No, she couldn't have had me. The bigger question is, why did he stay with her?

GEORGE GOBEL. An AIDS test? I think I took that test at the DMV.

JOHNNY. And you carry your score in your wallet. So Nancy, how did Joey take it?

NANCY. Well, his mouth dropped down to here. I don't think anyone had ever set the rules before he had started to play the game.

DEAN MARTIN, *pulling on jaw*. Did his mouth look like this?

NANCY. And number four, I told him, you have a son, I have a daughter, they come first. I just upchucked everything because I was so done with L.A. men and all their crap, and I had a baby at home who was way more important than that.

GEORGE GOBEL. I'm from L.A.

DEAN MARTIN. I own L.A.

NANCY. I told him I didn't want to waste my time on somebody who doesn't want to have a future with somebody. If you're just looking to get laid, go find somebody else. I'm not that person.

The audience laughs nervously.

DEAN MARTIN. Yeah, I'm busy too.

JOHNNY. And I guess he . . .

NANCY. The nonstop mouth stopped working.

JOHNNY. How did you decide he's the guy for you?

NANCY. OK, here's why I ended up marrying him. We started dating, and one day I was at his house. He was off somewhere, and I had my daughter, Melody, who was maybe five years old, and her best friend, so I walked them a couple of blocks to a little street fair.We had a great time, and we were on our way home, they're chomping on popcorn, Melody is proud of her brandnew sparkly shoes. We start crossing a boulevard and reach the median when the light turns, so we stop. Just then, Melody runs away from me.

ED MCMAHON, *to Johnny.* Sounds like a couple of your ex-wives.

NANCY. Now, Melody does everything by the book. She always looks to make sure everything's OK. So for Melody to run away was so out of character that I was stunned. Then in the corner of my eye I see a car coming. My mother's instinct kicked in: I pushed Melody's friend back, popcorn flying everywhere, and she landed in the median. Then I dove for Melody, and I got hit by the car. I was on the hood, and she was hit by the far end and went down. If she hadn't taken off, we would have all been smashed. What's interesting is that all day long she had been freaking out about wheels. We were at the grocery store and I just left the cart next to the car as everybody does, and Melody starts flipping out. "Mom, no! No! It's gonna hurt somebody. You have to put it back, you have to put it back." Freaking out. Never does she do that.

"OK, fine." I put the cart back. At the hardware store, the same thing happened. Here's something weird: A few months before I met Joey, I went to a psychic, who asked, "Does Melody have a bike?" I said yes, and she says, "I see her having an accident with wheels. It's probably the bike. She'll be fine." And that's all she said.

JOHNNY. Carnac the Magnificent knows this psychic.

GEORGE GOBEL. In the biblical sense?

NANCY. OK, now, in L.A., smart-asses try to beat the light by going around everybody. This asshole was doing that. So he was coming around trying to beat everybody, and he didn't see us. Melody sensed it, and she started running. I looked for Melody, and she was sitting there in oncoming traffic, which had slowed down. She was dazed and bloody and swelling. And one of her shoes was off. She tried to stand up and said, "My shoe, my shoe, my shoe!"

The fool driver stops. "Oh my God, oh my God. What can I do?" And I just scream at him, "Get her shoe!"

We were only two blocks from the hospital, and I made him drive us there. They took her to get X-rayed, and I called Joey. I didn't realize until the next day that I myself had a huge bruise. "I'll be there," he says.

JOHNNY. And he drove right over.

NANCY. No. In a few minutes I turn and there's Joey coming through the double doors, sweating like a pig.

"What happened to you?" I say to him

"You're blocking my car," he said. "I had to take the bike." He rode this rusty old bike that could hardly move. He hugged me, and I almost started crying.

"I can't, I can't lose it right now," I said. "Melody needs me."

When they let me go back to her, I saw that her neck was all swollen and a tooth was knocked out. But she was OK. Joey had to ride that awful bike back home. And that's the moment I fell in love with him.

JOHNNY. So he passed the test.

NANCY. Joey got that right. The next big test was his proposal. We'd only been dating a short time when we went out to dinner with his friend John Davis, who had just gotten married and was so in love. He started in on Joey.

"You're never going to find anybody like her, Joey," he said of me. "You're stupid if you don't marry her."

"I will if you pay for the wedding."

"OK, if you get married within a year, I'll pay for the wedding."

We got home, and as soon as we were in the door, Joey got down on one knee.

"Oh, screw you," I said. "It's just because somebody's going to pay for the wedding." I'd already discovered what a pain in the ass Joey is about money.

DEAN MARTIN. I was on my knees one time . . .

GEORGE GOBEL. I remember that time.

NANCY. The next time Joey tried, he showed me a ring. I looked at it. It was a bit beat up. It was his mother's ring, and there's a lot of history just lurking in it.

He was so proud. "Here's the family ring," he said.

"I don't think so!" I said. There was no freaking way I was going to put that on my finger.

"Well, you know what?" Joey said. "When Dani can walk down the aisle, then we'll get married."

The next time he asked me, Dani was not quite two, and he

actually went ring shopping. He probably asked me to marry him because of the deal he got on the ring! Anytime he gave me something, he would say, "Oh, you should see the deal I got on it." He never just gave it to me, he always had to qualify it, make it OK—I think more for him than for me. It's the whole anxiety about money thing, going back to Jersey.

JOHNNY. Jersey?

NANCY. Yeah, you know he thinks he's escaping Hoboken but his head is always there.

JOHNNY. He passed this test?

NANCY. I guess so. Then we started talking about a prenuptial agreement, and it was as though he walked into a final exam in calculus. Do you know what happened right before our wedding?

JOHNNY. I'm having chest pains.

NANCY. I always wanted an agreement, because I got screwed in my first marriage—

GEORGE GOBEL. You know, in my first marriage . . .

NANCY. Joey had no problem with a prenup and presented it to my lawyer. There was a line saying anything I do in the relationship with regard to home or our family is worthless. It actually said that. I was so upset with him, I walked out and just disappeared. I took Melody and Daniella and stayed with a friend. I said to my friend, "If he can't understand why I wouldn't want that in there, I don't want to marry this man. "Well, it was two days before the wedding and I wasn't anywhere around. He looked and looked and finally found me, and sent flowers. The note read "OK!" Finally, his business manager had gotten him to understand. We took the line out, we signed it and we got married. I don't know if he ever read it.

On my fortieth birthday, as a gesture, Joe lit our prenup on fire using the candles of my birthday cake! The lawyers screamed like little girls trying to stomp it out. Here's what I've learned since then: Joey is loyal to a fault, he's responsible. He would cut off his arm before he would allow his family to not be taken care of. Oh, he says, "I'll never pay for this!" or "I'll kick their ass instead!" But he doesn't follow through on those threats.

JOHNNY. OK, well, now we've got some idea of why you're with him. But why the hell did you agree to be in this dream?

NANCY. When he told me this book was going to be an exploration inside his head, my first thought was, maybe it will sell. People do like horror movies, after all.

JOHNNY. So what's it like now that he's exposed these maladies?

NANCY. Well, it's not as if his family didn't realize he had issues, but since he was diagnosed, there's certainly been a change in the intensity of JP's impulses. Joe doesn't come first anymore; he's put a lot of things before him. Me and our kids for one thing. It used to be Joey, his work, and then us. That's certainly changed. He used to go on location, come back and want to move to wherever it was he'd just been—the family came to expect this whenever he'd return home. I would be getting calls from at least ten realtors Joey had met. Now he's able to put the brake on, and I get only one call.

Another time, it was around my birthday, and Joey was car shopping. Of course I already had a car, but Joey couldn't decide between two cars he wanted for himself, so he bought them both and gave the second one to me as a birthday "gift," even though I didn't want or need it. But that way he was able to have both. Before the meds, Joey would go in to a dealership and come out with a car. Now he goes in and comes out with a card.

JOHNNY. One letter makes all the difference!

NANCY. Imagine this behavior when we renovated. We were all excited and trying to figure out where to put the furniture, and we couldn't agree. He went off to L.A. to shoot something and came back all excited. He'd bought all new furniture—he didn't tell me what he was buying—and he was excited because he got it all on sale. Forget about the fact that he had to ship it, which meant it wasn't a deal at all. Any female would know what I'm talking about. "What?" I said to him. "You bought what? The furniture came, and it was two chairs and a purple couch.

JOHNNY. A purple couch?

NANCY. A purple couch. And this furniture was not family room furniture, it was living room furniture. He put it and the two chairs all in this small space, because his perception of space comes from his growing up in Hoboken—walls have to be filled, rooms have to be filled, because that's how he grew up. But there was no comfortable space for anybody to sit, except for the person who sat on the couch, which was always him, and he'd spread out. So it just didn't work. It became a joke when he wasn't there. Whenever he'd leave I'd switch it with a different couch, and then when anybody would come in we'd say, "What do you think?"

The purple couch went back and forth for years. I mean years. I wanted to kill him. But that's Joey.

DEAN MARTIN. I had a couch like that once.

JOHNNY. Who manages the money in the house?

NANCY. You don't want to know. Because of the way his brain works, Joey is both a hoarder and a penny-pincher, and a compulsive shopper—he'll buy whatever he wants, then live in fear that he'll end up back in the projects.

For most of the years I knew him, up until a few years ago, he was like this. Every once in a while he'd go out and come back with bags full of clothes for me. But most of the time the bags of clothes were for him. Jewelry was never for me, it was always for him. Anytime he'd be on a big job, he'd be on a big high. As soon as it ended, he'd say we were broke. He'd go around turning off all the lights. When he left a room, he'd leave on the TV, but if somebody was there doing their homework, he'd still just turn off the light. He didn't care, lights out. We'd have to get up and turn them back on.

But we're poor and we don't have money, he was thinking. It was the fear of his luck running out. "I don't think that anymore," he said just recently. It was kind of a surprise for him, I think, that he's not as worried. "When I think about it there's always been money. I've always been able to pay the bills. I've never been late." He had a revelation.

JOHNNY. How did you put up with all of it?

NANCY. I'm talking about these manifestations of Joey's disease, not necessarily the true Joey. My husband is an amazing man! Supportive, loving, and giving, and well now. The main thing? He is my biggest fan in whatever I am attempting and always out there rooting for me. For instance, after having our daughter Daniella, I wanted to explore other avenues of work. I tried selling cosmetics, pottery (he even encouraged me to get a kiln and a studio), then I worked at a marketing company. Later I went back to modeling, because it was what I knew—but I was now older, a "classic," and not the size 4 I used to be. Finally I tried real estate, which is the one that stuck. I don't think he expected this particular career to work out so well . . . but he always encouraged me to try, to jump in.

JOHNNY. Sounds like he's a keeper, as well as a fixer-upper.

NANCY. Well, I have a history of needing to fix my man . . . that's its own book. One diagnosed schizophrenic, two suicides, one bipolar, and my hero, Joe. I seemed to recognize his broken soul and wanted to fix it.

GEORGE GOBEL. You could fix me.

NANCY. George, this is only an hourlong show.

Signs "Applause" and "Laughter" light up.

NANCY. Other men I've been with just couldn't be there for me, or for Melody. Very few men would have ridden a bike to the hospital. So I'll take Joey.

JOHNNY. He can keep the purple couch.

NANCY. He's dreaming, Johnny! He doesn't own a purple couch. Or an East Hampton beach house.

JOHNNY. What? This is a dream? Well, you deserve *three* Purple Hearts! We'll be right back.

CHAPTER EIGHT

These Are the Good Old Days!

In my early career I never took a moment to really stop and smell the roses of success. There was never a moment to rest. I was always out there hustling. An agent gets 10 percent of a thousand careers, and I get 90 percent of one. So I had to do 90 percent of the work. I defined success as being able to pay the mortgage soley as an actor, and anything after that was gravy. Starting out, when there was nothing to lose, it was easier. Now I'm a veteran with even greater challenges ahead, but I see my best work is still in front of me.

In 1993 I worked with Harrison Ford and Tommy Lee Jones on *The Fugitive*, where hustling meant you had to watch out for the swinging beam.

In *The Fugitive*, Harrison Ford plays a doctor falsely accused of murdering his wife. He's pursued by a team of U.S. marshals led by Tommy Lee Jones. I played Cosmo, one of four in Tommy's team. The climax of the movie plays out in a hotel basement, where the U.S. marshals have cornered Richard Kimble, Harrison's character, but the true villain is also lurking in the shadows, try-ing to take out Harrison before the marshals can get him.

Shooting was well under way when the director, Andy Davis, held a meeting to discuss his concerns about the final sequence of the script. The climactic scene was to take place in the laundry room after Harrison and the villain crash through a skylight, fall into an elevator shaft, and end up in the basement. The original script then called for TLJ to get hit on the head with a massive beam, momentarily knocking him out, and giving the bad doc-tor an opportunity to take his gun and kill Richard Kimble.

The general consensus was, "No one will buy this!" Every-one agreed. You can't have TLJ get hit in the head with a fucking beam and a few seconds later he shakes it off and saves the day. It's unbelievable, it's unrealistic, it would never happen! Andy and Arnold Kopelson the producer were great in that they had a lot of production meetings to see if a sequence we were about to shoot made sense. This one obviously didn't. So the big ques-tion was, how does this bad guy get a gun?

Everyone walked off in frustration, and I stayed behind and talked to Andy.

Keep in mind that before we started shooting, the U.S. mar-shals didn't even have first names. We'd rehearse at Andy's house, talking and discussing background. I dug in and made sure I was in that fucking movie. There was Tommy Lee and the four marshals, all of them good actors vying for screen time. I was absolutely shameless during the filming of that movie. I wanted in. I velcroed myself to TLJ and made sure I got screen time. If I had to make a few enemies so that I could tack some actual character onto an underwritten one-dimensional card-board cutout, so fuckin' be it. Like Dr. Frankenstein, I created a living breathing being. Cosmo was heard! Show business isn't about being nice. It's about survival.

Anyway, after they all left Andy's trailer, I turned to him and said, "Andy—hit me in the head with the beam."

"What?" he says.

I say, "What if I go one way, TLJ goes another, I get hit in the head, the bad guy takes *my* gun, TLJ saves the day?"

Andy smiles, and maybe a week later we're back at the Hilton. We were shooting nights, going in at 5 p.m. and later and working till the sun came up. Finally we were getting to the basement scene, and I got the rewritten pages and discovered that, *yes!* I'm in another scene! I get hit in the head with a beam! Great! But what's this? WAIT! I get KILLED by the beam? The writer has decided to KILL me? What the FUCK!

I went running into Andy Davis's camper. KNOCK KNOCK!

JOEY. Andy . . . Andy, they want to kill me? Jeb is killing me!

ANDY DAVIS. So what? We thought you'd be happy!

JOEY. No, no! Happy? No, please, you can't kill me!

ANDY DAVIS. Why?

JOEY. Because! What happens if . . .

And here time slowed, the room fell silent, and I said it. The sexiest word in show business.

JOEY. What happens if there's a . . . *sequel?*

By now Andy's laughing. "OK, don't worry," he says, still laughing, and puts a paternal hand on my shoulder. "Don't worry, Joey, we won't kill you. We'll just knock you out and send you to the hospital."

So we began shooting in the laundry room, working our way toward the rubber beam sequence, and we finally got to it late in the night. I'd just been hit in the head, I was on the floor, and we were filming the part where the bad guy leans down and takes my gun. I've got enough experience to know that I have to be moving in the shot, or they could just make it look like I'm dead. The shot is really tight; you see the bad guy's hand and foot along with my head and the gun. As he's reaching in to take it I'm moaning, my eyes open, my head gently moves left then right. When they cut, I suddenly saw another set of feet, and as I was looking upward, a slow reveal, my eyes panning up, I saw that it was Harrison Ford looking down at me. He too was moving his head left and right and he was wearing a little smile.

JP. What?

HF. You should be dead.

JP. I should be dead . . . Why?

HF. Because. Anyone gets hit in the head with a beam like that, a half ton of steel—would be dead.

JP. Well, now wait a sec. They were going to hit Tommy Lee Jones in the head with the steel beam, and it wasn't gonna kill *him*. He wasn't gonna die.

HF, *now smiling broadly and laughing, ribbing me*. What do you care, Pants Man? You'll get the sympathy vote AND a few days off!

JP, *nodding, acknowledging he's made a good point*. But Harrison! What if there's a sequel?

I may be embellishing my memory of the following interaction, but my recollection is of HF speaking his thoughts much the way the Mexican bandit in John Huston's film *The Treasure of the Sierra Madre* answers Bogie: "Badges? . . . We don't need no stinking badges!"

HF. Sequel? There ain't gonna be no stinkin' sequel.

JP, *confused, wondering how his plan could possibly have a hole in it*. Why not?

HR. 'Cause I won't do it!

WOW! He was right! That could throw the entire plan down the shitter! After a long thoughtful pause I responded.

JP. Oh yeah? Well—we don't need you. We'll just chase some other twenty million dollar asshole through the woods.

Harrison and I had a pretty good laugh about that one.

And two years later, sure enough (thank God!) our crew of U.S. marshals, with a little help from Robert Downey Jr., were chasing Wesley Snipes through the woods in the sequel. Two movie stars equaled one Harrison Ford!

Tommy Lee Jones, he is a force of nature. I love the man. I learned a lot from working with TLJ making that movie. He's a brilliant, cantankerous, big-hearted guy. And he was protective, very protective of his marshals. He made going to work fun. Cast and crew were on a charter flight from Cherokee, North Carolina, back to Chicago after finishing the train wreck scene for *The Fugitive*.

"Joey," TLJ says, "you like good food?" "Why yes I do," I say. Then TLJ says "We're gonna eat some good food while we're in Chicago. You like sushi, don't you?" Yes I do, say I.

"Well deputy, I want you to find the best sushi restaurant, 'cause we're gonna eat a lot of sushi. You ever watch TV late at night, lying in your hotel room, you can't sleep, and you see this actor in some episode rerun, and this poor guy, he's just horrible? That's 'cause instead of spending his per diem on a good meal, he's in front of some bathroom mirror, working on that fucking scene the whole night before shooting it. The poor bastard overworked it. He left his best work in the bathroom!"

"Well, we're not gonna do that," says I. "We're gonna have fun."

"That's right!" says TLJ. "We're gonna eat good food, and we're gonna eat some sushi. 'Cause let's face it—ain't nobody gonna win an Academy Award on this one."

Cut to a year or so later: "The Oscar for Best Actor in a Supporting Role goes to . . . Tommy Lee Jones!"

—m—

In 1996 the highly regarded film writers and directors the Wachowski brothers, Larry and Andy, hired me to do their film noir crime thriller *Bound*. I was chosen to play Caesar, a Mob accountant. The brothers wanted me but the famous Italian producer Dino De Laurentiis, who financed the film, didn't see it. He said I was a character actor, not a leading man. (Though later Dino said, "I love Joey Ponts. He is funny. He is handsome, he a leeedy man! I'm glad I picked Joey Ponts.") Luckily, the Wachowskis won out.

Bound was the first time I had a starring role in a good movie. My name above the title and all that. It was also the Wachowskis' first time directing. I loved the challenge of a difficult role, and the movie turned out so good—despite my tendency to paraphrase. If I forgot the lines I'd usually just make something up. No doubt any other poor screenwriter would've said, "What the fuck? Those aren't my words." But the Wachowskis were more forgiving, at least of me.

During the filming Jennifer Tilly once tried improvising her lines.

"Don't improvise, just say the words," one of the Wachowskis said.

She protested: "You let Joey improvise."

"Well, Joey can't remember—and he has to say something."

As I said, I hustled my way into Hollywood any way I could. Give me an impulsive, uncontrollable mouth, and I'll give you a fearless, spontaneous audition. Give me dyslexia and I'll deliver lines so fresh you'll think I made them up. Maybe I did.

The Wachowskis made *Bound* only to prove to Warner

Bros., which had already bought the screenplay they'd written for *The Matrix*, that they were capable of directing a $70 million movie. As writers they also wanted control over their own material. There came the time when they storyboarded the entire *Matrix* movie to show the executives frame by frame how the movie was going to come out.

The Wachowskis started talking to me about *The Matrix* during the filming of *Bound*. They wanted to give me the part of Cypher, the traitor.

Once again they championed me—the Wachowskis hired me for *The Matrix* even though the studio wanted then to cast somebody younger. They refused and they would not let up. They supported me, they were there for me, they were on my side. They succeeded in hiring me, but by that point we had only six months before we were to start filming in Australia.

After the casting was finished, the Wachowskis decided to have some fun with me.

One day Andy and Larry called me to say that they were going to cut the steak scene, and that Keanu Reeves, who had a starring role as Neo, thought they were making a big mistake. He *liked* the steak scene.

"Yeah, well, tell Keanu to get over it," I said.

They started laughing.

"What?" I said.

"You're in the steak scene, Joey."

"Keanu's right!" I said. "How dare you cut the steak scene!"

That's when they knew.

"You haven't read the script!"

So retarded, right?

A few weeks later, Carrie-Anne Moss, who was cast as Trinity, had a little party for everyone before we all went to Australia for filming. We were hanging out in Carrie-Anne's living room, and I was playin' around. I said to Keanu.

"You believe these fucking guys were gonna cut the steak scene?" I say.

"I know, I know," he says. "It's my favorite scene."

"Yeah, mine too. We're gonna be great in that scene."

You could hear a pin drop. Everything just stops. The Wachowskis are high-fiving each other.

"What?" I say.

"We're in that scene together, mate," Hugo Weaving says. "Just you and me."

Andy and Larry gave me up. "He hasn't read the script! Still hasn't read it!" They screamed, laughing then crying on the floor.

Now everybody was laughing, me included. I'd rather them laugh with me than at me! We weren't starting for another four months. Things change. What's outrageous to me is that I've been cast in two of the most trippy movies of all time! *The Matrix* and *Memento*.

Well, obviously by the time we shot the steak scene, nine months later, I'd read the script. Many times. That evening's work stands out as one of the most memorable experiences of my life. The actors asked if they could come to watch Hugo and me work on the scene: Keanu Reeves, Laurence Fishburne, Carrie-Anne Moss, and Hugo Weaving. Well, Hugo had to be there, but the rest came in on their day off. Their commitment and support of the work, their being there, made me so proud to be an actor. And reminded me how lucky I was to have been invited by these genius minds, the Wachowskis, and the rest. One of the things I loved about the Matrix Trilogy is how the Wachowskis are able to entertain their audience on a visceral, animal level. But then looking deeper, you see the script is a deeply thoughtful exploration of perception and reality.

—◊◊◊—

For most of my life I've been in some form of therapy—cognitive, primal scream, whatever—trying to keep the dragon at bay, to keep my genetic legacy from hurting anyone else that I loved.

But it wasn't until I met Dr. Kelly that I understood that the core of my problems was brain chemistry. After meeting him for the first time, I left Dr. Kelly's office with the knowledge that I had no one left to blame. It wasn't my mom's fault or Daddy's fault. I was diagnosed with a brain dis-ease, in my case clinical depression.

The good news was, this was not a conviction, a death sentence. Now that I had this newfound understanding of my emotional dis-ease and surrendered to it, I was feeling lighter by the moment. I was suddenly happier than I had been in years. I felt as if my head had had a colonic, scrubbing the prefrontal cortex walls clean of my traumatic debris. Maybe I could even find my smile! That night I slept better than I had in months.

The next morning, though, as I lay in bed half-awake, I decided to get a second opinion. Now that I'm officially crazy, I figured, I'm going right to the top, see the top dog.

I had a couple of friends who got me to the front of the six-month waiting list to see the world-famous father of psychoanalysis, Dr. Sigmund Freud. Sometimes being a celeb does help. They tell me he saw *Memento*, like, eight times!

It was a rainy Monday morning when I went to see him. The fall leaves were sticking to cobblestone roads, making it difficult for me to stay in my boots. I was afraid I was going to be late because my GPS hadn't been able to read all the German street signs. And Dr. Kelly's free-sample antidepressants hadn't kicked in yet.

Given the fact that Dr. Freud is the father of psychology and all, I was surprised by the size of his office. It was small for a guy who had achieved so much. I had just finished filling out the paperwork for my insurance when I noticed someone out of the corner of my eye sitting partially obscured by a plastic palm in the corner of the waiting room, checking me out.

I saw that he had it. The Look. I've seen it a thousand times. It's still odd for me. I don't wake up in the morning thinking I'm going to be recognized, so in the course of any given day when it happens it's kind of a surprise. I wonder if other celebrities go through that. I thought I'd talk to Dr. Freud about it.

There are many variations of the Look. There's the "Brad Pitt." That's the thirty-footer. As soon as they spot you, *bam*, they got you. But they pretend they don't! Then there's the "Harrison Ford." They spot you at thirty feet and they're smilin' at twenty.

Then there's the "Old Joey Pants." At fifteen feet they're thinking, how do I know this fellow? Then, as they're passing . . . *bing!* they zero in. But it's too late! They've gone past me. Ah, what price for the success of the minor movie star? My personal favorite look, and the one I aspire to, is the "Tommy Lee Jones." It can only happen in a restaurant. They spot you, but they have to be loaded or rush to the bar and get loaded before they have the balls to approach you.

The man staring at me was overweight, unkempt, used and abused. Clothes too small, stained and ragged. Face swollen and aged. I greeted the man.

JOEY. Hi, how are you?

MAN. Fine, thanks for asking, how are you?

The man has a funny look on his face, as if he is hearing an old song but can't remember the lyrics.

MAN. You sound familiar.

JOEY, *with a smile and a laugh.* Yeah, I get that all the time.

MAN. This is so weird. I feel like we know each other.

JOEY. I don't think so . . . you from Jersey?

MAN. Nope. Where did you go to high school?

Now, as I said, I get this thing all the time. It's time for me to put a pin in his persistence, so I smile and say:

JOEY. If you're not from Jersey, I don't think it matters, right? You probably know me from show business.

Just then the man lights up, and jumps from the couch.

MAN. Look at me . . . Oh my God, of course! Joey Pants! Who am I? Don't you recognize me? Take a good look—go ahead! What's my name?

JOEY. Take it easy, fella that's—it's okay . . .

Geez, this guy's too much. Take a couple of Xanax and call me in the morning! This was a first even for me. I've never seen any fan this animated, happy even.

Then everything comes to a screeching halt. The room is spinning, crazy. I wouldn't be able to pick him out of a lineup, and yet, something in his eyes . . .

JOEY. Are you . . . Cypher?

CYPHER. YES! You played me, Cypher McGillicuddy, in *The Matrix*! You remember! You interviewed me, we hung out. That's me! I'm Cypher McGillicuddy!

JOEY. How are you?

CYPHER. You've got to ask? I'm a mess! Look at me!

JOEY. It's been eleven years since *The Matrix* . . . you put on a few pounds . . .

CYPHER. A hundred pounds! It's the drinking! I'm not well. Not well at all. I went to AA, but I couldn't stop, then it was drugs. I lost my wife. I lost my house. And the bank don't even want it—I'm there till they throw me out. Then I fell in love with this stuntwoman from *Battlestar Galactica*. I thought she loved me for me, but she's just like the rest. It's been hard, Mr. P. I'm disgusted, let me tell you. That's why I'm here, hoping this Freud guy can help me.

This poor man. I played Cypher! I needed to defend this man— honor him, even. Cypher was the only character in that movie who had doubt. He was filled with doubt, fear, jealousy, envy. Everyone else in the movie had complete faith . . . in their cause, their mission and most of all in their leader, Morpheus.

JOEY. Cypher—you're a warrior! You took the red pill, you chose to see reality! Come on man, so you lost faith. Your humanity shows.

CYPHER. I should have stayed in my pod, plugged in, feeding the machine, dying a slow death and loving every minute of it, an average life, not extraordinary in any way. I had a good job in the Matrix, nothing special. I ran a video shop and I was good with computers. Yeah, I took the red pill. I woke up to reality. But who the fuck wants to deal with reality? You begin to doubt everything you ever believed in. So when I was offered the deal, to commit to the betrayal and not have to remember, no nightmares, no guilt, just go back to sleep into the Matrix, there's something great in that. Hell, yeah, I took the deal. Who wouldn't? But then my character gets blown away, and I end up being everybody's worst enemy.

JOEY. Look babe . . . I identified with Cypher, I LOVED PLAYING YOU. I was proud to defend you. My soul cries out for the price you had to pay. But lighten up! Look at Shakespeare, man! There are no better parts than the bad guy. The bad guy is always the most memorable, and he usually gets to wear designer clothes too! Everybody always needs the bad guy. The hero, the victim, the good guy—they need the traitor in order to be who they are. Everyone wants redemption. Our greatest lessons come from the bad guys.

CYPHER. Look at me! I'm a mess! I didn't mind it when the movie was a hit. People wanted to meet me. Chicks for the first time looked at me differently. I was getting laid, man. What the audience didn't know is that I didn't die. I could've come back, but they never gave me that opportunity. The Brothers dropped me like a hot potato! Everything was good until the minute I knew for sure that you weren't going to be in *Matrix 2* or *3* . . . Why did you have to tell them the *Fugitive* story about Harrison Ford and Andy Davis and sequels? I mean, it's a science-fiction movie for fuck's sake. They could've brought me back!

JOEY. I don't know, brother, but SNAP OUT OF IT! Come on . . . you can't blame them. IT'S ONLY A FUCKING MOVIE!

CYPHER. Yes I can! I've got nothing no more, moving from one ism to the next, searching for peace, validation. If this guy can't fix me then it's done . . . *(He starts sobbing on my shoulder!)* My line from the movie is still true for me—I didn't want to remember anything. I just wanted to be important, rich, and famous. Someone like you—an actor.

JOEY. Why? Why? Do you know what it's like wondering when and if there's going to be a next job? Playing the same one-dimensional, underwritten bone because you know how to put the meat onto it? Fuck, you deserve everything you got! You could've been anyone! The president, Michael Bloomberg, Bernie Madoff, even! You had one wish, and—of all the things and places—you chose to be an actor? Are you fuckin' nuts?

Cypher jumps up in a rage, grabbing me by the throat. We go flying over a chair, crashing into a magazine rack, knocking over a five-gallon water cooler that comes crashing onto the hardwood floor and Persian rug, shattering glass and shooting water everywhere.

During the commotion we hear screaming from the other room in German. Dr. Sigmund Freud exits his office, big stogie in the side of his mouth, smoke billowing out. Meanwhile his 3:15 client, Donald Trump, tries to leave without being noticed, walking on tiptoe so as to not get his shoes wet.

FREUD. Vas . . . Vas . . . is das? Knine it! Shtop, dumkopf, halt it now!

He looks stern with his wire-rim glasses leaning on the tip of his nose. His vest is open, revealing the buttons on the outside of his trousers and his suspenders. He takes his cigar out of his mouth to finish the last bites of the hot dog he holds in his other hand. There are visible specks of mustard in the grey of his beard. Cypher and I lie on the floor, wet and spent. Cypher is crying. I can do nothing but console him.

CYPHER. Why did he have to be right! Why couldn't he leave me aloooone?

It's odd to see his three-hundred-pound frame, this dude who looks like Joey Pants, now three times the size of me. And I'm next to him, soaking up water in my cowboy boots and jeans. The nice shirt I clipped from Bad Boys II *is ruined. We're both on the ground sitting in a puddle of water. The overhead master reveals Dr. F. and our wet figures on the floor.*

But in a flash we have changed position. As the camera pulls back and up we see that we are no longer in the waiting area, we're now looking into Dr. Freud's office. Now I'm lying down on Freud's couch, which is merely a tiny loveseat, and my legs hang over the arm.

Cypher is gone now and it's JP who has been doing the talking.

JOEY. Wait, what's happening? Am I dreaming again?

FREUD, *putting a kettle of tea on a heating coil.* I do love dreams. So what are we doing today, discussing your mother's relationships with Florie and Monk and you?

I look startled, and Freud sees he's hit a chord.

FREUD. You'd be surprised how much I know about you already.

JOEY. You seen me in the movies?

FREUD. No, I play bingo with your Mother every Monday, Tuesday, and Friday. She's so proud of you.

JOEY. It always leads back to my mother! (*Eruption like Cypher did a moment ago.*) When can I be free of her!

FREUD. Ah, very Freudian of you!

JOEY. Ha ha, gotcha. I was just goofin'. I had to see if you'd take a bite of that bait. (*Pause.*)

FREUD. Hey, it's your nickel, if you vanna vaste it . . . (*Freud now back at the burner, boiling more water, preparing to boil another hot dog.*) You vanna a frankfooter?

JOEY. No thanks.

FREUD. You sure? It's vegan—it's delicious.

JOEY. You got mustard? (*Freud nods and adds another hot dog to the water.*) OK then. Hey, Doc, sorry for being a dick and fucking with you like that. Please tell her I—(*the words are hard coming*)—that I love her.

FREUD. Joe, that is indisputable. She brags about you all the time. And she loves that you have a lawnmower.

I start to tear up, of all the things.

FREUD. So, in a nutshell. Give it to me. Vat are you here for?

JOEY. I want to know why, what happened? I was a happy-go-lucky guy. I was having a good time and then it started to change. I'm having such a hard time enjoying life, I worked so hard. Why does my misery feel so much more exciting? Why am I acting out? I feel that I got some gypped blood in me some way.

FREUD. Nine-Eleven didn't help. The earthquakes and floods and oil spills and nuclear plants in Japan blowing up everywhere. That's some depressing shit. It's not your fault.

JOEY. But what about sex? Nancy has thrown down the gauntlet! If I want to be with another woman, then I'm out.

FREUD. She sounds like someone your mother would approve of. How did you get her? Anyway, I don't really deal with sexual issues. My duty is to be a constant reminder that we are the descendants of apes. If you're being ruled by Ralph and the twins, for that you want to talk to Carl Jung.

JOEY. Oh, you mean the little head?

FREUD. Yes.

JOEY. Can you get me in?

FREUD. No, he's too touchy-feely for my blood. Plus, rumor has it he sleeps with all of his clients.

JOEY. Not bad work if you can get it.

FREUD. Those pleasures were just symptoms masking the real problem inside you. Take them away, and the problems come out. I take it you're better now.

JOEY. Yes. I get that my life is 80 percent chance, and that I'm powerless over everything. The sadness that was living inside of me can be overcome simply by asking for help and getting my head out of my past, and staying in the present.

FREUD. And what's the price you pay? That you can't be a baby anymore? That you have to be an adult? That your children look at you as someone who is imperfect and broken, just trying to do the best you can with what you've got? You would trade that for being a scumbag and liar and cheat? That's why you became an actor. Because you can be all of these people without consequences in real life. You have a rich family life, and you've chosen the appropriate work, but you just don't want to grow up!

JOEY. Easy for you to say, you fucking cokehead. I hear you smoked fifteen cigars a day to cure the throat cancer you got from smoking in the first place. If you can't get it right, how can I?

How can anyone? All these demands! Can't a guy make a mistake once in a while?

FREUD. A Freudian slip? I love that, by the way.

JOEY. I don't want to grow up! I don't want to grow up! Fuck you! I refuse! Why do I have to? Look at Clooney! Look at Pitt! They're doing great!

FREUD. I know George and Brad. They're friends of mine. Joey Pants, you're no Brad Pitt or George Clooney. Be you! God gave you the gift—or is it a curse? I keep forgetting. But the world needs people like you to ask questions. The weight of the world can get heavy, so you sublimate your life and turn them into characters that you can play. By the way, *Midnight Run* is my favorite movie. Will they make a sequel?

JOEY. You didn't see *Risky Business*?

FREUD. You're in that? Let's change the subject. What was that fight in the waiting room about?

JOEY (*pause*) Ask him—he started it.

FREUD. Schmuck! This is your dream! You are him!

JOEY. It's always been easier to be in somebody else's skin . . .

FREUD. Really, you should stay away from caffeine. You won't be having these dreams.

JOEY. But I like my dreams; I got to meet you.

FREUD. You're crazy.

JOEY. I think that's the second opinion I came here for.

CHAPTER NINE

Stuck on Stupid

Election night in 2000. At that time Tony Goldwyn and I were co-presidents of the Creative Coalition, a nonpartisan group of actors and creative types who want to highlight important issues of social relevance. Caroline Hirsch, a Coalition board member and the owner of the Manhattan comedy spot Caroline's, lent her venue for the evening so we could watch the results come in. TV sets were on, and there was excitement in the air. Come on, we all remember that historic night! The race was very close. Most of us in the building wanted Al Gore to be the next president of the United States, and we all thought he would be when Tom Brokaw announced that he had won Florida. Everyone in the room exploded with joy.

Ten minutes later, Al Gore was no longer the president-elect anymore, and after drinking Diet Coke all night I started hitting the vodka. I had to work the next day at 6 a.m. on *The Sopranos*, but I started in on the martinis—huge martinis. As the saying goes, it's the first drink that gets you drunk. Three drinks later, I was two sheets to the wind, smoking a Fuente Opus X cigar, wait-ing to hear if the polls had closed in California.

Martha Plimpton, whom I'd known since *The Goonies*, was al-ready mad at me for being a jerk and acting like one to Nancy, who was also fed up with me by that point. Nancy decided I wouldn't go back home to Connecticut as we had planned. My pal Tony Spiridakis had come at the last minute with his wife to Caroline's, and they decided that he would stay behind to watch out for me, and after the festivities he would take me back to Hoboken and tuck me in. My old pal Rosanna De Soto, who played Ritchie Valens's mother in *La Bamba*, was also on Joey duty that night.

Tony found out that the Weinstein brothers were throwing a victory party for Senator-Elect Hillary Clinton at the restaurant Elaine's, and Tony, Rosanna, and I wanted to go. Someone said we'd never get in, since President Clinton would be there with his Secret Service detail.

"Ah, well, let's go," I said. "You never know."

I didn't want to admit that I had already met President and Senator-Elect Clinton several times through Darius Anderson and Ron Burkle, and I had a better than average chance of get-ting in. So we went to Elaine's, famed for being the literary and celebrity dining spot. Anybody who was anybody had been go-ing to Elaine's for more than thirty years to get a glimpse of the glitterati. Elaine's was always packed, and this night they had car-doned off three blocks of Second Avenue. When we got there, the Secret Service guys recognized me and said, "Come on in." They ran a wand over the three of us and we were in. The place was packed, and there was no place to sit except for one round empty table, so we sat down.

A young woman who was a volunteer came over and said,

yelling through the loud music and screaming fat cat Hillary sup-
porters, "You can't sit here because, it's, uh, it's reserved."

JP. WHAT! I can't hear you!

YW. This table is reserved for the president and senator-elect!

JP. All right . . . But they're not here yet and there's no other
place to sit. So if they show up, we'll be up and out before they
finish "Hail to the Chief."

YW. No, no, no, it's reserved for the president.

JP. But he's not here. (I could not follow her logic and was
getting perplexed. I wasn't drunk-drunk at this point, just a little four-letter-word high. Looking for a fight. Now this young
woman—and I want to pause right now and apologize to her, if
she's reading this—is upset, and starts screaming at me.)

YW. Get UP, or I'm going to tell Harvey!

JP. (I was amused that this pretty young thing had blown her
top! Hey, I still had it! I'd found her button and pushed it. Where
I came from, this was foreplay!) You can tell anybody you
want—but the president's not coming. Look what time it is.
Hillary just won the election, they're three hours late! I'm sure
they're too busy to come. (I stood up nose to nose to make my
point. Tony pulled me back into my chair by my jacket, forcing
me into my seat as Rosanna laughed.)

Meanwhile, Jessye Norman, the opera singer, was sitting behind me, and she was very upset that I had a cigar, even though
it wasn't going. The cigar wasn't lit, I was. But the cigar had that
smell of having been recently lit, and she was upset.

"It's not lit," I said. "It's not lit, see?"

At that moment, Harvey got everybody's attention. "Excuse
me, excuse me," he said. "Listen, President Clinton and Senator-
Elect Hillary Clinton are not going to make the party. But a select

few have been invited to the Hilton. Everyone else, thanks for your support." In other words, fat cats come with me, we're going to be with Hillary. So off we go in Tony's Jeep. The Hilton's an enormous hotel, maybe forty stories high, and there must have been 4,000 volunteers working the party. I sized it up pretty quickly, and I said, "Let's go. The Clintons aren't going to come to this."

We were back in Tony's Jeep almost immediately, as the Secret Service had allowed us to park it right near the front. My God, how things would change in eleven months. The next party was on 42nd Street at the Hilton Hotel by Grand Central Terminal. It was about 1 a.m., and I had to be at work in five hours.

We walked into the lobby, Tony taking the lead. The entrance hall was enormous and filled with around 2,000 people. The layout was wide open, and from my training for the role of Marshal Renfro in *U.S. Marshals*, I knew that it was bad cover for a president, and there was no way that the Clintons would make an appearance. I had had enough and demanded to be taken home. As we were leaving the building, Tony spotted Harvey and Bob Weinstein, Ben Affleck and Gwyneth Paltrow, and all the other $200,000 high rollers who had contributed to the campaign, and they're all walking into the kitchen. "Let's go," Tony says. So we folded into the tail end of the group and blended in. The whole time I was still chewing on my half cigar looking like a drill instructor in an episode of *Combat*, and there were Secret Service dudes all around. These guys are watching us like hawks. This time they look different though because they have Uzis. *Uzis?* We stuffed into the elevator and were surrounded! It was too late to turn back now. We were in the elevator with the high rollers and the Secret Service dudes with Uzis. They looked like *Men in Black*. I'm thinking, *I'm Bing Crosby in a road movie and*

Tony is Bob Hope. Jessye Norman was standing next to me, and she was still staring.

"Ah—ah," she said, imitating a sneezing sound."Uh, sir, a cigar?" some guy said."It's not lit," I said. "See?" He seemed OK with that. Jessye wasn't.

Tony was between the two of us and was trying to calm her down, telling her that the cigar was not lit. I was also telling Ms. Norman, "It ain't lit, the cigar ain't lit!" and drawing more attention to us than Tony would like at this point.

We got off the elevator and two Secret Service dudes saw me and said, "Come this way, sir." They took Tony, Rosanna, and me into a very small one-room suite. There were several couches and in the far corner there was a table with a TV on the nightstand still giving election results and there were buckets of beer and wine and cheese and crackers. They left us there.

Tony whirls on me and says, "You motherfucker. We got us arrested, you fuckin' asshole. Why'd ya have to open your fuckin' mouth?"

"Will you relax?" I say. "Whaddya mean arrested? Look there's beer and wine here. They're not arresting us." Then (just in case I was wrong) I went to use the bathroom.

When I emerged from the bathroom I walked into mayhem. As if a magician had snapped his fingers, where once there were only three of us, now there were a hundred—and the president! I walked right into Chelsea Clinton and said, "Chelsea! Chelsea!" And then I was next to Hillary. I had the cigar in my mouth and I had my arm around Hillary, and I was saying, "Hillary baby, you did it! You did it!" And she said, "We did it!" They were taking pictures and I got in them. Tony and Rosanna were sitting by the round table and Tony was up against the curtain. He was trying to hide behind it because he didn't want anybody to know he was with me. Plus he was in sweatpants and a raincoat, because I'd invited him on the spur of the moment.

I had met President Clinton and Mrs. Clinton on previous occasions in photo lines and whatnot, and I was asked to host President Clinton's fiftieth birthday at the House of Blues (they were holding them in all fifty states; I did California). So I was like, Hey, me and the prez are tight! I went up to him and I was patting him on the shoulder, saying "Hey, Mr. President! Oh man, I'm gonna miss you, Mr. President." He was smiling, and saying thank you. I had my arm around his shoulder and gave him a hug around the neck, and I had a sense of joy and sadness—because I really did love this man, and I really was going to miss him as president. Soon it was obvious that he was done with me, he just wanted to watch a little TV. But I was crying, telling him this weepy shit, so he just kept saying, "Thank you, thank you very much."

Meanwhile for the last thirty seconds someone or something had been pulling at my jacket. I felt it through my drunken haze and finally realized I was getting the hook, so I signed off: "No sir, Mr. President, sir! Thank *you*! I'm gonna miss youuuu!" He was lucky I didn't french him! "Oh Mr. President! What a run we had, huh? What a run!"

By now Tony was furious with me. Rosanna was sitting on the other side of the table, hysterical with laughter, dumbstruck that I wasn't in a body bag. She was laughing so hard she couldn't say a word. Tony was whispering in my ear inches away: "Sit down! You crazy bastard, sit down!" He finally pulled me off the president with such force that his fingerprints are still engraved in the side of my ass. Then he pinned me in my chair. We were eyeball to eyeball, and I saw my reflection bouncing off the sunglasses he had put on, trying to avoid being recognized by anyone. I could feel Tony's nose pressing into mine, as he held me down with his pork chop arms on my shoulder. "You don't see these fucks? They're Secret Service. These guys want to shoot you. I'm going to let you go now, Joe, and if you try to stand up I will throw you through this fuckin' window! 'Cause I'll never work again if they fix me with you! So shut up! Shut the fuck up!" So I shut up.

Now everything was cool. Everyone was there. Jessye, Bob and Harvey, Ben and Gwyneth. The whole Rolodex that keeps on giving. We were listening to the only TV in the room and our president was concluding a running commentary on the poll results. "Now, what Gore's gotta do," he said, "he's gonna have to win Florida to win this election."

Well, at this point everybody understood that he was stating the obvious.

I leaned over and whispered to Tony, "If he would have kept little Billy and the twins off a navy blue dress in the Lincoln bedroom, Gore wouldn't have had to worry about Florida." The president shot me a look, and Tony suddenly had a handful of my balls, so I was done talking! With horrible clarity I realized our 42nd president must have heard me. My ears were ringing when I heard him say abruptly, "OK, got to go back to work. Thank you." And they left.

How the hell? How is it possible that I wound up in the singular most important moment in politics of that millennium? I was literally with the president of the United States and perhaps the future first-ever female president. And could I keep a thought in my head? No, it came sliding out of my mouth.

The following summer Tony and I were at a screening of the new Spielberg movie *A.I.* At the party, this big guy comes toward us, laughing as he's introducing himself. "Hey, Joe, how are you?

You might not remember me, I'm retired now, but I used to be on President Clinton's Secret Service detail. I was there that night at Hillary's election party."

I nearly choked on my heart.

"You know what? The president got in the car that night, and he was laughing. He thought you were hilarious. You were so lit up that night."

Can you imagine? How is that possible? How is it that I say something that stupid within earshot of our president then later come to find out that he wasn't even pissed at me? In another country, a dopey fuck like me who couldn't hold his liquor or his tongue in that situation would've been strung up before he got to the word *dress*. Thank you to all my angels, who must have been working double time for me yet again.

—m—

By August of 1999 I was working in Montreal and had five days off, so I took a road trip with my then eight-year-old daughter Danielle. We were driving to Connecticut, when I got a call from my agent. He said that David Chase, the creator of *The Sopranos* was casting a new character. Was I interested in maybe playing a part on the upcoming seasons three and four? Could we talk now? Sure!

David Chase is a wonderful man to work for; he's as honest and direct as they come. We had known each other from his *Rockford Files* years, and had a mutual friend, Larry Konner.

In that first conversation David told me, "You're on the short list, Joey. Do you know the show?" No, we didn't have HBO. "OK," he said, "I'll send you the best from season one and season two." I had no idea how good it really was.

"He's a scumbag, Joe," David said of the character, Ralph Cifaretto. "But they're all scumbags. We'll want him to be funny, but he'll become a thorn in Tony's side, and in the end he'll lose out to Tony." He said it would be a two-season job.

I just said, "David, HBO has a terrible rep for being cheap, and I don't do cheap. If there's a budget, the agent will tell you what my quotes are, and if you can't come close then knock me off the table, because I don't want to waste your time."

So I didn't get the job.

Meanwhile, Nancy and I were moving back east, to Connecticut. We had picked out a house, negotiated and closed, and I would be leaving California in a week. I had to go there first while Nancy and the kids loaded up the old house. One evening in that last week I went out to meet Chazz Palminteri at Aggo, Paulie Herman's restaurant. It was busy—it was always busy— but it also happened to be awards season, and the casting awards were that night. Paulie had no room and needed to double up some folks, so he was asking all the people that knew each other to sit together. He asked me if it would be OK for Georgianne Walken and Shelia Jaffe, her casting partner, to join us. They were nominated that year for best casting directors for *The Sopranos*.

They showed up and for some reason it didn't occur to me that Georgianne had had something to do with David Chase asking me about the possible role in *The Sopranos*. They were already on the third of ten episodes of the show by this point. Apparently the guy they had picked wasn't to their liking, even though he was and is a great actor. (I've been fired off pictures before. They always tell you the same thing, that you're not really being fired, you're just being replaced. It's the same thing! But here's the upside: you still get paid. So I like being fired every so often.)

We had a great time talking that night. Everybody was laughing and telling stories on each other. Georgianne and I bonded when I'd told her I was about to move to Wilton, Connecticut and where it turns out she had been living for thirty years.

The next day my agent, Nick Stevens, called. "They're going to give you what you want on *The Sopranos*," he said. "We've got you tied into Michael Imperioli."

I knew I wasn't top tier, but I wanted the same perks as Imperioli—the same dressing room, salary, photo approval, and the like. I had learned about this stuff from a former agent, Pat McQueen. She was my mentor and also one of my most important angels. I've always known how to keep my eyes open, but from Pat I learned the most. She was the one who schooled me in the art of contract negotiation.

So I said to Nick, "What's the hurry?"

"They need you there. They have to shoot three episodes to catch up."

"They're expecting me to leave in two days? For two years? This is a complete hardship for my family!"

"What the fuck? You're leaving in two days anyway."

"Yeah, but HBO doesn't know that!" (Of course, Georgianne and I had just talked about my move so they probably knew I was heading back east, but they wanted me enough that they closed the deal.)

So it worked out that HBO paid for our entire relocation. They flew our nanny Christina, Nancy, the girls Dani, Izzi, and Melody all first-class and paid for the moving van. They really stepped up to the plate. I wanted to work hard for them because they considered me important enough to offer me the part and give me what my agent asked for.

It's hard for an actor to come into situation already under way, but HBO, David and the actors all made me feel at home immediately. When we were building Ralph's character, I asked David if I might make some suggestions based on my own life experiences. He was wonderful to work with and gave me free rein.

My character, Ralphie, was a gangster, so he hung with

goons and lowlifes, but he could also sit across the dinner table with governors, senators, and bankers. He could be in either of those places. He could fit in. I saw him, like I saw myself, as a chameleon: he was different things to different people. I could put my whole life into him.

I felt that I really understood this character. I remember how affected I was by *West Side Story* when I was young. Well, the same was true for Ralph when he saw *The Godfather* at age thirty-five. When he heard Michael Corleone in that movie, in his mind Michael was telling Ralph that he would be the godfather, the Don, *il capo di tutti capi*. He resented Tony and coveted his position. He wanted Tony's spot! He felt smarter than Tony and envied him for being born into this dynasty.

Ralph had some big secrets. He was damaged, completely insane. Beaten and abused by his own sick and demented mother as a kid, he was fueled by shame, and fated to reenact his past. Ralph had also been raped and beaten by his mother's boyfriend, which played well into the fact that he wanted to see people suffer. It also left him searching for a father figure, which may be why he wanted Tony's respect so badly. Toward the end he was addicted to cocaine and hanging out with a young, sick girl who was a prostitute just like his mother and possibly pregnant with his child. But on the outside, Ralph looked like a fully functioning gangster.

Ralph worked his ass off through college. He had a college degree and a mind for business, which made him very valuable to the Soprano bunch. I wanted his look to reflect that. The costumer, Juliet Polcsa, put Ralph in ascots and gave him penny loafers and Paul Smith vests. He was very Brooks Brothers looking. We got really crazy with it. The first day I showed up for a set rehearsal already dressed. Everyone assumed I wasn't in wardrobe yet.

So Jimmy Gandolfini, who played Tony, was perplexed. "That's your costume?"

"Yep, I'm dressed," I said.

"You're wearing *that*?"

Because I used to live in Hoboken—the epicenter of Goombah Land—I was concerned that I would be spotted once the episodes started. I wanted to distance my real self from my character, so I said I wanted to wear a wig. We had the hairpiece designer model one after the director Chris Nolan's hairstyle. I always loved Chris Nolan's hair. I showed pictures of Nolan to Irwin Hoopnick, the best hairpiece maker I've ever worked with. The hairpiece showed up and needed to be combed a certain way, but David didn't like it so he kept having the hairdressers change it. A wig requires a lot of maintenance, and because I have ADHD I don't like people nitpicking over me. I couldn't stand still. I didn't want any touchups, no makeup, so in dailies this wig became the bane of everyone's existence, including David's.

I loved my *Sopranos* character because he was such a bastard.

Audiences remember the bad guys! Behind every great hero there is a greater bad guy. History remembers them. We will always remember the "takers"; the takers write their own history. They fight to the death and do whatever it takes to make their own way. In my real life I don't have the stomach for that, I never did, but I could, in my fantasy world, embody these characters and become them on film and stage.

How do I want to be remembered? I know I will be remembered for playing bad guys, one bad guy in particular. Look at all the good guys I played—nobody remembers. So now I have a legacy. I can be remembered. I guess that allows me to do good things that might help somebody, because I'm recognized.

Unfortunately, somewhere along the line bad guys are always

made to suffer, so I've been beat up a lot on set. And when actors get hurt, there's always a doctor to prescribe painkillers. In the second season of *The Sopranos*, I got my first visit from Dr. Feelgood. I was shooting a scene in a steam room with Peter Riegert and Jimmy Gandolfini. They used real steam. I walked by it in bare feet, and I got first-degree burns on my ankle. The pain was unbelievable. A doctor prescribed Percocet for the pain, and he gave me the whole sermon on the drug, which amounted to: "Be careful." I was in so much pain that alcohol wasn't enough. Percocet felt good. It did the job. People can understand physical pain. It's emotional pain they have trouble with. But oh, that doctor knew, when he warned me about Percocet. He knew I'd start loving it for the way it dealt with the emotional pain.

Every time you're on a job, drugs are accessible. If you need something, people in the crew, usually the drivers, they get it for you. For them it's prestige: "Yeah, I take care of so and so." The doctors, too. I was in Florida once and needed some Vicodin. The doctor who gave me the prescription was also building a rehab center. He could get the client hopped up on the shit, and then make a fortune getting him off of it. Fucking brilliant! What a business model!

I had been prescribed painkillers before, but it wasn't until 2000 that they became a habit. When I turned forty, in 1991, a friend I've known since we were twenty, Bobby Moresco, along with Paul Haggis, Fisher Stevens, and Matt Dillon, decided to take me out on the town. The town happened to be Chicago. Fisher was there working on a pilot, Matt had come out to visit his childhood friend, Brian Collins. We were drinking and going from bar to bar, restaurant to restaurant. They are eight or nine years younger than me, and we found ourselves on a sidewalk between bars.

"Last guy to the corner has to buy the drinks," Matt shouted.

My only thought: I don't want to have to buy another round of drinks. So I take off running, and Matt cuts in front of me. I trip over his foot and down I go. Everybody heard the pop. I get up, and I'm concerned about my Japanese suit. Did I tear my pants?

"Oh my God," Fisher said. "You went down. What was that noise? Joey Pants, you're the man."

"I'm hurting," I said.

"Don't worry about it, Joey. We'll buy the next round."

The next morning I was in shock. I had been so anesthetized by the alcohol the night before that I didn't feel the full force of the pain. Now I couldn't get out of bed.

I called my friend Dr. Andrew Feldman, who is the orthopedic surgeon for the New York Rangers, and told him what happened. When I walked into his office and he looked me over, he laughed.

"I'm going to save you the money for the x-rays," he said. "You have a third degree clavicle separation. It's very common. Skaters get it, hockey players. If you were a leading man or woman I would operate and put a pin in there. It's seldom necessary, but they demand it. But you're a character actor, so I'll leave it. It just has to heal."

Andrew knew best. My clavicle healed just fine by itself. But hey, if you don't want to give me an Oscar, at least give me a pin for my clavicle!

About eight months into my relationship with Nancy, I fell off my roof. I had bought a nice piece of property in Santa Monica, and I was going to tear down the house to build a new one. I took a buddy up on the roof to show him the view the new house was going to have. Just look. There it is. All mine. I was on the top of my world, I thought. But I was really slipping and falling. We were coming off the roof, and I fell straight down the ladder. I grabbed the rain gutter, but my leg was caught in the rungs. It has never been the same. Years later, my leg still talks to me when I'm getting out of a chair or getting up. So now it's my clavicle and my leg.

When we were filming *Memento*—the psychological thriller about a guy with no short-term memory who tries to solve the murder of his wife—Guy Pearce has me on the ground in the beginning and end of the film, holding a gun to my mouth. I had to elevate myself a little during the scenes, and later when I was trying to get up I felt a ping. I told them I had to go to the emergency room. Call for an ambulance. It was so embarrassing. They put me on a stretcher, and I felt like a idiot. They X-rayed me and sent me back to the set.

So now it's my clavicle and my leg and my back. Later in *Memento* there's a scene in the hallway where we get into a fight. So that I could do it, they gave me a whole bottle of Vicodin and told me to be careful. I took two of them but I wanted to have my wits about me during the scene. Even so, I got pushed up against a wall and my lip started bleeding. Blood was coming down my face, and I don't even know it. They cut.

"Why did you cut?" I said.

"Your lip is bleeding."

That was my introduction to Vicodin. I realized that it was taking care of my back pain, but also doing something else. I never felt high the way I did with alcohol, but I just felt good. I started to take three a day, one every six hours.

Vicodin just put a bounce in my step. It made me feel alert, alive. It gave me energy. In the beginning, the feeling would last for five or six hours. If I wanted to I could get off the pills for six months, but then my back would go out and I would be back on them. Eventually I started taking more, and had two doctors filling prescriptions. I got sick twice and I thought I had the flu. I didn't know I was a junkie, a Vicodin and Percocet junkie.

Up until then, alcohol had been my vice of choice. I drank only to get loaded. I never went out and had a single glass of wine. I would drink because I felt I needed it, because I needed to feel good. The alcohol helped to bridge the gap, it helped me to have a better time. Often my drink of choice was martinis. I wanted to feel good quick, and as I said, I was always concerned about calories. But then once I discovered painkillers, I stopped drinking alcohol and just did Vicodin. I was going around for three years saying I was an alcoholic, and I didn't drink. I thought I was sober.

—m—

The morning of September 11, 2001, I got a call from my assistant, Maureen. "My God!" she screamed. "Oh my God, Joey. I'm watching people jumping out of the building!" I had heard that a plane crashed into one of the twin towers in New York. But she was calling before the grisly details had been reported, so this was my first realization that people were dying.

Nine-Eleven turned out to be a profound turning point for me. I suddenly realized I had taken everything for granted. I felt my personal security threatened. I was responsible for four children, and that thought created panic. I had basked in blissful ignorance until I was forty-five, and I was awakened to my disastrous past when 9/11 happened. From the moment that second plane hit that second tower, I had the fear: What have I done? What kind of world did I bring my kids into?

"You know, this is war," I said. I'm thinking, Who am I? Where am I? What am I? My inner turmoil started to churn, this mental dis-ease that I didn't know was in my DNA began to surface. My mother's DNA was all over me—her tremendous fear of being hurt almost to the point of schizophrenic paranoia. Afraid I'm going to get struck by lightning. Afraid I'm going to get hit by a car in the street. This tremendous fear was starting to obsess me. I couldn't shake it. My children were going to get hurt, my wife was going to get hurt.

I thought everybody was feeling what I felt. I thought it was absolutely universal.

In September 2001 I was doing a two-part guest-star role on *Roswell*, a sci-fi show about aliens and monsters. I was an alien. I was starting my first episode and had planned to be in L.A. for three weeks.

But when news of the attack reached me, my first thought was to get myself and Nancy home. Everyone feared what would happen next. God only knew if Al Qaeda, whoever the fuck they were, were going to attack us again in the following days. I felt compelled to stay and finish filming *Roswell*, but we needed to get home. Meanwhile all the airports had been shut down, and even if we'd wanted to drive all the way back to Connecticut, there wasn't a car to be rented. I had met a guy from a product placement company who gave me a Cadillac truck to drive while in L.A. (They like to do that with celebrities—it's an endorsement. It's good for them and good for us. More success equals more free stuff.) But I had already given my truck to Tony Spiridakis so he and Chazz Palminteri could drive home across the country.

The next day, September 12, was my fiftieth birthday. I found myself in a chair in the makeup trailer on the *Roswell* set. The television was on, playing scenes of the disaster over and over. I thought about bolting, but then in my head I heard Mickey Rooney talking to all the kids in Judy Garland's barn, saying: "The show must go on!" I could hear Mickey Rooney in his young voice, with his passion, his talent and energy, with that big movie star smile on all five feet of him. "Come on! We ain't quitters!" I was thinking that too. How could I walk off a Paramount show on a stage floor that Mickey Rooney and Judy Garland probably danced on? Mary Centrella didn't raise no quitter!

Even so, I was frantic. My anxiety was spiralling. What could have happened to my children? I didn't know where Marco was at first, but I knew he had to go to New York City that day, around that time in the morning, and he had to take the PATH train from Hoboken into midtown Manhattan for a meeting. I knew that he wasn't scheduled to be downtown, but my brain immediately went to what if he had gotten lost, or had accidentally boarded the World Trade Center train instead of the Penn Station train. He hadn't lived in the Hoboken area that long, and it could have happened. I'd gotten on the wrong train so many times over the years. There would be nothing he could do but ride it right into the World Trade Center. When it happened to me I'd just change trains or simply walk uptown. What if Marco wound up at the World Trade Center station with the thousands of young professionals going to the financial center of the world?

I was envisioning the scenario in my mind, building it bigger and bigger and bigger. How could I find my Marco? The cell phones were down, and he wasn't answering the phone in our apartment. On the TV in the makeup trailer I could see the towers being hit over and over again.

Finally I got up and stepped out of the makeup trailer. I saw our director and my friend, Jonathan Frakes, talking to the executive producer, and he was speaking to someone on a cell phone. They were nodding. Then Jonathan called out that they were shutting down the set until further notice. The news came as a tremendous relief, but now, how to get home?

Finally one of my angels came to my rescue. We were in Sonoma, California, for our old friend Darius Anderson's wedding, which nobody had wanted to postpone. Ron Burkle, the billionaire supermarket financier, was Darius's best man. Ron mentioned that he and his staff would be leaving to fly back to New York, and I jumped. "Do you have room on your plane?" He said he did. Nancy and I looked at each other. "But we have to go back and pack."

"No, we'll take care of that," he said. The next thing I knew, Nancy and I, along with some other guests, were at the Sonoma airport getting on an amazing helicopter like the one the president flies in. But this one was a cream color, with beautiful leather and wood trim. It was magnificent. The helicopter took us to San Francisco airport, maybe a twenty-five-minute ride, and we landed next to Ron's new plane, which was a converted 727. It was a house. Literally, a two-bedroom house with wings. The beds had cashmere sheets. "That's President Clinton's," Ron said, pointing to one of the bedrooms. We were assigned to the front seats in the boardroom, which sat thirteen or fourteen people around a large conference table. The table was on a hydraulic system that could bring the table down to the floor of the airplane if necessary. Nancy and I used the occasion of that flight to join the mile-high club—or the half-mile club, since we didn't go all the way. We decided that if we had to be airlifted out of someplace in an emergency, this was the way to go.

—m—

When I got home, my drinking started to dull my senses like a film of melted wax.

On the outside, I was doing great. I had more success than a kid like me from the projects could ever dream of having. I had kept that promise I'd made to myself back in 1961, that I would be far from P.S. 8 and in show business by this point in my life. Production was starting up on *Sopranos* season four, my movie

Memento had ignited college kids in Europe first, then in the United States, making it a global success and the most profitable and critically acclaimed independent film of the year. So I had both a hit TV show and a hit movie, and I had had other massive hits like *The Matrix*, a groundbreaking movie with the top directors in their field. I was lucky to be where I was, but still the inner pain was creeping up on me.

This deep depression had hit me before, again when I was doing so well on the outside. It was in 1983, my *Risky Business* glory days. Back then I was filled with love. I loved to have parties. I loved bringing people together. I was a tremendously faithful friend. But something inside me just shut down. It came on slowly. I'd get up in the morning and I'd go to the Rose Café in L.A., then I'd start my day, and I found myself going back to the house and staying in the house, watching TV, taking a nap.

I knew 9/11 had something to do with this current malaise. I had lost three friends—Joe A, Mattie, and Randy—in the attack, and I felt as though something inside me fell along with the towers. It was around this time that my doctor said I'd done so much damage to my hip and back from the years of running that I had to stop. He told me the condition would just get worse, so he forbid running and told me to use an elliptical or some other low-impact option. I couldn't go out for a run anymore, which had worked for so long as a balm on my psyche. His recommendation was a right hook that caught me directly on the chin when 9/11 already had me heading for the floor.

I kept taking the Vicodin, more and more each day, and as I did, there was a part of me that knew if I took enough of these, I'd die. Spiritually and emotionally, that's what I wanted.

Around the same time, my cousin turned me on to Xanax for the first time. He mentioned at dinner one night that he was taking it as a sedative to help him sleep, and offered me some.

Eventually I got my own prescription and added it to my personal pharmacy.

Meanwhile, the stint on *The Sopranos* was coming to a close. I had only been contracted for two seasons, so I was prepared for the end. Still, I was sorry to hear David Chase say the inevitable: "Joey, we racked our brains, and it was a painful decision, you've been a pleasure to work with, but we're killing you."

There was a tradition on the show that nobody talked about plot developments. David would make a statement about how hard we worked, and how leaking the story ruins the experience for the audience, so he'd appreciate it if we didn't share details with friends or family. People honored that. It was never a demand, always a request. So when we'd find out a guy was going to get whacked, we'd just take the guy out to dinner. I was less than happy when my turn came.

My career was on an upswing, but I was back on the market.

I called my agents. "Get me out to California. I need a job." Gary Foster was producing the action film *Daredevil*, and they wanted me to play the reporter. I thought the role was a great idea, because the character was a good guy, and I wanted to play a good guy. When I got the offer I called David and asking if he could kill me off *The Sopranos* earlier. "I'm unemployed and need to feed my family," I explained.

David was gracious and accommodated me so I could do both. He called to talk to me about how I'd get whacked. "You OK with us doing something where you lose the hairpiece?"

"How are you killing me?"

"We're going to throw you in a wood chipper."

I had been thrown in a wood chipper in the movie *Downtown* and I didn't want to make a career of being thrown in wood chippers. That's how they came up with the whole bowling bag thing. In the episode that became my Emmy submission, Tony kills me in the kitchen and has someone cut off my head and hands and stuff them in a bowling bag. On the whole, I'd rather be in Philadelphia . . . but at least I didn't go the way of the chipper.

—✷—

In the fall of 2002 I was invited to perform a two-actor Broadway play: *Frankie and Johnny in the Clair de Lune.*

This was a personal best for me. Joe Mantello, a wonderful actor, would be directing us. People were coming out to see us every night. I got everything I ever wanted—my name in lights on Broadway three blocks from where Frank Sinatra had performed. Two Hoboken boys making good. But the experience ended up being anything but good.

—✷—

There are two emotional parts to a play: the foundation of the play that's being unfolded and the emotional life and the journeys of the actors, directors, writers, and producers, with all of their stories going on in the background. It's a lot easier when the character you're playing and your real-life character are on the same trajectory. I experience a lot of fear and anxiety whenever I am taking on a new role. The four questions I was taught to ask as an actor are: Who am I? Where am I? What do I want? And, how am I going to get it? Those were Dennis Stanislaviski's four questions that every actor should ask when preparing for a role. I got his book and studied with acting teachers who were influenced by the teachings of Stanislavski, the Russian guy from the Moscow Arts Theater.

So here I was, going into a play I had seen and wanted to be in. I understood this character. I had been invited by Edie Falco, who had performed it with Stanley Tucci, to the opening. Now they had completed their production, and the producers were replacing the cast. I was meeting an actress I didn't know, Rosie Perez, and she seemed nice enough. The director Joe Mantello I already liked. Everybody seemed raring to go and it all sounded good.

This is a two-character play. The curtain went up on two people and I was one of them and was onstage the entire evening. There was a moment during the performance when Rosie got to go to the bathroom where she was able to make a costume change, but I had no break. The show was rigorous, and an emotional challenge. The press were there, meaning that we were to be reviewed again as a new production. I wasn't seeing a doctor at the time and thought I was doing really well. I had just finished shooting *Daredevil* with Ben Affleck. I mean, what would I need a doctor for? I didn't realize at the time that I was really into the heart of my sickness. I just didn't know it.

The first performance was January 1, 2003, after only three weeks rehearsal. It was all so very exciting. I was starring on Broadway with Rosie Perez, an Academy Award–winning actress who came from the same humble background I had. Our pasts paralleled each other. She was a ball of energy. Joe Mantello, the director, was great, and I felt his warmth and enthusiasm. I was even upfront about my dyslexia, but I actually didn't know what it really meant. I would tell people I had dyslexia the way I would tell them I had high cholesterol. This play had a lot of dialogue, and learning dialogue is just matter of memorization, and memorization is relatively easy for me. I never worried about it. For me it was a form of repetitiveness. I never worked on learning lines. I would just read scenes over and over again, but I would read them because I was breaking down the character. And for the first week with Mantello we just read the play over and over again.

At home, Daniella would help me practice. I would read the play once a day, making little marks on top of the script, and ended up reading it some thirty to forty times. During production they found me an aspiring thespian to help me run the lines. And I had Nancy read the lines into a tape recorder without any emotional overtone or punctuation. I would put it on a tape recorder and go to sleep with it.

The play was intense. Kathy Bates and Ken Walsh had created these roles in the first production done off-Broadway. Edie's and Stanley's performance of the play was the first one on Broadway. The curtain opens to complete blackness. You hear two people making love to orgasm, and they're naked. We were naked for maybe the first eight pages of the script.

There was a point of truth at the beginning when I realized, I have to be naked! (This was my first Broadway play so people told me the protocol. You were supposed to give wardrobe a $50- to $75-a-week tip. I had no wardrobe for eight pages, but I was supposed to tip them!)

At the beginning of the play, after Frankie and Johnny are done with their lovemaking, Johnny starts laughing hysterically while they're both still in bed. He's trying to stop but can't, so what's a girl to think? Laughing was always hard for me to get into. I felt very self-conscious. In addition, I'm in this show where a guy and girl are walking around naked in front of eight hundred people. I actually put in the Playbill a bit where I told the audience that, if they must compare me to the others who played this role before me, to please give me a two-inch penis credit due to shrinkage. It was the middle of winter, for crying out loud!

Acting is the ability to be completely private, as if there is no one around you, even when there are 150 crew members picking their noses nearby. It's the ability to maintain a quiet reverence, as if no one's there.

I'm so self-centered that it's all about me. I may not be much, but I'm all that I think about. I woke up one day and all of the sudden I was an old man. I was fifty-one years old when I did this play. Nine-Eleven had happened and New York was a scary place with the towers going down and the effect that had on my psyche. There was a smell down there where the towers had been. I understand now that it was the smell of death. We were all supposed to get over it and move on. To paraphrase *The Wizard of Oz*, "Pay no attention to the people who died behind that curtain."

By the second week I was filled with fear, and was competing for attention with Rosie. She rubbed me the wrong way. She also thought I was lazy and she was mad at me. She kept telling me that I wasn't holding my own or working at her speed. She was clocking me at every turn and paying too much attention to what I was doing. I wasn't attracted to her; she reminded me of all the girls in Hoboken who weren't my type. I was also being told I wasn't loud enough. All I kept hearing was that I wasn't good enough and didn't belong there. By the time the curtain came up, I almost felt that I had to apologize. I had to let everyone know how miserable I was.

Joe Mantello was a good director, but he got frustrated because it was becoming obvious that his two actors didn't like each other. The play is about a chance for happiness and love, but Frankie doesn't want to take that chance because she's been burned too many times. And Johnny's attitude is, so you get burned, put a little butter on it and keep moving.

At one point he cleared the room except for Rosie and me. He felt frustrated that he couldn't get these two people to like each other and planned to give us a serious talking to. He said, "I can't do it, you guys have to do it." Mantello took the tough love approach, and since I came from tough love it didn't bother me.

The rehearsal hall was just a big old room with fluorescent lights. When we got our talking to, Rosie was wearing a house-dress over her jeans. Joe said, "I'm done. I don't know what to tell you. It's a play about two people who love each other, and I don't know how to get you two to do something to get that to happen."

We weren't talking to each other at this point. It seemed like Rosie was holding back, talking in a very measured way. I was numb the entire time, and if I wasn't numb I was sobbing.

Joe said, "Well, Rosie? I think . . ." but he never got the chance to finish his sentence. Already Rosie was like The Hulk transforming, this little 5'2" person, her brown eyes turning fiery red. Like a runaway train she started slapping and kicking at the makeshift set, tearing at her dress and kicking at the set pieces on the stage. As I went toward her she started slapping at me, and picking up a piano stool, cursing the whole time: "Okay Mr. Hoboken, you think you're so tough! I'll show you some *Brooklyn*!" Joe hid behind his chair. He told me to quickly hide in a nearby bathroom as she tore out of there. For several minutes all we could hear was Rosie kicking at the elevator that still hadn't come.

Great, I thought, *we don't have to do this*. I thought the play was over. But it wasn't as easy as that. Poor Rosie didn't know the button she had pushed. She thought I was lazy, and it was the worst thing for me to hear, because that's what I'd heard my whole life. She brought back my worst memories of elementary school. She reminded me of that uncaring teacher who told my mom I was lazy. Now it was ten days before previews, and I was preoccupied with what had happened.

Later I got a call from Rosie wanting to apologize. It was hard for her to say she was sorry. But at the time I was so miserable I wouldn't accept her apology. I wanted to punish her. I felt she didn't say sorry the way I wanted her to, and I couldn't let it go. I convinced myself that she wasn't really sorry after all, that she was just saying it to come back in to the play. She was wrong to call me "Mr. Hoboken." I was little boy Hoboken.

Somehow the show went on, and we pulled off opening night. We got a standing ovation. Afterward I went out with friends and had two martinis, my first alcohol in a year.

But for the rest of the production all I wanted to do was count the days until the thing was over. Every night I just knew someone in the audience was thinking I was horrible, so I would telegraph how I felt about my own performance. I was never able to take a curtain call with gratitude. I blamed everyone in that building for my own unhappiness. I boasted by putting up a calendar and counting the days until we would close. I hurt so many people's feelings. My children and my wife wanted me to quit the role, because they couldn't live with me. I even asked my agent to find me a pilot so I could get out of the play and ended up taking the first piece of shit I could.

Much later I tried to make amends with Rosie. She was really wonderful and warm and graceful—all of those things I couldn't see when I was so sick.

Maybe the play struck too close to home. It was the story of two lonely middle-aged people. Men thought the wife was hot. Me, lonely with a wife men would kill for? Maybe Rosie was right. For better or worse, you can't leave your life behind. In so many ways I'd never even left Hoboken. I could still smell the perfume of the urine in the fire escape stairwells. I had prayed that I could escape those stairwells for so long, and I never did.

CHAPTER TEN

The Great Depression

As I succeeded in my career, and succeeded and succeeded, it was only then, when I realized that I had all of these things and they still weren't enough—they were never enough—that I started to self-destruct. I was 800 IMDB points from true happiness, and then came the depression. The real depression.

Ironically, in 2005, just as I was about to hit bottom, I started working on a movie about BD called *Canvas*. In the film I was John, married to a schizophrenic. Anyone watching it can see the exhaustion and resignation in my face, the sluggishness in my walk. Talk about affective memory—boy, would my acting teacher have been proud! I was certainly using my personal experience for this guy! What was inside of me served my character well.

Toward the end of our pre-production on *Canvas*, two days before the start of shooting, I got a call from my old friend, actor Charlie Rocket. Charlie was not only a brilliant actor and comedian, he was also a self-ordained minister. Charlie had married Nancy and me, our ceremony like a comedy sketch on "Saturday Night Live." He surprised me, Nancy, and our 300 guests by pre-

siding over our nuptials in his magenta tuxedo and rose-colored
John Lennon glasses. He spoke of those rose-colored glasses as a
metaphor for married life in his wonderful deep voice, sounding
like the voice of God Himself. In fact he was so funny that director Andy Davis cast Charlie on the spot for his next movie,
Steal Big Steal Little. Charlie was my go-to man for many of my
problems. So when Charlie called out of nowhere, I was glad to
hear that voice. In our fifteen-minute conversation, we shared a
couple of laughs, and made plans to get together with mutual
friends over the Thanksgiving weekend, some eight weeks away.

On my second day of shooting Nancy called to tell me that
Charlie was dead. He had slit his throat with two kitchen knives,
one in each hand. He didn't leave a note. I thought, how could
this be? I just talked to the guy! There was no evidence that he
was troubled in any way. How angry must he have been? Later
I learned that suicide without warning is actually very common.
People experience a wave of despair and/or fury, sort of like a
stroke, and they seize on the idea of suicide and *just do it*. A permanent solution to a temporary problem.

The thing is, I had had friends commit suicide in the past.
I remember being angry at them for choosing that way out, and
for leaving such a mess. But I didn't feel that way with Charlie.
Not this time. I felt an overwhelming sense of compassion and
empathy. I became scared. I remember thinking that suicide
might be a reasonable way of ending my own pain. When I had
that thought it stayed in my head, and I could not shake it. Kind
of like an out-of-body experience, I sensed my unconscious
mind floating above me, contemplating my physical self's next
move. Charlie's death coupled with all the emotional dust that
was being kicked up throughout the filming of *Canvas* had me on
the ropes. To think that I, of all people, now that I had everything

that was supposed to insulate me from bad feelings, would really want to commit suicide…the idea left me white-knuckled and frozen with fear.

Depressed as I was, working on *Canvas* changed my perception of mental illness. I began to realize that mental illness is something different from the way it's typically portrayed in the movies. One day my costar Marcia Harden and I went to a mental clinic so that we could learn the mannerisms, the rhythms. After talking awhile with some of the patients, I said, "You folks are very nice, but where are the crazy people? You know, the ones who talk to trees?"

"We are the crazy people," they said.

There was something else in making the movie—the way Marcia was building her character. Everything Marcia was doing in front of the camera was dead on for my mother, and Marcia had never met her. It was like the scenes in the movie were scenes in our cold water flat in Hoboken. I always thought Mommy was just a character in the first-generation Italian-American melodrama I grew up in. Now I began to realize that my mother may have had BD.

BD is subtle. It isn't always seeing elephants or hearing bells. The way Marcia portrayed her character was very real. Her behavior didn't look like out of the ordinary. In one scene her character says, "I don't want to go there, I don't want to go to that house." She reminded me of my mother when there was a thunderstorm, and she was afraid afterward that I would fall into quicksand. She had a million reasons for not allowing me to hang out with my friends or have a sleepover or go down to the shore with my friends, or insisting that I call as soon as I got there, and if I didn't she'd be screaming and calling the cops.

But even as I was recognizing my mother's mental illness, I didn't have enough perspective to see that I too needed help. I was racked by despair and anesthetizing myself daily with painkillers. My director, Joseph Greco, would say, "Cut," but the feelings stayed in me; I couldn't shake 'em.

Meanwhile I'd make offhand remarks about the painkillers I was taking for my various ailments, or mention my many doctor visits. Apparently Greco had been observing me more closely than I thought. He texted me at one point and said, "I don't care if you get mad at me, I'm worried and scared and I have to tell you, I'm afraid you're going to kill yourself using these painkillers."

Schmuck! You want the whole world to know?

I stopped whatever I was doing and went directly to his hotel. We were in Hollywood, Florida, which had recently been hit by Hurricane Wilma, and now a different type of storm was brewing. I burst into his hotel room and grabbed him. I wanted to nail him to a cross!

"Are you fucking *nuts*!" I screamed in his face. "You never text shit like that to me, putting it in writing! Once you hit that button you're making my life public knowledge! Words live on forever!" (Like the words I'm writing right now!) I kept ranting at full tilt. "You motherfucker, how dare you. Don't ever text me or anyone else about my personal affairs!"

It took balls for Greco to confront me . . . and it had to be said. I had lost my smile and I couldn't find it anywhere. Greco cared about me so much he ran the risk of alienating me completely.

The truth is, by getting hooked on painkillers and letting my health deteriorate, I was repeating family history. My mother became addicted to prescription drugs, tranquilizers, but we didn't know that in those days. How could you know that in 1965? We just knew that she needed her "fuckin' tranquilizehs." My mother's other vices were cigarettes (three to four packs a day), coffee (with three scoops of sugar), and gambling. Mommy's death certificate read coronary thrombosis, but no doubt the tranquilizers, cigarettes, sugar, and later diabetes sped her decline.

There was a report put out by the Substance Abuse and Mental Health Services Administration (SAMHSA) a few years ago that really got my attention: it said people with undiagnosed mental dis-ease will die twenty-five years younger than those in treatment. I started on the pills at fifty; Mommy was fifty when her downward spiral began. She died at sixty-three. My aunt Tillie, a drug addict and alcoholic, died at fifty-nine; my grandfather, an alcoholic, died at fifty; my grandmother died at forty-nine (although my uncle Pete, who really suffered from gambling addiction, lived to be ninety-three!).

When the movie was done and I went home, I knew something was going on inside me. Something was up. The movie was in my head. So was my friend's suicide. So was one of the first characters I ever played, Billy Bibbit, who slit his throat like my friend.

I lived in the bedroom, which became my cave, like an old dog who knows his time to die is drawing near. I could see how empty my life had become, even though I was surrounded with the pretty things meant to define me. I pushed everyone I loved away, or scared them, thinking I was teaching them a lesson. I withdrew from everything that I had accumulated in my past, and I was ashamed of a tomorrow that hadn't even come yet.

NANCY. Well, at first, everything at home was great. There was no distinct moment when all of a sudden, boom, there was this different person in my life. It was a slow slide. You know, things happen in life. I would attribute a change in his mood to a TV series being canceled. So, he's a little depressed, no big deal. He's a little angry, or worried. Then the next job comes around or the next good thing happens and those bad feelings would go away. Same with the drinking. If it got to the point where it felt like Joey was drinking too much, all I had to do was say something and he would stop. And that was true for a long time. But the drinking periods got longer and longer until it got to the point where it seemed like it was always tough to be together. Everybody was on pins and needles.

For example, he'd be coming home from somewhere—he'd have been gone for a month—and what he would do is come in and he'd inspect every corner and find something wrong with everything. But I didn't understand why at the time.

Before one homecoming I went top to toe everywhere, outside, inside, everything I could think of, and had the house perfect. In he comes, and he's looking around, going to each room and he can't find anything wrong and it's making him crazy. There's nothing out of place and it's totally messing him up. This is when I realized what was going on.

He went to his office and walked around. Then finally he was outside, and he went way down in the backyard, down the steps, behind the garage, way in the back to a deck where none of us ever goes. We had furniture piled up. We never put the furniture out because we never went back there. The furniture was still piled up from the year before. Joey comes up. "I can't believe you didn't put the furniture out!" And blah blah blah. We all started laughing because, oh my God, he actually found something.

"Why are you laughing?" he said.

The routine used to be, whenever he'd come home he'd have to find something and scream at somebody and make it all OK, right? So we would all scatter. But this time we were so sure we did it right that we were watching him. And he was just storming. We just laughed. But it was very serious business. I told my therapist about it, and she said, "It's about him feeling out of place and needing to feel in place." And that was his way of doing it. It's kind of like a dog pissing on a bush. It's his imprint.

The more depressed I got, the more dogs I got. When I was at my sickest we had ten dogs. Nancy joked about me being a dog hoarder. I loved the dogs. I let them kiss me. The kids would say, "That's disgusting!" and I would reply, "Have I ever gotten sick?" (My dad once told me that a dog's tongue is clean and healing. A human tongue has 600 percent more microbes and it's filthy. And yet people French kiss each other on the first date! Meanwhile dogs are 600 percent cleaner and they don't french me.) Why was I working to surround myself with so many dogs? Because they understood. My dog, Bogie, named after Humphrey Bogart, was my higher power. My dogs loved me unconditionally, and I never had to apologize to them. Unlike my human family, they never talked back or suffered hurt feelings when I behaved badly. And the more depressed I was, the worse I behaved.

At our house we have a bell that goes off when you come into the driveway to let us know that people are coming. That bell would go off when I drove up, and the dogs would come out to greet me. The kids would say, "He's home." They'd gather their stuff and go to their rooms so they wouldn't have to deal with me.

—◊—

In one of my darkest moments, I found myself in a DC hotel room confessing all of my transgressions to Nancy. All of my failures as a husband, all the betrayals I'd committed during our marriage. She needed to know what kind of person I really was.

I remember confessing my sins to the figure behind the white lace shower curtain while watching the warm water ricocheting off the vinyl below. I had surrendered my arsenal of deceit. My petty crimes were a repeat of the same broken record, the rusty needle going round, scratching out the same predictable song my mother taught me with white lies of omission. Mine was a dis-ease thirsty for attention and deaf to the volume of harm.

I lay back in bed with my head up on the pillows. In this position I could see the bathroom I had just left after finishing my confession. I could see the silhouette of Nancy's lean and shapely body reflected in the large bathroom mirror above the sink, still steamed up, her shower sounding like rain as it bounced off the porcelain and drowned out her muffled weeping. What would be my penance for my petty crimes of passion?

Nancy entered the room still wet from her shower, her eyes red from crying. She was now covering herself, turning from me, embarrassed, not knowing me anymore. I had admitted my laundry list of transgressions, hacking away at our foundation of trust and respect.

When I met Nancy, she was already successful in fashion and print. At twenty-eight she was a veteran model and a single mom.

She spent two years in NYC, then went on to Paris and Germany for five years. Nancy wasn't naïve; she had literally been around the world; she had had her share of heartache. But in this hotel room, twenty-five years later, my confessions spewing out had hurt her deeply. My Nancy folded over, sobbing. She couldn't hold herself up. She was crumpled up on the floor in a ball. I was standing there realizing the magnitude of pain that I caused her, seeing the effect of all my lies and my desires on my wife, the woman I love. And the fucked up part was, I did love her. I loved her even as I hurt her by showing how unworthy I really was. I despised myself, and part of me must have despised her for loving me.

—∿—

I needed a way out of this pain. I couldn't eat, I couldn't sleep, and nothing seemed to satisfy me or bring me joy.

I was already on antidepressants, and checking in regularly with the doctor who prescribed them. When I finally told him about the depth of my despair, about how suicide now presented itself as a viable option, Doc listened to all of this. He said I needed to see someone. *Oh, no kidding.* He wrote on his prescription pad names and numbers of three different psychiatrists.

I waited a few weeks and went to see Dr. George Kelly, a shrink. He has an office in Norwalk, Connecticut, not far from my home. When he called me in, the first thing I noticed was his poof of white hair, like the cumulus cloud I saw floating out there in the sky, framed by the vertical white blinds.

I walked over to the window and looked out. Wouldn't you know—a funeral parlor. I know funeral parlors. They were our entertainment when I was growing up. Mommy dragged me to every funeral and she made me look at the dead people. I thought that was normal.

Dr. Kelly with his hair was straight out of central casting. If you've ever been to one of these therapist guys, you know they like to sit there and say nothing, to wait till you talk. Well, we were a perfect fit. I don't know how to stop talking.

People have always said, "Jesus fucking Christ, this guy, there's no edit button with him. What hits the brain comes out of his mouth." That's a good trait to have as an actor. They call it spontaneity. To be immediately spontaneous, go with whatever's flashing in your head, to be fearless. To be dumb enough, stupid enough, that you have no fear. That's great in acting, shitty in the real world.

The pills, the booze, the betrayals, Mommy, the despair, I told him all of it. When I wake up in the morning my first thought is, "Fuck, I'm still here." There is no reason to live, I said, and it's a cliché unless it's you who's thinking it. If this is what my life was going to be, if even these pills don't work, I'd rather be dead. Then I ran out of words, and there was a silence in the room, and I was thinking, *That's your cue, Doc.*

"It's not your fault," he said.

I didn't understand what he was saying. I tried to explain. Doc, I lie and cheat—I was taught to lie and steal as a kid. I do booze, pills, women, clothes. I am those bad characters I play in the movies.

"It's not your fault," he repeated. Of course I have to take responsibility for my actions. That's not what he was saying. What he was saying was that I had something inside me that I didn't put there. I had a mental illness, a brain dis-ease.

It's depression. There are three degrees of depression, he explained. The clinical is the toughest. That's the one that lives inside of me. It's in my genes. And it was nursed along by everything I experienced as a child. It was in the script I wrote as a kid to explain my world and me to myself. Those lines keep coming back to me decades later. It's like I can't start a new movie. I just keep reciting the old lines.

So that's it, I thought, when the doc told me. I'm crazy. Not Hoboken Italian crazy, but there's-a-diagnosis-for-this crazy (He didn't actually say I was crazy. I think he called me a "lovable neurotic.").

I felt as though I'd hit the lottery. It's not my fault. I had been saying to myself forever: Shame on you, Joey, shame on you. What else do you need? What else do you have to have? You've got all this and you're mired in quicksand. Now I didn't have to feel that way anymore.

On hearing that they officially have BD, many people take a room at the stigma motel. I didn't. I was hitting my bottom— a term I would eventually learn is used in Twelve Step Programs—but it was a bottom that offered a rope to climb out. None of this made a lot of sense at the moment, but now these flying monkeys in my head had a name: Depression—Capital D Depression. They have therapy for that, and pills for that, and they can teach you how to manage that the right way.

As Dr. Kelly and I sat there in silence looking at each other, I realized, I'm fifty-five years old and suddenly my life has an explanation. This is an epiphany. You don't get many real ones in life, and when you do, you gotta grab 'em. It was the beginning of a Twelve Step journey.

Dr. Kelly said that what we would do is delve into my past and look at the stories and situations that have been unresolved. My stories were not very flattering. What was my past like? One incident sums it up nicely. Six months before he died, my father, Monk, was arrested for getting into a fistfight with a candy store owner who accused him of stealing a sixty-cent cigar. Which he had done.

I can still see me surrounded by all of that Italian madness. All those symptoms, living in the neighborhood of the Deadly Symptoms. The gambling, cheating, lying, addiction. Those are the symptoms. Let's call them Symptomotron. I was assembled on the character-defect factory line. I was an emotional second, couldn't be sold as a primary part. I was in the discount department.

The fact was I never had the tools for proper living, because my family never had the tools, and I thought the entire human race was like that. The gambling, the lying, the stealing, the addictions. My mother was fucking my father, and she was fucking her cousin Florie. They never got divorced—my father and mother broke up and Florie never got divorced from his wife, Marcia. This is what I think life is like.

That first session with Dr. Kelly started me off on a journey to look squarely at my life.

Getting here was a combination of things. The drugs—Mommy's "tranquilizehs"—I took to be tranquil, to be able to live in my own skin. But then I built up a dependence on those drugs and they started losing their effectiveness. My mind would race and I would want to jump out of my own skin. It was making *Canvas*, meeting Marcia Gay Harden, seeing my friend Charlie take his life, thinking, for the first time, that it might be an option for me. It was the misery and shame I felt, having accumulated all of these amazing things, setting enormous bars for me to hurdle. I was achieving that. Now, I'm no Jack Nicholson, I know, but I was regarded as one of the top character actors, and that made me uncomfortable.

I am now a walking potato sack of diagnoses: I've been diagnosed with ADIID, dyslexia, and now depression and PTSD. ADHD and dyslexia, yes; depression, yes; but PTSD?

I was telling the doctor, "But I'm an actor. I never went to war."

"It doesn't matter," he said. "Trauma is trauma. And trauma to a child impacts like a bomb over Baghdad."

PTSD, posttraumatic stress disorder. Before I started working with my shrink I believed most of the stressful, traumatic times from my childhood were just funny anecdotes from my past. I knew they were dark, and twisted, and black humor at best. However, I never admitted to myself that what I called "antics" or "hijinks" often were violent, abusive acts.

Now I understand what posttraumatic stress is. When I was a little boy, two boys who were much older, maybe eleven or twelve, held me down and urinated on my face and all over my clothes. How did that affect me? It's not funny. Well, it sounds somewhat funny. But mostly it was horrible and scary and traumatic. I was only six.

Another time a friend threw my ball down a sewer. He did it on purpose, but mostly just to fool around. My dad took the sewer cover off and grabbed this kid by his ankles, a twelve-year-old kid, and hung him upside-down to grab my ball. I thought my dad might kill my friend, and I was screaming, "Daddy, stop, Daddy, stop."

I used this trauma. I meditated on it and wallowed in the pain to create characters with depth. In many ways it was indispensable to my career. In acting school, in auditions, onstage and on set, I was rewarded for my dysfunctional life.

I guess you use what you're given. I didn't hesitate to capitalize on the emotional trauma of my past to create emotional characters. Growing up, emotion was acceptable in our house. In my family, bad feelings were expressed without hesitation. Talk about living in the moment. In a lot of ways we were seizing the moment, *carpe momentum*, because we didn't carry resentments. We said it. All of it. Our kitchen was ringside, ready to ignite. Mommy vs. Daddy, Mommy vs. Florio, Florio vs. Daddy, Mommy vs. me, or a neighbor, a stranger, or a bookie. Our cumulative blood pressure could have fueled a power plant.

We'd want to kill each other. Then ten minutes later it was, "Joey, you want some coffee?" You just lay it all out in Italian families, especially in Italian families infested with mental disease. I thought the entire human race was like that. So I had a gift. In acting school that's what they called the ability to relive a traumatic experience. I was "gifted."

Lucky me.

—〰—

The great irony, that my madness may well have been part and parcel of my success—I'm obviously not the first to think of this. Old man Socrates beat me to it:

"Madness, provided it comes as the gift of heaven, is the channel by which we receive the greatest blessings. The men of old who gave things their names saw no disgrace or reproach in madness; otherwise they would not have connected it with the name of the noblest of arts, the art of discerning the future, and called it the manic art. . . . So, according to the evidence provided by our ancestors, madness is a nobler thing than sober sense. . . . Madness comes from God, whereas sober sense is merely human."

Well, which came first, madness or creativity? God didn't give the gift of madness to everyone. And it *is* a gift, you know. The scientists have linked ADHD and creativity. And I was able to find a craft that was exciting to me, that held my attention. Until I found acting, I couldn't focus on anything for long before it became boring. Discovering acting was like finding a key that would take all my defects and turn them into assets. As a performer and storyteller, I found a use for all the pain and emotional trauma that dogged me over the years.

Confucius say, "He who would pursue a career as actor has to be a few sandwiches short of picnic." Because, financially speaking, as an actor you can't make a living. To survive, you have to make a killing!

Everyone working on a picture leaves a part of himself or herself—their pain, their soul, their spirit—in that project. Example: *On the Waterfront.* Iconic film. Shot in my home town. Imagine the filming of that classic scene of two brothers in a cab, arguably the most memorable, discussed, imitated, and acted scene in movie history. Brando and Stieger are sitting in the rear of a severed taxi—what we folks in show business call a picture car—that through the wonders of movie magic seems like it's in motion. (Remember,

King Kong was only three feet tall . . . but I digress.) So, two thespians sitting in the rear end of a severed cab inside some garage in Hoboken. Lights, camera—and now some crewmen start shaking the cab, creating the elusion the cab's driving on its way to 427 River Street—then director Elia Kazan says *action*!

That scene is a creative collaboration between two actors, a screenwriter, a director, a photographer, and a composer (the music, especially when created by Leonard Bernstein's brain, plays a starring role). All complicated men, from different socioeconomic backgrounds. Their individual lives, their secrets, personal experiences, some even traumatic, are sublimated into the material and transmitted through the actors into that cab scene, a frame at a time.

In the end the film is really a magic carpet made from pieces of everyone who contributed to it, and we the audience play our role too. We bring our own life experience into the mix as we experience the scene. As Brando and Stieger speak as two brothers, Terry and Charlie, their performances affect us deeply because we identify with them; we're reminded of our own emotional past. Everyone has regrets, has made mistakes. We all want redemption as we watch those flickering images. The actors' affective memories conjure up our own. Because we coulda been somebody too.

The thing about madness is that it gives its gifts to those of us cursed with the need to express ourselves. All actors, all artists, have a pinch of madness that pulls us toward them. We empathize with them. Through their words, music, paintings, and acting, we identify, we see ourselves in them.

This is true of our greatest actors—if I dare put myself in that class. Consider the stories of such brilliant performers as Fanny Brice, George M. Cohan, Paul Muni, John Garfield, Glenn Ford, John Wayne, John Ford, Ward Bond, Spencer Tracy, James Dean,

Marlon Brando, Marilyn Monroe, Montgomery Clift, Rip Torn, Judy Garland, Robert Young, Cary Grant, Laurel and Hardy, Abbott and Costello, the Three Stooges, William Holden, Alan Ladd, Grace Kelly, Frank Sinatra, Dean Martin, Henry Fonda, Elia Kazan, James Cagney, Humphrey Bogart, Peter Laurie, Walter Houston, John Huston, John Barrymore, Drew Barrymore and her great-aunt Ethel Barrymore, and uncle Lionel Barrymore. And the television actors of the '50s and '60s like Robert Young, Gig Young, and Robert Blake. They all had great qualities, but they all had their own dis-ease, their own deadly symptoms. I could feel myself in them, in their pain, which is what made them great stars. River Phoenix, Heath Ledger. The list goes on and on and on.

Why did I want to be like Spencer Tracy? Why did I love Cary Grant? I adored Cary Grant because I sensed his pain, and he made me laugh. I think Cary Grant is the greatest film actor of our time. Cary Grant suffered greatly from depression, and tested psychotropic drugs. Spencer Tracy, oh my God, was such an alcoholic. He just couldn't get life. He just wasn't good at it. Ava Gardner was a mess with alcoholism. Frank Sinatra was manic-depressive. Dean Martin was depressive.

This is the company I have kept in the asylum, where I was rewarded for my dysfunctional life, manipulating my brain to dredge up emotional trauma from my past, or to create emotional trauma through my imagination. I was getting paid for it, meaning it had some value for someone. People pay to see me do this.

Mental dis-ease never leaves you. If you don't deal with it, it gets you. And so much of its causes are subconscious. I didn't have a clue about where it was coming from or what the root of my problem was. To deal with it, you first have to see it, and it can be such a part of you that you can't see it, like the fish can't see water. Sometimes you need a Dr. Kelly.

CHAPTER ELEVEN

Twelve Steps out of the Mile Square

When actors get parts in movies, they also get a physical. For insurance purposes, actors and other players of importance—directors, producers—are given checkups to make sure they're healthy. I must have had over a hundred in my humble career. Now, only after you check out to be healthy will the insurance company cover the bet on you in the event something happens and "the show can't go on" without you. It's not complicated: you do paperwork, see the doc for five, and you're out in fifteen. They check your blood pressure, your heart rate, listen to your lungs, they want to know if you have any family history of heart or lung disease or diabetes or cancer. The doctor will ask these routine and mundane questions such as . . .

DOC. Do you drink?

JOEY. No.

DOC. Smoke?

JOEY. No.

DOC. Use illegal substances?

JOEY. No more.

DOC. Are you still taking your Lipitor for your cholesterol?

JOEY. Yep, 10 milligrams.

DOC. Great stuff. They should put it in our water (*both laugh*).

I'm just getting my shirt back on.

DOC. Oh Joe, are you taking anything else?

JOEY. That and the baby aspirin . . . Oh, and an anti-depressant.

DOC. How much?

JOEY. Ten milligrams a day.

So I check out fine and I'm on my merry way. Except . . .

Phone rings.

MY LAWYER. Yeah, Joey, we have a problem. It isn't the movie company. OK, they're pissed too; I've been on the phone with Business Affairs all morning *and* the insurance company.

JOEY. Paul, can you get to the punch line?

LAWYER. You're an insurance risk. You can't do the movie—

JOEY. ???<*&^ ſ*$%ing.

Paul is laughing now. After twenty-five years of working together he knows my moods pretty well.

LAWYER. Will you wait a minute! You can't do the movie un-less you sign a waiver.

Paul breaks it down as I listen.

JOEY. Motherfuckers! So their solution is that I have to sign a waiver and cover their ass! So, if I have a "mood attack" and do a Peter Pan off the George Washington Bridge or suffer a Charlie Sheen, anything that prevents me from performing my duties, any-thing that might slow down or shut down the movie due to my inability to perform my duties, then . . . ?

LAWYER. Then their expenses would be your financial re-sponsibility, correct.

JOEY. But it's costing them $150,000 an hour to shoot this—I would be financially ruined in a matter of hours!

LAWYER. *THAT'S NOT GOING TO HAPPEN.*

JOEY. What if I have a heart attack?

LAWYER. What?

JOEY. I have a history of heart disease, just like I have a history of mood dis-ease. I'm taking Lipitor for my heart health, just like I take antidepressants for my emotional health. The antidepressants lower the risk of any kind of job-endangering emotional implosion, which by the way I've never experienced in my thirty-three years in show business . . . So why are they *insuring my heart but not my brain?*

Well they didn't have a good answer . . . and I did sign that waiver in order to do the movie. And don't ask me which one it was, 'cause I ain't talking.

—m—

I started seeing Dr. Kelly on a regular basis. He educated me about clinical depression, which was a truly enlightening experience. I had pretty much stopped drinking by the time I went to him, but I was still taking the painkillers, and each morning I still had trouble coming up with a reason to live. Life was still completely unmanageable. The dis-ease had won. I realized I couldn't get off Vicodin even with Kelly's help—I needed to hand the reins over to someone, or something, bigger.

So I went back to AA.

I went by myself on a Friday night, and I sat and I listened. And I finally connected with these people. I saw myself in them, I saw that we were all, in one way or another, battling the same demons. One of the first things I heard in the rooms was someone saying, "I always felt there was a hole inside of me." Wow. I could describe that hole. He was talking about the hole in me! How the hell did he know about me?

I also witnessed the solace so many had found when they surrendered to their dis-ease, and connected to a higher power, whatever they considered that to be.

I had a lot on my mind on the drive home, and I found myself thinking about my mother again. How both she and I were sick; how we shared a dis-ease, not necessarily the same character defects. How I'd made a dreadful mistake in the way I'd been characterizing her choices all these years. I pulled into the driveway and parked. As I was walking up the drive, looking up at the starry sky, my cell phone rang. It was a bad connection. I heard someone say, "Hello? Hello this is Mom . . . This is Mom, can you hear me?" And then nothing. It was one of those moments that seemed less like a coincidence and more like, well, a spiritual experience. Was my mother trying to tell me something, or was . . . God?

I started attending meetings every day.

I've been lucky to be in the glittering rooms under chandeliers and klieg lights—winning an Emmy, yukking it up with a president—but I'm at home today in different rooms with people on a journey like me. There are other actors in there, and lawyers, and people who drive around in Mercedeses, and there are people who were like me when I was growing up, who would know my streets in Hoboken, whose biggest worry of the day is getting a part for their rusty car so they can get to the welfare agency.

"Hi, I'm Joey. I'm dual diagnosed."

I say that a lot these days in Twelve Step meetings, in "the rooms," as they call them. I've been to them all: rooms for alcoholics, dieters, spendthrifts. Often Bogie is lying on the floor in front of me. Bogie has been my higher power for so long. He's a Wheaton terrier, a soft-coat Wheaton. I couldn't get in the car, I couldn't go into New York, I couldn't take a meeting without Bogie being with me. In some of the rooms he's allowed in. He's part of the group conscience. Well, Bogie thinks so. People don't seem to mind that he's there, especially those who know his role in my recovery. The people in the rooms are seeking a higher power, and they're not too picky about what that means to someone else. For all of them, it's something greater than themselves. Because, like for me, "themselves" didn't work out so good.

I was in a meeting recently, and one fellow starts talking about how his sister is dying of cancer, and he's dying of cancer, too. He knows he's going to die. She's drinking a bottle of vodka a day, but he's got the program. She's saying, "Aw, this" and "Aw, that." She couldn't surrender. She couldn't let go. But he's got serenity. He has a spiritual foundation for his life now. He's got peace of mind. That's what I'd always been chasing, when, instead, I found myself wanting to die.

Jimmy's my sponsor (I almost wrote "my agent"). A sponsor is a sounding board, a second opinion. Big Jimmy makes the rounds of the rooms and has for years. He was an Irish kid who grew up on the streets in the South Bronx—he knows from stickball—and I wish I'd had him at my side on the Hoboken streets. He was a cop at one time, and I don't think you'd want to mess with him.

With everything in my life I now count to ten. I don't do anything, I don't make a call, I don't push a button without counting to ten. I call Jimmy and I say, "I'm thinking about saying this to my wife. What do you think?" That's what I do, because once I let the toothpaste out of the tube, it's out. Big Jimmy is like the prefrontal cortex I never had to edit the rumblings in my alligator brain. I'm getting better at not having the words pop out. I don't know what it is. There's no blocker—my mother didn't have it, my daughters don't have it. A thought hits my brain, it comes out.

So today I have these warning signs to regulate, manage, and stay on top of my *sette bello* symptoms. I have my support team, my doc, and God, as I understand Him.

I'm now guided by the twelve simple steps, which is a style of living that's made the most sense for me.

In the first step I came to understand the powerlessness over it and that my life has become unmanageable because of it.

In the second step I learned of a power greater than myself. Because I'm a spiritual guy, I believe that power to be God. And so in the third step, I believe that I surrender to God and that I am powerless over everything. It's a magnificently simple concept: I take the leap of faith that is daily living and trust that something will keep me from falling, and that something is my higher power.

For me, the problem with group therapy was its absence of faith. In group therapy, the group leader wanted his power to be godlike, but what really helped me was simple faith. Having faith in God, or the gods, or the universe. Faith that you will be provided for by working hard at what you want. You know the saying, "God helps those who help themselves."

Surrender is letting go, letting Him help you. It was only when I surrendered to my dis-ease that I was able to find peace of mind. It's surrendering to win. It's having the courage to believe.

I've spent a lifetime perfecting my emotions. I have character defects, and I know how to use them, as people in the rooms say. I've earned a living from them, and it's not easy giving them up. Take sex. (Thank you, I will.)

Today I'm practicing to change my thought patterns. Now

my first thought in the a.m.? *Your will be done.* So just for today I'll ask God to please do for me what I can't do for myself.

The whole point of these Twelve Step Programs is coming to an understanding of your dis-ease and seeing that you are powerless over it. What I've learned is that I'm powerless over *life.* I had been trying to control all of this for so long. It was my responsibility, and I was going to make it happen. But the first moment of surrender was my discovery of recovery. My life had become unmanageable, and I had to stop trying to manage it. Instead I just surrendered to it. This thing we call life is just one goddamn thing after another. For me now, what matters is how in the moment I'm going to deal with that one goddamn thing.

—⚏—

It took me two years of meetings to finally grasp the fact that I had to give up everything—deny all of my seven deadly symptoms—in order to keep my emotional equilibrium. No drugs and no alcohol, for starters. No starving or bingeing or spending, and of course no women. Even now my symptoms are constantly on my mind, always whispering in my ear, but as they say, I take it one day at a time.

The symptoms still live in me, but I don't act on them. It's a choice today. When I'm under stress I feel like I want to drink, but instead I do yoga.

When I was beginning this book I got robbed. The thieves took a whole month's worth of my clothing from my car. Heirlooms! Three pair of my favorite cowboy boots. And a couple of those Barelli jackets. Silver buckles and knives. I had left my luggage in the car because I had an early flight. The car was at a friend's house in a four million dollar neighborhood. When I realized what had happened, my first thought was, I wanna get laid. Not get drunk. Get laid. I told Nancy about it. Alcohol and sex are my two greatest addictions. And being under the influence always made it easier for me to be unconscious in betraying my wife.

Starting this journey with the shrink and Jimmy and my new friends in the rooms was crazy for a while. I still wanted the seven deadly symptoms. I put alcohol and drugs away, but I wanted to shop for clothes, so I had to give my credit cards to somebody to keep me from using them. I wanted ice cream. I wanted women, obviously. And then a funny thing happened, the higher power thing. It wasn't until I had surrendered to the idea that there was a power greater than myself that could restore me, that could fix me, that it all clicked. At that point that I experienced a spirituality that I had never had before.

Why is it that with alcohol I need a power greater than myself? I knew it was bad for me. I said I was going to stop, but I kept on going back to it, because it worked. Alcohol was my medicine, the best for the problems that I had.

I am what they call a high-bottom alcoholic. Alcohol didn't ruin my life. I never lost a job over it. The first time I went into a twelve-step room, when I was twenty-nine, I decided it wasn't for me, because I needed that medicine, and I didn't have the cognitive skills to see it differently. I just said, I've got to be able to drink occasionally. And so I drank occasionally when I was excited, when I had good news.

This is the first time in memory, ever, that I'm going with the flow. I surrender to whatever happens. Every morning I ask God to help me to surrender. I get up, and the first thing I do is, I say, "OK, I'm here. Thy will be done. You got my back." God is the Universe, the Sun, the Force. It's a spirituality that connects all of us. I believe that. And it's in control of this thing sitting on top of my neck: Spaceship Joey.

I realize now that I have to "act as if." I have to find that blissful ignorance again if I can. I don't worry about drinking or drugging today. I know I'm not going to. I can't. It's not even because I might not be able to stop. It's because it'll mess with the chemistry in this brain! I have a different way now. I work the twelve steps. I exercise. I do yoga, and in trying to do the poses my mind stays focused. I also take a minimal amount of pharmaceuticals to regulate my brain chemistry. I could play Ralphie and all the other bad guys so convincingly, because I knew that life. I'd seen it up close. I can explain to you how to do the seven deadly symptoms, if you don't already know, because I've lived them up close. I've had a lot of practice. And they got me where? Today I've decided to give something totally different a try. Every day I try—OK, I *try*—to live by the prayer of St. Francis.

> Lord, make me a channel of thy peace;
> That where there is hatred, I may bring love;
> That where there is wrong, I may bring the spirit of
> forgiveness;
> That where there is discord, I may bring harmony;
> That where there is error, I may bring truth;
> That where there is doubt, I may bring faith;
> That where there is despair, I may bring hope;
> That where there are shadows, I may bring light;
> That where there is sadness, I may bring joy.
> Lord grant me that I may seek rather to comfort than to
> be comforted;
> To understand than to be understood;
> To love than to be loved.

For it is by self-forgetting that one finds; It is by forgiving
   that one is forgiven;
It is by dying that one awakens to eternal life.

I'm pretty sure you'd get beat up in Hoboken if you started reciting that on a street corner.

—— *m* ——

Another legacy I'm working on is No Kidding, Me Too! (a.k.a.
NKM2), the organization I founded to remove the stigma at-
tached to brain dis-ease through education and the breaking
down of societal barriers. Our goal is to empower those with BD
to admit their illness, seek treatment, and become even greater
members of society.

This is how I got the idea for NKM2: Whenever I'm at the
airport, my customers (fans) will ask: JP, where you going?
What are you working on now? At the time it was *Canvas*, and I
was flying to L.A. to work on the edit with Joe Greco. I'd tell them
about the movie, how the main character has BD, and the response was always, "No kidding! Me too! Really, my mother (or
my brother, or I got) . . ." I started to feel that I was a part of
something, and that we had to lead with humor!

While making my documentary *NKM2* I came to understand that BD was shrouded with discrimination, bigotry, and
shame, and that's in essence why millions suffering from undiagnosed BD won't reach out for help.

The research I did for the documentary wasn't much different from what I'd do when building a character for a role.
When developing a character, I'll reach out to the person the role
is based on (if it's a biopic, for instance), or dozens of people
who have shared similar experiences. Throughout my career I've

been invited into worlds so vastly different from my own. I got to meet history face-to-face, hear incredible people's opinions, their passions, fears, what they like or disliked and why. They were sharing their secrets, opening their hearts to me. Sometimes it was more beneficial for them than me. I would then interpret them through the part I was playing. I realized how much I'm like these folks. It was a common bond I shared with people from so many walks of life. Sometimes they invited me, JP, a little snot-nose kid from the projects into their souls! And that would not have been afforded to me if I were just a regular Joe! So I had a certain reverence, a responsibility to get this right.

—m—

In the *No Kidding! Me 2!!* documentary, we examined the shame and bigotry surrounding BD. In interviews with six diverse (socioeconomically, financially, agewise) individuals, Casey, a high school student who was suffering from depression, tells of her experience in the ER while being treated for a self-induced cut that the esteemed hospital where her father and grandfather sat on the board. Knowing that the cuts were self-induced, her doctor unethically penalized her by not giving her an anesthetic while sewing her up. He wanted to teach her a lesson. Like that would somehow cure her, like sticking a dog's nose into the spot where he peed. This professional was punishing her for something she clearly had no control over. These kinds of reactions happen all the time. People with BD might be dismissed as GOMERs (Get Out Of My Emergency Room). They'll even write it on a patient's chart, a label used to warn others working in the hospital that these patients aren't worth the trouble. People with brain disease entering an ER have a big *S* painted on their foreheads, for *stigma*. Even doctors in emergency rooms, who see BD all day long and can read the symptoms of BD and their coexisting addictions that occur 75 percent of the time, act as if they don't know anything.

I talked to Dr. Robert Campbell, a board-certified thoracic surgeon who had suffered from bipolar disorder and other mental problems, and he told me: "As a resident I hated taking care of suicide attempts, and I was demonizing them as much as anyone—until it was me and I was saying, 'What can I do to end this pain?' For me—and I've gone through two back operations—there's nothing as great as the psychic pain I've felt."

Campbell had a psychotic breakdown while working out on his treadmill, the result of his undiagnosed bipolarity. "I'm watching the Pope on TV, when suddenly I decide I'm going to fly to Rome and kill him!" That was when he finally recognized that something was really wrong and sought help.

When I started work on *NKM2*, I thought I was making a movie about the shame around mental illness, but then the movie started having a mind of its own. And there was a force, a pull: it wanted to say more about shame, discrimination, and bigotry toward the All-American Brain. It wanted to prove that our brains should have constitutional parity with any other vital organ. Insurance companies should treat our brain dis-ease as they would gallbladder disease and acute appendicitis. It's a question of basic human decency.

I spoke to people with BD from all over the country. I'd meet them when I spoke at the clubhouses, twelve-step meetings, and luncheons, and interviewing these amazing folks was fascinating. Never monotonous. Have you ever worked on something that you couldn't get enough of, you just had to keep going? That's what this was for me. Their stories were so compelling, they fueled my desire to go on. All of the people I interviewed were charming, charismatic, excited, and talented. They were eager to talk, to open up. They were never afraid to show their emotional disturbances. That's a form of heroism, of hope. I think heroism is having the courage to be candid about the problem, and accept the help that's available; in some cases of BD there is a recovery rate upwards of 80 percent! When I see a film that romanticizes or demonizes BD, that's when I "jump the couch." People with brain problems are not weak, or evil— they're just people. I see the future of BD as a time when stating your "brain style" won't be a matter of bravery, simply a matter of fact.

In *NKM2* I wanted to bring these people's amazing stories to the forefront. They had thought that there was no hope. No chance of recovery! I wanted to bring hope to all those suffering with shame that they couldn't get out from under, or for those who didn't know they were sick, they just felt life draining from them and believed that hope and optimism could never exist for them. To them I say, What the fuck? That's just not true! Knowing you have BD is when the healing begins.

I've found that the more chances I take sharing my secrets the lighter I feel. I was amazed that once my secrets were out, I no longer relived the trauma of my past. I could move on with my life. The way I manage and gauge my mental sobriety and sanity has been derived from a lot of things I have learned from the doctors at McLean Hospital.

McLean is a psychiatric hospital noted for its groundbreaking neuroscience research. They have more than 4,000 human brains with which to do research and send to other hospitals all over the world. McLean is the bank, the center.

When we were filming the documentary my crew and I were there off and on for over three weeks, shooting, asking questions, becoming involved. When I first interviewed these top doctors they weren't about to give me the key to the ranch. But they had time to size me up, and I had time to gain their confidence. They came to discover that I was making a documentary that would be helpful to both patient and caregiver, and that I wasn't gonna go Michael Moore on them.

On the morning of my last day one of the top research guys in the world pulled me aside, as if we were in the *The Bourne Identity*, and whispers to me about the white rat. Have I seen it? I have to see it! The hitch was that I couldn't photograph anything. No wires. No audio, No video, no nothing. So I went down to this basement at McLean Hospital, in the tiniest building on the property. And I had to leave my crew behind. I was in the basement of the world's largest brain bank. Then I was introduced to the white rat. I became fascinated by this little guy. He weighed in at eighteen ounces and was about eleven inches tall. I can see him in my memory bouncing around there now! The cutest pink eyes you ever did see, like a tiny bunny rabbit, a pet. The doctor told me that their brains function very similarly to ours, so the experiment was to examine how his prefrontal cortex reacted to stimuli.

The white rat was in a glass-enclosed case, maybe one foot by one foot. There was a pedestal he jumped off of, some water to the right, then something that looked like a basketball hoop, but instead of the hoop itself, there was just the backboard and a white light. Under that there was a pedal like a gas pedal. They had surgically removed the skin and his skull around his prefrontal cortex, so there was a hole in his head, and in that they stuck an electrical rod that the white rat wore like a football helmet. The white rat had come to understand that every time he hit that lever he felt wonderful. He got a boost of electricity that stimulated the prefrontal cortex, which is where the pleasure zones are, and he was addicted to that feeling.

In fact, the research went even farther. They'd discovered that if they starved him for two weeks and then put him in a cage with the lever and a meal that would rival the most savory Thanksgiving dinner, he wouldn't eat. He'd go for the lever instead. He'd refuse food, even water, until he was dead. All he wanted was that feeling, that high. They were also experimenting with having the white rat abstain from sex for six months, then they put him in a cage with a beautiful luscious female mouse, and he'd deny her! He wanted the new love in his life, that lever! And it killed him . . .

My first thought? *How do I get one?* I couldn't get it out of my mind! Oh boy, look at me now! In a suit and tie and a really cool electro derby wired to the base of my brain, continuously smacking my lever, busting the much-needed dopamine to rattle my cage. I saw the images of my life flashing before my mind's eye, my home movies playing backward and forward: Mommy, Daddy, Nancy, coming, going, crossing paths. Big memories coming out of storage, some conscious, most not . . . These surreal images belonging to me. The verdict was in! I was ready to give it all away! Give it all back, for one more jolt at that lever in the rodent's cage!

Then . . . wait. Why did I feel so sad? I realized that those behaviors and substances that gave me this feeling of well-being lasted only for a moment. The food, ego, shopping/shoplifting, success, sex, alcohol, and prescription drugs are for me, and the millions like me, what the lever is for the white rat.

Something must have clicked in my unconscious mind, because I suddenly understood why I needed to be an actor.

Acting onstage gave me a rush of dopamine. Acting was always exciting, back when I didn't know what was gonna happen from one moment to the next, or as I started gaining success. For a journeyman actor like myself the three greatest words in the world are "You got it." Because actors are like salesmen. Let's say I'm selling rat shit. Let's say it's the white rat's poo poo and I go into an audition and I lay out my rat shit. They can buy rat shit from anybody. Great actors are a dime a dozen. They can buy my rat shit or another actor's rat shit. So what makes me special and different from any other actor in the business with the same product? People hire me when they see that I'm closest to the character.

When an actor goes into a room to audition, the casting directors want them to do well; they're looking to cast that role. So what do you do in those five minutes? That's really the core of what acting is. It's five minutes that you're an actor representing that part; you have that part for five minutes. Once you're fortunate enough to hear the words "You got it," well then, the rest is gravy. That's where the fun begins.

My doctor has made his diagnosis. He's convinced that there's a method to my madness, to this whole Joey persona, brand, or whatever it is that I use when I get into a room to get that job. It's not just about the acting. It's about convincing these people that I'm gonna be a pretty decent guy to have around for the next fifteen weeks. I'm gonna be part of the solution, not the problem. That's when I get the biggest boost of serotonin and dopamine—and it's that natural high that I've been after all along.

An Open Letter to the Late, Great Frank Capra

Dear Mr. Capra,

I've been meaning to write for fifty years. Finally, my mind is clear as a bell; no longer rambling, splashing through the murky waters of my past. My memory is a scary place: you need a flashlight and a gun so as not to get mugged in there—and I'm stuck with these images.

In the first sentence of your memoir you wrote, "I hated being poor!" Boy! Could I relate!

These preceding pages were moments tucked into the crevasses of my past. Most were never meant to see the light of day; unfinished fragments flickering in my minds eye, like the flickering black and white images that lived inside that Zenith twelve-inch TV set in Mommy and Daddy's bedroom. You were behind the cameras creating one image at a time, telling stories through the accumulation of images, turning them into secret dreams that I held close to my heart, that I never dared to share with another soul until now. I saw the future that awaited me as a giant hook grabbing me by the neck and pulling me into that Zenith!

It's clear to me now that your tales played an important part in my life.

Perhaps because your movies seemed so real, I paid desperate attention to them. They showed me, frame by frame, what America was. What it looked like, sounded like, its food and music, which was different from what I knew. No one in Hoboken talked like Jimmy Stewart. I had no other reference for the real world. I took your images and sounds as gospel.

You were a beacon in my mind, my heart! An Italian-American classic. In the 1930s, when my family and millions of immigrants like them were starving, your name was above the title. By the 1960s I sat in front of my parents' bed, watching your movies, listening to my father saying, "That guy's Italian!" Your stories taught me to see through the thick fog of poverty, bigotry and prejudice. Through this young boy's shame and secrets. I was afraid I couldn't catch up, that my situation was my fault. But your movies gave me hope, made me try harder. Now in my autumn years, traveling my arduous journey gleefully with the newfound enthusiasm of a child, I still think maybe, just maybe, my best work is ahead of me.

Mr. C, your movies influenced the road I chose to travel. I made it to my destination, and believe me, Hollyweird has gotten crowded. I'm no Frank Capra. I wanted to make a killing, but I make a living instead. My older kids were the victims of my miserly fear of failure. Some say I wasn't there for them . . . they're right. I was too consumed with the love of my life: success, its sweetness drowning out the noise of my poverty. Failing was not an option for me. But as a result they've lived a privileged life. No way would they experience the poverty I suffered. They'll never know life without gas and electricity, having to sleep in three coats. I've been broke, now I'm wealthy. Wealthy's better.

I always felt encouraged because you were Italian-American. Maybe I too could succeed. I remember every Italian filmmaker and actor and the movies that swept me off my feet. Guys like Lou Costello from Paterson, and Frank Sinatra and Jimmy Roselli. They grew up on my block—I'd see my Mom talking to Jimmy, that felt special. I loved the comedians, out of all of them—W.C., Buster, Lloyd, Groucho, Chico—my favorite was Harpo Marx. Harpo made me laugh. At age eleven I would see my aunts and uncles crying with laughter in Uncle Mario's kitchen watching The Marx Brothers on a borrowed twelve-inch TV. Harpo spoke with the wisdom for the ages, never uttering a word. A clown. His ballet of behavior could make you laugh, make you cry. Harpo Marx opened my eyes to the great characters. Anyone that funny had to be Italian! (I thought he was a left-wing Italian.)

I had to devise a way to get inside that TV. I fantasized what it could be like to get out of the gutter. Your movies represented the Average Joe. I was below average, but I had heart and guts.

I bought in—hook, line, and sinker—to your vision of the American dream. Those images were my history lessons, the flag I pledged allegiance to. As Thornton Wilder wrote, "Ninety-nine percent of the people in this world are fools," and most of the time I'm dangerously close of falling into that category.

A lot has changed since you passed on. In 2001 New York came under attack, and thousands of people simply evaporated, leaving behind only dust and bits of gold Rolex watches. We were told that we had nothing to worry about, that we should go shopping. I was eager to please my country, for shopping had long been an answer for me, but what I couldn't pay for, I stole. I started to accumulate stuff I felt would make me feel whole: I surrounded myself with symbols of status. I believed the TV commercials with all my heart. I felt that those material things I was being sold defined me.

Now millions of Americans have lost their jobs, and the middle class of America, your core audience—those often inspired by your movies—has been annihilated.

Hollywood was a place of serenity and comfort for me: an asylum to which I committed myself. My training taught me to effectively use my experiences, which were similar to the fictional experiences created by screenwriters. And then I sublimated my traumatic past into theirs.

So now I'm learning to separate myself from my fantasy: Hollywood fantasy from human experience. God has blessed me with a compassionate wife and a loving family. I've also been blessed with an inquisitive spirit and undying desire to succeed (which, in the beginning, meant at all costs). I realize that the sadness that lives on is, in fact, an inside job. No more do I surrender to the anxiety of tomorrow. I make adjustments, moving a muscle, changing a thought, trading a positive behavior for a negative.

And no more secrets. I was so sick from being the canister for many generations of humiliation, pain, and disgrace. I realize now that I'm not alone. I now understand the genetic link to my mother's trauma and her father's too, and how he had to drown it in Guinea red. I no longer fear I'll turn into my grandfather. I love myself now, and I can be emotionally intimate with another soul. I've learned to show myself. No more hiding. I enjoy your movies, not as a historical document of what was, but more as a vision of what could be. I have peace of mind. I like the way it feels. It truly is A Wonderful Life.

Sincerely,
Joey Pants

Book Acknowledgments

Firstly, my thanks to everyone who helped me put together my proposal. And of course to Brian Flynn, thank you again.

To Eddie Mo, my Capo, we began our journey, again, me telling my stories to you over many cups of coffee, tea or even some hot lentil soup. You transcribing and translating remnants of my fragmented past, from the badlands of Fairfield to the swamplands of Gainesville, then finally winding up shacked up with me and Bogie in my humble 100 square foot home in Hoboken. Hundreds of hours covered in black dust, mining through dark passages in the caverns of my unconscious misery, turning it into a shiny diamond, tiny but flawless.

Also, a big thank you goes out to Sarah Lueck, for your tremendous helping hand (. . . and arm and leg). You surrendered it to help me make sense out of my messy past. To Terry Kirkpatrick, my Project Mole and friend.

Thank you goes to my creative partner Ben Churchill, who helped with the edit and assisted with the photos for this book. Most importantly, he introduced me to my girl Friday, Navigator Natalie Nightwolf.

To Nancy Sheppard-Pantoliano and Patti Arpaia, for their participation in my book. Thanks Patti for your great photos, and thanks also to Tom and Morgan Kellogg, for your assistance in formatting the photos Morgan loaned out for this book.

To my old friends, Michael Kell and Peter and Roberta Wallach.

Marco, my boy, thank you—for your assistance and the valuable research you did, and for encouraging me to learn to practice yoga and for all the benefit this would yield me. And God bless my other kids Melody, Daniella, and Isabella (and Queen Christina, our Nanny Wrangler).

Thanks John Hook and all my friends at NKM2!

I am humbled and grateful for my recovery, which enabled me to surrender these portions of my life, which I'd normally dread to share.

To our family shrink, Dr. George Kelly, and my friendly shrink Dr. Robert Irving. Not to mention Dr. Richard Lerner and his wife, the beautiful Dr. Jackie Lerner, and Dr. Bob Campbell: thank you for your 100% open and honest approach in all that you do.

Also to my friends Dr. Stacey Gruber and Patricia Cornwall, and to my friend Wendy Richardson, thank you for writing *When Too Much is Not Enough*, and for your official diagnosis of my ADHD (or is it ADDH?).

Thanks also go to Ben Schafer and everyone at Perseus, Tony Hagopian and everyone at Weinstein Books, and to Bob and Harvey Weinstein, a big thank you for not having F.O.B.'s Secret Service cap me on election night, so I got a chance to write this fucking book.

Another big thank you to my agent David Vigliano.

And to my manager, Estelle Lasher.

Thank yous also go to my yenta/mentor, attorney Paul May- ersohn and fellow shark Jamie Coghill: you boys clocked way too many hours over an anemic five percent of this advance. Next time, the voild!

Finally I'd like to thank Judy Hottensen: you believed in me, this non-writer, as a writer. Your calming presence and patience helped me to continue, my dyslexic brain missing deadline after deadline. Most of all thank you for assigning Amanda Murray as my editor. Her beacon was so bright, guiding me, understand- ing my choices, and clarifying this non-writer's scribbles. I think without her I would have been lost at sea. And now that she has graduated from being my editor to being Editorial Director, I'm really glad I didn't piss her ass off along the way, because I have a hell of a pitch for our next book.

Index